# BLUE-EYED IN LUHYA-LAND

Gunilla Fagerholm

Published in 2010 by New Generation Publishing



First Edition



Book cover by Ela Sawosko and David Wettergren

Swedish Edition: Blåögd i Luhya-land
Translated into English by Gunilla Fagerholm

My Heartfelt Thanks go to:
Mrs. Lindsay Johansson, Sweden, for her wonderful work correcting my English, and to Mr. Andrew Ashdown, England, for his tough job pointing out paragraphs needing correction or clarification.

*This book is dedicated to:*
*Bertil, my husband,*
*my brother Per Erik,*
*my sons Christian and David*
*and my dear friend Susanna*

This is a true story about the years my husband and I spent in the Kenyan countryside. The purpose of the book is not to accuse anyone but to show how Kenyan village life, as late as around the turn of millennium, was still a mixture of old tribal traditions and beliefs... and modern life with the ever-present corruption - so common in many countries all over the world. Therefore I have, in order to protect individual privacy, changed names, places and details.

I want to emphasize that we love Kenya and the Kenyan people and that we have never regretted our adventure, once we'd come to terms with the shocking departure.

To find out more about our life in Kenya, visit our website: www.medialib.se

# Prologue

(May 8th, 2001)

"Mr. Lindstrom, please wait a moment."

I looked round to see who was calling. We had a taxi waiting outside the hotel to take us down-town for some shopping and it had already been waiting for us for quite a while. Over at the reception desk, I saw the receptionist signalling to us. We went over to him to see what he wanted.

"Mr. Lindstrom," he said. "There was a phone call for you earlier today. He's left a message." He handed Bertil a paper.

I staggered. What was this? I'd spoken to my family in Sweden a moment earlier so I knew the message wasn't from them and nobody else knew where we were. I felt a sense of imminent danger – that I was falling into a black abyss. Oh God, my pulse was going up; I started shaking and hyperventilating. With a comforting arm around my shoulders, Bertil held the paper so that both of us could read it at the same time. Having read it, we stared at each other. It was from Kakamega; from Noah, who had helped us to sell our computers. The message in itself wasn't important but how on earth did he know we were here? We'd certainly never told him we'd stay at the Boulevard. We'd actually lied to him and told him we were going up north, to the Turkana area on vacation and then we'd secretly sneaked off to Nairobi instead. And in order to fool people, we hadn't booked a direct flight to Sweden but instead one via Italy and Spain. I felt kind of creepy inside. This didn't feel good. We'd decided nobody in Kenya was to know we were heading for Nairobi. I mean, after all our lives had been threatened and now people had found out where we were; if Noah had figured it out, it was quite possible others had also.

In fact, this made us so nervous that we immediately took a taxi to the Swedish Embassy, where we explained what had happened and that we were very worried. The female Embassy official offered us a security guard from the Embassy for our remaining day in Kenya. We declined the offer, not wanting to seem hysterical. She advised us that if we felt in the least worried at the airport, we should contact the Embassy security officer on duty there. To make sure we'd recognise him, should we need his help, she called him into her room.

We had by now lost all interest in sightseeing and shopping and went straight back to the hotel where we kept close to other European hotel guests. Maybe they'd help us if something happened. We both had this strange feeling that people wanting to harm us were watching and following us.

At early dawn, we caught a taxi to the airport, where we waited anxiously for the hours to pass. We were still feeling very uneasy as if, at the last minute, someone would catch up with us and prevent us from leaving the country. It was an irrational fear but nonetheless very much present.

We waited for boarding time, hovering in the vicinity of Immigration. For a couple of years we'd been longing for this moment to come – the moment when we'd leave Kenya. I felt somewhat relieved when I saw the security officer from the Swedish Embassy making sure we got safely on our way. But when I looked at the

Immigration officer in front of my queue, my relief disappeared. He looked so stern; it was quite possible he'd stop us. Who knows, it might be forbidden to leave the country while a court trial was going on.

"Bertil," I said, "couldn't we switch to another queue? That officer up front seems awfully stern."

"No, we can't, that would look extremely suspicious. We have to remain in the queues we've chosen. See you on the other side. Don't be afraid."

It took such a long time at Immigration. I sweated and had difficulty in remaining calm. I wanted to shout, "Hurry up."

Suddenly it was my turn. The immigration officer looked at me, while he slowly leafed through my passport. He stared at me again until I felt I couldn't stand it much longer.

Then he said in a serious voice, "Madam, you're not allowed to stay any longer in Kenya. Your entry permit expires tomorrow."

"Yes, I know. That's why I'm leaving today," I answered in a pathetic voice.

"Have a nice trip," he concluded and handed back my passport.

I turned around and noted that Bertil had now also passed Immigration. Through the window I saw how the Swedish Embassy security man waved farewell to us.

"Gate number 12 is now open for boarding." What wonderful words.

Tears ran down my cheeks. "Thank God, we're alive!" I said. "We made it..."

I hiccupped, laughed and cried; all at the same time. In spite of laughing, I felt totally ragged. I felt as if I'd just barely avoided an accident, with waves of adrenaline flushing through my body. An enormous fatigue. Limbs weighing tons. Almost incapable of moving.

By my side on the plane just taking off from Nairobi's international airport, sat Bertil, bearded and sweaty; also he had tears in his eyes. He put his arm around me and gave me a reassuring hug. It was thanks to him I'd made it through all the tumultuous events we'd experienced.

"And now, some champagne," he said. "Let's toast the future and celebrate we're on the plane."

"But Bertil, I'm so…"

"Sh, sh, don't think about the bad times now. Let's plan the future. And – who knows – maybe one day we'll also remember the good things."

I saw below us the dry plains in the slum areas on the outskirts of Nairobi and the national park. We were leaving Kenya, a country which had been our home for five years and the place we'd intended to spend the rest of our lives. We'd only packed one suitcase each on this trip. The rest of our belongings remained at Riverdale Gardens, our Kenyan home.

We toasted and then Bertil drifted off. I thought about our dogs, left behind in Kenya. I missed them so much: Rufus, my liver-brown flat-coated retriever we'd brought from Sweden when we emigrated in 1996, his beloved bitch Merry, and their puppy Musse, a sweet black rascal.

My thoughts also dwelt on the paradise we'd left. Riverdale Gardens with all its beautiful flowers, bushes and trees, lots of tropical birds in different colours and thousands of butterflies, and all the fruit trees. The wonderful weather. How on earth would I be able to live without all that?

But, on the other hand, we were through living with thieves and violence around us. I wanted a normal life again. No more checking over my shoulder to see if someone was too close; if someone followed me; if someone looked dangerous. I wanted to disappear into the crowd; not stand out as different and consequently a target for others.

And… Oh God, what would we do once we were back in Sweden? We'd handed in our notice when we left for Kenya five years ago, and we'd certainly not get our jobs back after such a long time. We'd also sold our house and I'd, once again, have to live with constant pain because of Sweden's cold climate; one of the reasons for leaving Sweden. No work, nowhere to live, no money, no belongings …

When the steward had brought me a glass of whisky, I leaned back in the chair. I felt better now; my blood pressure was once more almost normal. With my eyes closed, I tried to concentrate on positive feelings, but it was so hard.

Bertil woke up, stretched and, scratching his beard, said, "Why on earth did we believe the village chief, when he said the villagers would celebrate us upon our arrival?"

"We're probably the most blue-eyed people on the universe. Bertil, why can't we ever learn?" Thinking of the chief's words, I felt my blood pressure going up again.

"Yes, and imagine; if it hadn't been for the gold, we'd never have been in this situation."

## 2. Gold on the savannah

Our Kenya adventure began with a trip to Masai Mara at the end of 1995, when I found a stone containing gold on the savannah. When I showed it to Herman, the camp chef, he told us about his home town, Kakamega, and its gold rush. A week later, we found a description of the Kakamega gold rush in an atlas of Kenya. Bertil, being an old gold-digger, went back to Kenya a few months later in order to plan future gold-digger trips together with the camp owner and Herman. Then, in May 1996, Bertil and I made an expedition to the Kakamega district where we found villages living on gold panning. We had a marvellous time panning for gold in the rivers together with the villagers. Everything was beautiful and people were so hospitable. And then, one morning, I looked down on the green valley from our hotel in Chavakali and said, "You know how we've been talking about leaving Sweden and our dull life, and find a place in a better climate. This is where I want to live."

And Bertil answered, without hesitation, "Then we'll do just that."

We returned to Kenya in August that same year and spent time bumping around on almost non-existent roads in search of a plot. It felt like hundreds of kilometres and we got bruises everywhere from the potholes on the roads. We seldom had food and we almost never had time for sleep.

But then we suddenly found our green valley. Peaceful and beautiful and, as an extra bonus, close to the rainforest. Here and there, clay huts, scattered between tiny fields. A stream at the bottom of the valley and a small area with remaining rainforest on the opposite ridge. Cheerful laughter from the people working the fields. It felt right, from the very moment we saw it.

At the purchase ceremony, we spent five hours sitting on chairs in boiling sunshine, together with half of the villagers, all the village elders, the local administration and the chief himself and - of course - the vendor in his mauve robe, with a big cross hanging around his neck. He looked like a true prophet. All the presents and the money we handed over, all the prayers in kiluhya-language, all the surveys and all the translations. Shortly after all this was finished, into town for the sales agreements, witnesses signing with their fingerprints, all the stamps and lots of other boring details. When all that was done, the domains were at last ours: twenty thousand square metres of land, used previously as maize fields, with old clay huts. I was so happy then.

Back in Sweden, we sold our terraced house and paid off our bank loans. That way we managed to amass a few hundred thousand Swedish kronor in cash. On December 6th, 1996 the moment for our emigration finally arrived. And so we left, with the blessings of our grown-up sons and our parents, to start a new and better life. Full of optimism, we still remembered the farewell words of our nice future village chief: "The whole village will dance and sing the day you come back!"

## 3. Jomo Kenyatta International Airport

(December 7th, 1996)

The luggage line started with a whining and screeching sound. Everybody's eyes automatically turned towards the monitor close to the ceiling. Yes, it was our luggage that was on its way. My stomach was churning. How had it gone? Where was he? How was he?

I looked towards the line. I wasn't at all interested in our suitcases and other things. My eyes searched eagerly for one specific item. Suddenly I heard a murmur from the crowd of fellow passengers and a surge of people approached the line and my package. A couple of men pushed their way through the crowd, lifted my item off the line and carried it towards me, accompanied by lots of people. I slumped down onto the stone floor in front of the grey box and, surrounded by a circle of inquisitive people, I carefully opened the door of the box.

He was sitting in there, still half-drugged by the sedatives administered to him before the flight. Our beautiful young dog Rufus. He tottered out of the box into my arms and gave me a hasty kiss on my ear, followed by a big yawn. The spectators asked anxiously if he was OK. They'd, in fact, been present at Arlanda and overheard our discussion with the aircraft crew as to whether Rufus would be transported in a heated storage room or not. They'd also heard my threats of not entering the aircraft, unless we had an absolute promise it would be heated. It seemed as if all these unknown persons were as delighted as we that everything was OK.

When Bertil had assembled all our things, we moved together towards Customs with an over-loaded luggage cart. I had Rufus on the leash and in the other hand I carried an envelope full of different official and stamped documents. We chose the Customs exit marked with red and hoped we wouldn't have any problems.

The two Customs officials were talking to each other, their backs turned on us. I cleared my throat several times in order to catch their attention. After some more coughs and a long wait, one of the officials turned round and asked in an irritated way what we wanted.

"We've brought a dog and veterinary certificates to declare," I said.

"Go through," was the brusque answer.

"Where to?" asked Bertil.

"There," the official pointed towards the Exit hall. "Now then, move on."

Astonished, we stole through Customs to the freedom outside. What on earth had happened?

We'd had so much work with the Customs documents regarding Rufus´ arrival in Kenya. It was important to fill in the right papers. And then, a couple of days before our departure, we discovered the dog documents had been put in our ship container by mistake. It was impossible to get hold of them. It had been a true feat, succeeding in getting copies by fax. After all that work, nobody at the airport was even interested in looking at them.

Out on the pavement, we tried to exercise Rufus close to some dazzling flowerbeds. Not a chance; big balls of rusty barbed wire, hidden among the flowers, prevented Rufus from sniffing around. Seeing us, the passers-by recoiled, looking frightened at the brown monster on our leash.

Although it was still early morning and a little chilly, the air was filled with the fragrance of the *frangipani* - temple trees - and the blossoming flowers around the airport buildings. What a change to the Swedish weather; we'd left Sweden during a blizzard with the streets completely covered in snow. Now, just hours later, here we were in the beauty of the tropics, in a wonderful climate. The people around us looked so friendly – albeit curious at the sight of our great heap of luggage. The women were so beautiful, many of them clad in fantastic African dresses. They walked with a majestic posture. And people were laughing and joking: that also was very different to Sweden.

In a taxi, loaded almost to the point of bursting, we arrived at the only hotel in Nairobi accepting dogs. Our entire luggage was carried into our room, while I exercised Rufus in the hotel garden. The exercise came to an abrupt end, when a wasp stung him on the nose. Our poor dog probably already hated his new home country. Later, an embarrassed reception clerk explained to us that the new hotel owner the previous day had decided dogs wouldn't be allowed any longer. Crestfallen, we had to leave the room occupied a moment earlier. Now we had nowhere to stay.

Together with a friendly taxi driver, we tried for hours to find a hotel accepting dogs. It proved impossible. Finally, he took us to the estate outside Nairobi where we'd visited a Swedish friend on an earlier trip. After a search among hundreds of houses, we at long last recognised her house and could press the bell. What a relief when her house girl remembered us and invited us in and to stay in the house along with Rufus. The house girl told us that although our friend would be in Masai Mara for another week, she'd be happy to see us on her return.

Our first long period in Nairobi was dedicated to shopping for things to take to Kakamega. We rushed back and forth between the estate and the shops in the centre of Nairobi, overloaded with new and required equipment. Actually, we had neither any idea what there was to buy up-country nor at what distance we'd find shops.

We were soon able to find our way around in Nairobi without a map but, once in a while, by mistake, we ended up in the slum areas. What we saw there was awful. People starving, dying; deformed bodies, crippled children, street urchins intoxicated by sniffing glue or solvents … It was more than I could bear; I walked with tears in my eyes. A horrid stench emanated from the garbage heaps where people rummaged about looking for food. It was all so inhuman. A jarring contrast with the world of the well fed and clad Africans we'd seen at the airport.

Christmas Eve was spent with another Swedish friend, who invited us to a marvellous Swedish Christmas buffet in her beautiful house.

A few days later, just before New Year, we loaded our newly bought Land Rover up to the roof with canned food, tools, dishes and cutlery, cooker, refrigerator, gas cylinders and generator and with Rufus on the back seat; we started the northbound journey to our new home in Western Kenya.

## 4. Towards an exciting future

The journey up-country was exciting but long. Pressing on, we watched eagerly as the landscape slowly passed by the windows. It was impossible to press our overloaded Land-Rover onto any higher speed so we had, in other words, plenty of time to look around and enjoy the view. We'd, of course, travelled the same way on earlier visits to Kenya but not at the same snail's pace.

Earlier I'd imagined Kenya as a flat country with reddish soil. Acacias scattered on the plains. Here and there groups of round clay huts with grass roofs. Roaming giraffes and zebras, some lions, and lots of vultures both in the air and eating carcasses on the plain. And it's like that in Masai Mara among other places, but up in the western highlands of Kenya it is quite different.

While we climbed the western side of Rift Valley, I thought about the stories of how tough immigrants at the beginning of last century climbed these steep, at that time road-less, mountain slopes, in many places 2,000-3,000 metres high. After much hardship they managed to force their carts, pulled by oxen and overloaded with household goods, up the mountains in order to colonize the area west of Rift Valley. An area much more fertile than the plains they were leaving behind. A hilly and green landscape with streams curling in the valleys through the then existing big forests. Today a huge part of this forest area has been converted into enormous tea plantations.

With Kisumu, the capital of Nyanza Province, behind us, we climbed slowly northwards onto the plateau, which lies at an altitude of 1,600-1,800 metres. The road traffic was heavy. It was a tarmac road but with lots of big potholes in it. In many places on the descending parts, bumps had been built in order to decrease speed, but even so, fatal accidents were extremely common.

After about twenty kilometres, we crossed the Equator - marked with a signpost - and entered the most densely populated area of Kenya. The marketplaces were close to each other and alongside the road, commerce was intense. Everywhere there were swarms of people walking, cattle, bicycles and cars. People wore a huge variety of clothes. Some women looked as if they were going to attend a ball in their silk dresses. They carried their shoes on their heads in order to avoid dirtying them. Some men wore only a loin cloth, whereas others looked very neat in their suits, white shirts and ties.

In Chavakali, we saw the view that had made us choose this region for our new life. An undulating, green scenery. Ridges and valleys penetrated by streams. Along the roads, round grass-thatched clay huts and here and there houses with tin roofs. The huts were hidden in banana groves, among flowering bushes, tea plants and sugarcane. It was so beautiful and looked so tempting.

From one second to the next, it became pitch-dark. Nightfall comes so suddenly this close to the Equator. We realized we couldn't possibly find our domains on our own. They were somewhere out there, to the right towards the rainforest - but where? After long discussions we decided to try to find our friend Timothy's house.

Timothy was the man, who had driven us around in the district for days on end in August in search of a good plot. He was a cousin and close friend of the Member of Parliament, representing our new village. We knew more or less where he lived and asked people for road directions. Since Timothy was well-known in the countryside, we eventually got proper directions and found his house without any mishap.

The hospitality shown by him and his family, in spite of us being unannounced guests, was unbelievable. They quickly gave us a room in Timothy´s mother's house. It was an original brick house, built during the gold rush in the 30's and bought by Timothy´s father, who by that time was a most respected and popular chief.

The following day we went with Timothy, to our plot in Wuasiva village. After a couple of hundred metres on the narrow village road, we came to a stop. In front of us we saw a ravine with huge sharp rocks and hardly any space for the wheels. The whole ravine declined towards a tea plantation. If we tried to move on, the Land Rover could tilt over among the tea bushes. But Bertil rolled up his sleeves. We had to pass. Centimetre by centimetre he forced the rocks and after some horror-filled minutes we arrived at the far end with our lives and car intact.

"We drove here last August in an ordinary car. How is it possible the road looks like this already?" I asked Timothy.

"There's been a rainy season since then," he answered, "and the road has collapsed even more."

"One thing is certain," said Bertil, "I don't feel like passing this place every time we go shopping. We'll probably have to make improvements on the road. We must talk to the villagers along it and find out if we can repair it together."

Rumour must already have spread via the grapevine, since the village chief, accompanied by assistant chiefs, village elders and lots of others, met us at the plot. We'd earlier decided we'd live in the lower of the two clay huts on the land, so we parked the car down there and the men helped us unload it.

Before Bertil and I could move into our hut, we needed a toilet and a shower, a fence and a couple of guards –"askaris". Since the plot wasn't fenced, Timothy was concerned about our security and wanted us to rent a villa in Kakamega to begin with. Our own chief opposed that and repeatedly declared, "Your safety is my concern." However, as we understood it would be difficult to have Rufus running loose without a fence, we decided to accompany Timothy to Kakamega to look for a villa. After a several-hour-long search even Timothy understood we wouldn't find a suitable house. They were all let for a minimum of six months to a year and we were, of course, not interested in that. The heat was agonizing and Rufus, who was hungry, hot and thirsty, became increasingly restless.

Suddenly Bertil remembered a small hotel, where we'd had lunch during one of our earlier visits to Kakamega. Fortunately enough they had a room for us and also accepted we'd bring our dog. The problem now solved, we decided to stay there for some days, until the workers had put up the fence on the plot.

We spent New Year's Eve over a tasty Kenyan dinner with champagne on the hotel lawn. Above us thousands of billions of stars twinkled in the pitch-dark night. We felt very confident, with lots of plans for our exciting new life that would start the following day.

## 5. Challenges

I was too tired to sleep. So many new impressions and such a lot of sunshine had worn me out. Now my body couldn't relax. But it didn't matter as I was so happy. Everything was progressing on our land and we would finally move into our small clay hut tomorrow. It was such a challenge to make this adventure work.

My thoughts drifted to my earlier life; what I'd done before meeting Bertil. Suddenly, I realized that our African adventure wasn't the first challenge I'd accepted in my life. On my own, I'd actually once before exchanged a secure existence for a very uncertain one.

I'd been working hard for many years within the Swedish travel trade, having finally obtained a reasonably high position with a good salary. My work was prestigious and opened doors for me. I travelled a lot to different countries, always staying in the best hotels. Everybody seemed to think I was an important person. My life was really comfortable; I bought shoes in the Philippines, clothes in Hong Kong and had new outfits made for me in Bangkok. I had Singapore Slings at Raffles in Singapore; I visited Alice Springs in Australia – a place I'd wanted to see all my life; I went to Borneo and stayed with the head hunters in a long house…

During my vacations, I was quite another person. Walking barefoot at the summer house, fishing, roaming the forests for mushrooms…

One day, I started thinking about the future. Would it always be like this? Would there never be anything new in my work? Would I do the same boring work year after year? Was it enough to be regarded as an important person?

No, it was not enough. I decided to climb down the ladder. I needed a real challenge.

In my work, I'd started using computers, in a very simple way. I actually didn't understand them but saw that there was a potential in them. I bought one - 640 kb RAM - and started learning some fundamental computer programs. But these couldn't do all I wanted done. I needed to know more; I needed some programming skills.

I quit my work and the wonderful monthly pay check was history. With trial-and-error and a lot of computer courses, the machine suddenly obeyed my instructions. I was programming. My small company got a few important projects at a big company and I managed to survive on the money coming in.

Life was once more fantastic. It was such a wonderful feeling having to strive again. It didn't matter that I no longer could afford to travel abroad or all the other things I'd had for such a long time. I felt alive.

A couple of years later, I bought a new computer. It didn't work well so the company sent a man from their technical team to help me. We started talking and it didn't take long before we discovered that we had a lot in common. Both of us loved Australia, both of us had been in Borneo... He had been several times in Australia, digging for opals and panning for gold.

This man was my future husband, Bertil. He moved into my house and a couple of years later we got married at the Swedish Embassy in Bangkok. Christian and David, my sons from an earlier marriage, were our witnesses and accompanied us on our honeymoon trip in Asia.

Now, a really strenuous life began with work around the clock. Bertil was working full-time in a news agency. Night time he helped me with my computer company. But it was fun to work in a team. Whenever we could take some time off, we went gold panning in the northern part of Sweden and Norway – a hobby that I'd come to love.

Our major problem was that we didn't know how to balance work and leisure. Work occupied more and more of our time. Since I was also suffering badly from fibromyalgia, worsened by the Swedish climate, I was getting depressed. Would I always have this ache? Work was too much. Too little freedom. Too little time to enjoy life. Reading the newspapers was horrible. Everywhere on the globe, people were suffering. We wanted to help them but were regarded as too old. How could we change our way of living? Get more out of life.

One day, we had a wonderful gift: a three-week tour for two persons to Kenya. And that was actually the start of this new challenge of ours…

## 6. Our African home

While carrying our suitcases into our "banda" (clay hut), we couldn't help glancing furtively at each other. I felt certain Bertil, like me, was wondering what we'd embarked on. Would we be successful in this huge adventure? The difference between this and our terraced house in Täby was unbelievable.

Our new home was both very small and extremely African. A traditional round banda, thirty years old, with a roof covered with brown grass, tilted towards one side. The diameter was just over five metres. We'd have to share that small area; two grown-ups and a dog. But it would work; I was sure. The rest of the villagers lived in similar bandas and those families were mostly much bigger.

Part of our land was now fenced in. We also had a simple wooden shed for the shower and toilet a couple of metres from the banda. The shower consisted of a 70 litres black plastic tank on the roof, a tap and a hose. It gave us sufficiently hot water, assuming we asked someone to fill the tank. Of course, sunshine would also be necessary; otherwise the water would be too invigorating. The toilet was a pit-hole toilet, a deep hole in the ground. In order to feel more civilized, we bought a proper seat for it.

After our first night in the banda, we had to call the carpenter for urgent assistance. He had to put papyrus mats on the walls of the shed in order to prevent people from seeing us through the big gaps in them.

Timothy lent us a low table and a couple of office chairs to put outside. Since the small papaya tree, close to the banda, didn't offer us any shade, we had to move the furniture around the hut in daytime following the shade.

The askari problem had been solved. The village chief and Timothy, who didn't seem to be best friends, had finally compromised and chosen one askari each. Timothy, cousin of our Member of Parliament, chose the chief askari, Jim. This man had earlier worked as security guard to our M.P. and was an intimidating person but since he probably knew his stuff, we'd have to accept that. Our chief selected Nick, one of his cousins, as guard number two. A small, simple shed was built for them and our chief helped us to shop for the things they'd need for their household.

Apart from the two askaris, we employed Johannes as "shamba boy" - garden boy. Probably we wouldn't have chosen him of our own free will, since he didn't speak one word of English, but the reason for doing it anyhow was that we, one of our first days in the village, received an official letter from the Chief's Office. In this letter, the chief told us Johannes was very poor; his wife had recently died and he couldn't afford to get her body from the morgue. The chief asked us to lend Johannes money for that purpose and to let him repay us by working for us. We felt sorry for him and gave him a loan and temporary work. Every payday we deducted a small part of the loan. In that way, he still had some money left to use for food for his little daughter.

There were moreover loads of day-workers on the plot busy with fencing, compost digging, preparation of a vegetable garden and lots more. Top-speed everywhere and at the end of the day the queue of people waiting for their daily salary was long.

As our household goods in the shipping container wouldn't arrive for a long time, we had to make innumerable shopping trips to nearby Kakamega. We'd indeed bought a lot in Nairobi but had completely forgotten to buy essential things like kerosene lamps, mattresses, blankets and similar household items. We went to town almost every morning, with long lists of what to buy. And we returned almost always without having been able to tick off all the items on the list. Everything was so time-consuming.

Something as simple as opening a bank account took several days. You couldn't just walk into the bank, asking for an account. No, first you had to be recommended by other bank customers. Then the issue was to be discussed at a board meeting and only thereafter, if you were lucky, could you get an account; this being a big privilege.

It would have been difficult to cope with all these new things without Timothy's help. He assisted us almost daily, showing us around, introducing us to people and explaining Kenyan customs.

## 7. My former life

I looked up from the book I was reading. I saw Bertil further up on the compound talking to a couple of the workers. He looked so alive and happy, not at all like the tired and worn-out husband he'd been during our last year in Sweden. He didn't seem to miss his computers; he didn't even talk about them any longer. His mind was engaged in finding technical solutions in order to improve our existence. He'd even started commenting on birds and flowers; he'd started noticing nature and its wonders. He was really happy. He hadn't agreed to move to Kenya just to make me happy; he, too, had obviously really wanted that change in lifestyle.

I was so happy that both my sons had given us their blessings before we left Sweden. They were both very fond of Bertil and since he was such a secure and reliable person, they were convinced he'd take good care of me, and I of him.

It was maybe not so strange that David had given us his blessing since he had the same longing for adventures as I. A couple of years ago, he'd actually taken a break in his architectural studies to go travelling in India and South East Asia. He'd spent quite some time there, going twice with his friends. On his travels, he met and worked with Mother Teresa in Calcutta. He'd also travelled the Indian Himalayas on a motorbike. He was an adventurer at heart. I mused when I thought how much he resembled his father in his physical appearance but he had inherited a lot of his character from me. He was really a true mixture of both of us.

Also Christian, my eldest son, had given us his blessing. He had led quite a different life from his brother. He was now a civil engineer with Computer Science as speciality. From high school he went straight into a serious relationship, living with his girl-friend. Both of them studied hard and soon finished their education, after which they both found good jobs. They'd still not seen much of the world outside Sweden, but I hoped they'd visit us soon.

Ulrika, my sweet baby girl, had died in cot death at just one month old. Had she lived, she would now have been one year older than David. Losing her was horrible. I'd been almost out of my mind; if it hadn't been for Christian, who was three years old at the time and needed me, I wouldn't be here now.

I'd met the father of my children, and my first husband, when I was studying languages at Stockholm University. He was finalizing his studies in Economics. I'd just come back from Spain, where I'd spent much of the past few years. I lived with my family until the day I got married; moving in together was out of the question in those days. Courtship, engagement and marriage, it all followed the rules of etiquette – so important at that time.

Immediately after my wedding, my parents moved to Sri Lanka, where my father led a UN project. They left their big flat for us to live in, while they were abroad. It was enormous: 275 square metres, located in the affluent part of Stockholm. So there I was, a newlywed, without anyone to ask for advice. I didn't even know how to boil an egg. I didn't know how to polish the parquet floors; I didn't know anything at all about a household. I'd never lived on my own and had been sheltered from reality by my loving parents.

It was unbelievable how different my first marriage was to the life I now had with Bertil. Dinner parties, cocktail parties, dances, bridge evenings. Evening dresses, dinner dresses, mandatory high heels and painted nails, beautiful hair arrangements. I had two seamstresses making new dresses out of all the wonderful fabrics my parents sent me from Sri Lanka and India.

It was a fabulous life, at least to begin with. It soon, however, began to pall and feel shallow. When the children arrived, things changed a bit, of course. My husband was the centre of the family and there was no team work at all. In that respect, our marriage was very old-fashioned.

After twelve years, our marriage ended and my sons and I moved to a terrace house to start a new life. It was tough. In order to survive, I had two jobs: one full-time in the daytime and one part-time at night, when the children were asleep. I loved my children and wanted them to have the things their friends had. I also tried to compensate for their absent father. He was too busy with his new life to care about his sons and there was no contact.

Thirteen years passed in a never-ending struggle. I was lonely and it was tough bringing up two teenagers by myself. No one to talk teenage problems with. No time to relax on my own. My parents, who were back in Sweden, helped all they could, but they were getting old. Nor did they have much patience with teenagers.

And then suddenly I met Bertil and the loneliness I'd felt was over.

## 8. Interlude in Nairobi

It was a real nuisance that, after only two weeks in our village, we had to return to Nairobi to arrange our entry permits. However, it had to be done, so we packed some clothes and Rufus into the car; picked up a Kenyan couple we'd promised a lift to the capital and were on our way.

With Kisumu and Lake Victoria behind and driving towards Kericho, the engine stopped suddenly in the middle of the countryside. We were stuck on the road in the heat without any means of finding shade. Thank heavens we'd brought a Kenyan man in the car. He darted about like mad by "matatu", or minibus, in different directions all afternoon in order to find a car mechanic and spare parts.

The later the day, the hotter it got. It was dangerous that Rufus refused to drink in the increasing heat. I was so happy when he, several hours later, finally accepted some fresh pineapple, brought for the journey.

Just before sunset, a village mechanic was successful in making a temporary repair and we were able to start the car and continue our journey, although with a very weak engine. To stay out there in the darkness would have been dangerous. The car didn't work well at all and the headlamps hardly gave any light. It was really scary going at snail's pace and with poor visibility in the rainy weather up the hills to Kericho. At intervals, we had to shine a torch in front so that Bertil could see the road. The surroundings are notorious for road pirates and at our low speed it would have been easy to board our Land Rover.

In Kericho we put up at a hotel for the night and the following day we managed to drive all the way to Nairobi.

After the troublesome trip, we spent approximately three weeks with paperwork in the big capital. A couple of our friends had promised to arrange our entry permits before our arrival in Kenya, but had filled in the wrong papers. To our consternation we'd discovered on arriving in the country that we had no valid entry permits. Most of our first week in Nairobi was dedicated to waiting for people, who didn't show up at the agreed time, on different floors of Nyayo House - the building where entry permits were issued.

It seemed hopeless to get the permits, so we finally decided to contact our Member of Parliament to ask for his help. That was easier said than done since this man also worked in the President's Office, which meant that whenever President Moi was in Nairobi, our M.P. had to be close to him, thus being impossible to contact.

After a lot of waiting outside the Parliament building, we finally succeeded in getting a meeting with him. He sent us to different authorities and ministries in order to solve the problem. Days were spent on a never-ending back and forth. The hopelessly corrupt administration made the issue even more difficult for us. And the many cautioning remarks we got from resident Europeans gave us butterflies in our stomachs when we thought of the adventure we'd embarked upon.

Our documents were at last approved on Bertil's 50th birthday. By that time we were so tired we didn't have the strength to celebrate properly. The only thing on our minds was that we'd soon be able to return to our village.

Having waved goodbye to the friends we'd been staying with, we drove through Nairobi city centre in order to leave the city on one of the big bypasses. With us on the journey was Betty, our future house-girl, recommended by some friends of ours.

With a sigh Bertil asked me to help him read the map, saying, "I've more than enough, trying to cope with these perilous roundabouts."

I spent a while studying the map, giving small hysterical cries when other cars were almost hitting ours, but then, at last, we were finally leaving Nairobi with its smell of garbage dumped in the streets. We were once again on our way to our home in the Kenyan highlands, in the western part of the country – where the air was so much fresher to breathe. Betty sat in the back of the Land Rover with our two dogs, Rufus and Merry. Merry was our new young family member: a ten-week-old adorable black schabrador puppy we'd bought in Nairobi. I was happy that Rufus, just over one year old, now had a little girl friend to romp and play with.

After some time on Uhuru Highway going towards Naivasha, I snuggled down and started to relax. We had a full day's journey ahead of us and it would be dark when we arrived. Hopefully, the car wouldn't break down again.

I drifted off for a while but woke up, as Bertil drove into a big parking lot. I recognized the place. In front of us, we had one of the most beautiful scenes in the world: the view over Rift Valley. We bought a Coke each and walked Rufus and Merry, enjoying the fresh wind and the wonderful view. It was hard to understand that the villages down there at the bottom were almost a kilometre lower down. It was really unbelievably beautiful.

The journey continued downwards to the bottom of Rift Valley. It became increasingly hot in the car. In the neighbourhood of Nakuru we stopped for a meal and also took the opportunity to buy some bougainvillea and jacaranda plants at a nursery alongside the road.

"We'll have to make a turn here," I said suddenly a few hours later. A moment earlier we'd left Betty in her village, since she wouldn't start working for us until next week.

Bertil turned off the big road onto a dusty gravel one. It was swarming with pedestrians, cows, goats, pigs, matatus and "boda bodas", or bicycle taxis. An unbelievable hustle and bustle. Red dust was whirling around, covering everything. We realized suddenly that we were now in the real Africa. We'd been on the road all day long and the sun would soon be setting. The distance to Nairobi was only about five hundred kilometres, but it could just as well have been several thousand, judging by how tired we felt.

Half an hour later we turned onto our small village road. Bertil stepped on the accelerator and almost in flight we passed the horrible road section with the ravine; fortunately still in one piece. After another few hundred metres we saw the village public plot. Bertil turned to the left and stopped the car. We jumped out, with Rufus on the leash and Merry in our arms, eager to see the view of our beautiful valley. Home again.

## 9. The maize field

With our entry permits approved for the next two years, we were itching to start making our dreams come true. We'd, in fact, already been in Kenya for a couple of months and were longing for real work and we actually had a lot to take care of. It was still the dry season and only a few dry blades of grass were seen here and there, protruding out of the hard clay. Dust was whirling above the ragged soil. We walked around as if in constant fog with our spectacles covered in fine-grained clay and a thin layer of it covering all our belongings.

How would we ever be able to turn this dusty maize field into a flowering haven? The project seemed hopeless, but we knew it was possible. Upon our arrival in the village, at the beginning of the year, our shamba boys planted wild hibiscus outside our banda. They put some dry seedlings into the soil and poured some water on them a couple of times a week. Those seedlings had already developed green leaves and red buds. And, during our stay in Nairobi, they planted around 250 banana plants, sweet bananas as well as cooking ones, along both the long sides of our plot. These had also done well and we were already able to harvest some of them.

According to our calculations, our yearly banana production was going to be approximately four tons. Two bunches were always hanging in the shower: one with sweet bananas, which we ate for breakfast, and one with cooking bananas, which we boiled or fried. Cooking bananas tasted even better than the best potato. Bananas grow like weeds and they're easy to plant. You only need to dig a hole, put the plant in it and give it some manure and water. Six months later the plants are between three and six metres high, carrying up to twenty-five kilos of bananas. When harvesting a plant, you cut it off and within a short time a couple of sister plants come up, as compensation. This way the number of plants becomes increasingly higher.

We were enormously lucky finding, at an early stage, a gardener in the neighbourhood. His name was Petrus. He had an undying interest in both flowers and vegetables and had a big greenhouse on his compound. He was whole-heartedly dedicating his time to help us get started. We got truckloads with flowering shrubs and trees from his home and, with his help, we also found excellent manure for the plants.

Days on end, people were digging, sowing and planting everywhere on our big plot. The lower part of it, stretching all the way down to the valley bottom and the small stream, had been assigned as a vegetable garden. We'd have all kinds of vegetables there, since we needed to be self-supporting. Up here in Western, beyond the tourist tracks, you couldn't find much to buy other than carrots, tomatoes, onions and "sukuma wiki" (kale). That's why we now had small plants of squash, eggplant, sweet paprika, sugar peas, haricot verts, cauliflower, cucumber, red cabbage, spinach and mangold, tomatoes and much more growing in our seedbeds and in the remaining part of the vegetable garden we'd dug down potatoes, sweet potatoes, casava, yams, maize and groundnuts as well as sugar cane.

The sun was burning and so hot it became important to protect the seedlings from it so we built small tables out of branches and banana leaves above the seedbeds. It was good to have staff that could descend the steep slope to the valley bottom in order to get the necessary water for the plants, but we realized we'd probably have to find a better long-term solution to the watering problem.

We also worked hard ourselves and our working days began at sunrise. I removed stones and cleared away maize stub from the fenced part of our land, while Bertil was building a shed for the generator. It would supply us with the electricity we needed and therefore it had to be well protected. It was hot already early in the mornings so our working hours were short. When necessary, we rested down in the shade we'd built out of poles, with roof and walls of papyrus mats. It was a luxurious feeling no longer having to move around the banda in search of shade.

As soon as our employees began their working day, it immediately became much noisier. We had to give instructions and check earlier tasks. And we were constantly being watched. Outside the fence, around the part of the land where our banda was located, there were always hordes of villagers, watching and laughing at us. Lots of people wanted to meet us. The excuses to visit us were many. Some people probably only wanted to be able to say they'd visited a "mzungu" (European). Others wanted us to employ them or wanted us to pay the school fees for their children. They expected both this and that from us, because white people were rich.

As a consequence of all these visits, we never had time to sit down and plan. We'd therefore decided our askaris would have to restrict the number of visitors. This wasn't easy. They couldn't say we were busy or out since the potential visitors could see us. It was also important admission wasn't denied to the wrong people, such as the chief, assistant chiefs and village elders who should always be made welcome.

Late afternoons, when the day workers had left, we enjoyed sun-warmed showers after which we changed into clean shorts and T-shirts. Then it was time to find something to eat. We'd by now finished all the canned food bought in Nairobi, and fresh food was problematic. You could find bacon, tasteless sausages and cheese at a high price. Because of the drought, vegetables were scarce and you could only find deep-frozen fish once in a while. It seemed the only things the Kakamega shops were selling were marmalade, fruit drinks, spaghetti, flour, cooking-oil and margarine. But fillet of beef was cheap, if you found a butcher who knew what fillet was. Alas, most butchers cut meat into small pieces and therefore it was quite impossible to find a roast or a nice steak. You just had to choose between fillet and meat for mincing. And minced meat was out of the question for us, since our mincer was packed in the shipping container, which hadn't yet arrived. We usually wrapped the meat we bought in papaya leaves and left it in the refrigerator to tenderise. If we didn't do this, it proved inedible. My parents, who had spent many years in the tropics, had taught us this.

Evening time, we went outdoors and relaxed in the glow of a couple of kerosene lamps. Down in the valley, frogs were croaking and glow-worms and fireflies were dancing an exotic ballet. The starry sky was showing millions of stars and the white male flowers of our papaya tree were emitting a wonderful fragrance.

We talked endlessly. We had time to do that now. We'd promised each other there would be no more discussions about computers or computer programmes. And we didn't have to worry any more about client support. We were freed from all that. We would instead dedicate time for us and for each other, plan our future and enjoy life. And in this wonderful environment that was really easy. Yet another reason for feeling content was that I no longer had any problems with aching joints. I felt great after having suffered for many years.

Rufus and his girl friend Merry were resting on a blanket at our side. They, too, enjoyed the lovely evenings. Daytime was often so hot they preferred to stay in the shade or inside the banda. When it was cooler, they amused themselves immensely, running loose on the plot which we'd now fenced to approximately five thousand square metres. At night, we left the back door to the banda open, so that they could come and go as they pleased.

We mostly went to bed around nine, since we got up before sunrise in order to watch it. After tucking the dogs in, we strived to get into the camping beds in our pitch-dark and cramped bedroom. We'd lie there for a while, listening to the sounds from outside. In the neighbourhood close to our banda but on the other side of the fence, we sometimes heard the sound of a team of oxen, ploughing the neighbour's field in preparation for the sowing of maize. After that, we slept soundly in our small clay hut beneath our mosquito net.

Yes, we'd really commenced a Spartan life. But it seemed so right. Days and weeks passed quickly, but we didn't care what day it was or time. We had no idea what was happening in the rest of the world. We had neither newspapers nor radio or TV. We actually only cared about what was happening in our own village. Nothing else was of importance.

Happy laughter was coming from the other side of the valley. At this time of year, everybody was out preparing the soil on his or her tiny fields. You had to hurry with the preparations. The rains would soon start and then the maize must be sown immediately. It didn't matter how old you were. Everybody was at work, swinging his or her "jembe", or pickaxe. Children, too small to lift the jembe, collected sticks and other things that could be used as firewood for the stove and carried home big loads on their heads. Some young boys were driving the family cows and goats to their bandas, sadly with stabs and blows. We'd already noticed they didn't treat animals well and that many were limping. This wasn't strange, since their front legs were normally tied together. When walking, they were dragged by the rope, thus in principle being forced to walk on three legs.

The village women passed on their way to and from the fresh water spring, balancing water tanks on their heads. I wanted to see the spring and therefore I went down into the vegetable garden, in search of Johannes. I found him carefully watering our small plants. It was rather strange to see him, a poor illiterate who didn't even speak English, care that much about everything growing. Why was he so lazy when it came to his own home? Why didn't he plant bananas and avocado on his own land? You could get those for free and they didn't need watering. Doing that, he'd have something to sell and his daughter would get vitamins.

"Merembe, Johannes," I greeted him, when he came to meet me with a smile. I asked him some questions slowly in English. Despite him answering "yes" all the time, I grasped that he didn't understand me, so instead I started to try body-and-sign-language to explain to him what I meant. I could see he was delighted and proud that everything was growing like mad in spite of the drought. In many cases, the vegetables were ones he'd neither seen nor eaten. I'd make sure he and the rest of the staff would be taught how to cultivate them. They'd get seeds from me.

Johannes and I descended the slope down to the little stream, which wasn't more than a small dribble now during the dry season. It constituted the lower boundary of our land. He pointed down into the water, drawing a fish with his hands, and started laughing. I understood it was here he, yesterday when fetching water for the flowers, found the mudfish, a twenty-five centimetre long fish looking like a small catfish.

So, the fact that there were mudfish was the reason why everybody kept insisting we build a fishpond down here. Well, that would have to be another, later project. As it was, we had quite enough to do.

I explained to Johannes I wanted to see the fresh water spring, about a hundred metres from our compound. On our way there, he pointed to another place in the water, saying something sounding like "pesa". I didn't understand him and then he pointed to a yellow flower, making rolling gestures with his hands. I suddenly realized what he wanted to tell me and was absolutely delighted by the thought. Gold here in the stream. How wonderful, gold on our own land! It was a fantastic feeling. I laughed happily, showing I understood him.

A group of women were standing at the spring. When we arrived, everybody stopped talking and looked curiously at me. I got friendly answers to my greeting in luhya language and everybody wanted to shake hands and greet me properly.

Part of the spring was made of concrete and the water coming out of the pipe looked clean. Many families didn't fetch water from the spring. Instead they took water from the small stream, soiled by both animals and humans. Most of the villagers didn't boil the water; one of the reasons for the many cases of waterborne diseases in the countryside. We, of course, boiled all drinking water, even from the spring.

I said goodbye to the women and went back up into the shade for a rest, before Bertil´s return from Kakamega. My legs became increasingly heavy on my way up to the banda and I started dripping with perspiration. It was extremely hot and it got hotter for every day. The cracks on the ground, caused by the drought, were getting deep as well as wide. According to the newspapers, Eastern Kenya now had famine and no rain was in sight although the rainy season should have started by now.

## 10. The curse

For once, I woke up depressed and thoughtful. Not even the beautiful sunrise over the opposite hill could better my mood. I shuddered. I felt uneasy because of yesterday's incident. What a horrible night it had been. The most incredible nightmares about witches and sorcerers.

But it wasn't perhaps that strange. When lying in bed last night, I felt despair, fear and anger. And the nasty short man Makuso in his white Salvation Army uniform had caused it all.

Makuso was the villager who had shown us around in Wuasiva when we, along with Timothy, were looking for land, finally finding it in the village. Later he wrote us a letter, asking when he could fetch the matatu we'd promised him. We answered we'd never either promised or talked to him about a matatu. We weren't rich people able to give away presents that expensive.

Last week Makuso turned up at our gate, accompanied by a big horde, asking to see us. He was allowed to come down to visit us at our banda but without his companions. We talked for a while, without discussing the issue of the matatu at all. He's a rather unpleasant person, so I was almost pleased when Rufus managed to dirty his chalky white uniform.

Yesterday we suddenly had lots of visitors. Many of them looked at me in a strange way and asked after my health. Of course I answered that I was quite well. The local chief of the Salvation Army requested, when also he had asked about my health, if we'd allow him to put up a local office on our plot. He and his soldiers would then take care of the gate control and also hold daily prayers with our employees and us. We rejected this offer in a diplomatic way.

Eventually, our friend Timothy turned up. When he, too, inquired about my health, I asked him for an explanation to all those inquiries.

"Well," he answered, "unfortunately Makuso has visited the village medicine man, paying for a curse to be put on you. Now he's walking around in the neighbourhood bragging that you'll soon die, having suffered from a lot of body swellings. Are you sure you don't have any swellings, Gunilla?"

"No, I haven't," I answered indignantly, because I most certainly didn't want to tell him I'd awakened with a gum swelling that hurt. He might then think I believed in sorcery.

"Why does Makuso want to kill me?" I wondered.

"Makuso wants your land," Timothy answered, "and he's planning that if you die, then Bertil could marry one of his daughters. Then they'll murder Bertil and Makuso and his family can take over the land."

"Oh, my God!" Bertil exclaimed, "So I wouldn't have any say in the matter?"

"It isn't funny," I continued, tears in my eyes. "Of course, I don't believe in these things, but I think it's awful people can be this malicious."

"Even if the two of you don't believe in witchcraft," Timothy commented, "you'll notice it's widely spread here and that people can be dangerous. You grab what you can, even if you have to murder in order to get it. I do beg you never to buy food locally. Never buy unpacked milk; never eat bread or anything else without a sealed package. It's quite probable they'll try to poison you."

When Timothy had left, we both remained silent. What had we embarked upon? Yes, we had, of course, heard some atrocious stories about things the villagers had done. One mother, still in prison, had poured kerosene over one of her children and then set him on fire. The reason for doing it was that the hungry child had stolen some “ugali” - maize porridge - just before dinnertime. You poison your neighbour's animals, you poison one another. You stab people to death. It’s irrelevant whether you’re doing it to family members, friends or enemies. People sat among the banana groves, drinking illegally brewed "chan´ga" (local spirits) and once they got drunk, they started…

So, last night we went to bed feeling very ill at ease, suddenly not feeling like confident Swedes any longer.

## 11. Problematic Patrick

I was sitting in a comfortable position in the shade with my feet resting on another chair and a glass of beer in my hand. I'd been working in the heat in the vegetable garden and was awfully tired. I really needed a rest now.

"Hello ma´m. How are you today?"

I jumped up, spilling beer on my blouse. Patrick, one of the former landowner's sons, was standing close to me. My body stiffened. He walked on our land wherever or whenever he wanted. My pulse rose. We had no privacy at all. This had to stop.

"Hello Patrick," I said, trying to sound friendly, "don't you know you've to tell the askari, when you want to see me? I was resting and you're disturbing me."

As usual Patrick looked completely indifferent. He'd evidently not understood his family had sold their land to us. Whenever I walked around on the plot, he turned up like a shadow, walking at my side, talking incessantly. I felt as if he was the one showing his land to a visitor. This had to change.

"Ma´m, I've come to fetch the school-fees and I also need a new school uniform," he continued unconcernedly. "You've actually promised me that."

"No, Patrick, we haven't," I objected. "But come back at six o'clock in the evening, when Bwana Bertil is back. Then we can discuss the matter with you. Leave now, so I can get some rest." As he obeyed my order, I called to his back, "And don't forget to register at the askari´s desk when you return."

I settled in the chair for a moment's rest. But memories started immediately spinning around in my head. I thought of Patrick and of how we'd come to know him.

The boy was sixteen years old and as a matter of fact, a rather nice youngster. When we bought our land, he asked us to help him pay his already over-due school-fees. That was in August last year and at that time we promised to help him with the fee.

When we returned to Kenya in December 1996 to take possession of the land, we found Patrick living in one of the bandas on the upper part of the land. He didn't seem to have any intention of moving out. Furthermore he persistently asked for school-fees, as soon as we met, and during our stay in Nairobi he even invited in a lot of friends. He showed them the whole compound and told them he'd become foreman at our place.

A couple of weeks ago, the former landowner's family had arrived on foot. They wanted to celebrate "memorial day" for one of the deceased daughters in the banda Patrick was occupying. Since luhya-traditions are most important in connection with death, funerals and similar occasions, we had to accept that. During a couple of days lots of people lived in that banda; dancing and singing all night long. Daytime everybody walked around as if they owned the compound. And we ourselves felt like intruders.

We had to find a way to solve this problem; make Patrick with family understand their time on the land had come to an end and that it now belonged to us.

We'd just finished our dinner in the sunshine outside the banda when Patrick returned.

"Have a seat, Patrick," Bertil said. "Bibi Gunilla has told me you came to see her earlier today, wanting school-fees. Why?"

"Yes, but… You've promised to pay for my education."

"No, we've never done that and you know that very well. The only thing we've promised was to pay the school-fee for last term and we did that."

"But how will I be able to go to school in that case? I've no money and you're so rich."

"But Patrick," I interposed, "firstly, we're not rich at all. Secondly, you're actually neither our child nor our problem. You've taken care of the school-fees before without our help. How have you been able to do that?"

"Well, I suppose I've worked during my vacations… and I've been saving up. Well, I don't really know." He seemed a little uneasy, hearing my question.

Bertil and I discussed the issue for a while. We felt a bit sorry for the guy. He was clean and neat and eager to study. We should maybe reward something like that. But, in any case, we had to make him understand he couldn't come and expect money from us. Bertil asked Patrick to fetch his school report from last term from his banda, together with documents showing the amount of money he was talking about. Looking relieved, Patrick disappeared and soon returned with the documents we'd asked for. In the meantime, Bertil and I had found a possible solution.

Having studied the papers, Bertil uttered in a serious voice, "We're talking about a lot of money, but I can also see your grades are quite good. As you know, we don't think we can afford to give you all that money, but we've a suggestion," he continued. "Bibi Gunilla will tell you about it."

It was my turn. Now I had the chance to get Patrick off our compound, while helping him at the same time.

"Well Patrick, we can help you but this means you'll also have to help us. If we pay your school-fees and your clothes, you'll have to work here every Saturday and Sunday. Sundays you'll come immediately after church. Your tasks could be anything from fetching water and cutting grass to guarding the gate. You'll have lunch here those days."

Since Patrick looked very happy, I added, "Remember, we're only talking of the fee for this term. If your grades are good and if we are content with you, we'll have further discussions later on."

"By the way, there's something else you should know," Bertil continued. "We need to start planning the upper part of the compound. That means we'll have to tear down the banda you've temporarily been staying in, so you'll have to move. I've heard there's an empty house on the other side of the road. A nice house with a 'mabati' roof (tin roof) the owners want to rent out. We can rent it for you for this term."

The boy seemed displeased. He probably felt he was losing his foothold on our compound. I felt immensely relieved the old banda would be gone. No more invasions by the former owner and his family.

We finished the discussion by telling him he could come down to us, once a week, to get a week's supply of tea, sugar and maize flour. We offered to lend him a small piece of land down in the vegetable garden, where he'd be able to grow some maize and "sukuma wiki" (kale). He'd have to prepare that land and take care of it, when school was over for the day. Finally Bertil affirmed he was willing to help Patrick with physics and chemistry; his worst subjects.

Well, the long and the short of it was, as always, that we were far too generous. Our hearts had won over our brains. But it was anyway a content youngster, who walked off into the now dark night.

## 12. An unforeseen obstacle

Morning dawned with sunshine and bird song. At breakfast, beneath the sunshade, Bertil and I discussed our plans for the day.

"I've to go to the Water Ministry in Kakamega to hurry the men on," said Bertil.

"Do you think we'll ever get water?" I wondered pessimistically.

"Yes, probably, but they're more corrupt than I thought possible, so it'll probably take a long time" Bertil answered. "But we mustn't give in to corruption. Otherwise everybody will only ask us for more and more money."

When Bertil had left for Kakamega, I sat down again with a cup of instant coffee, pondering our problems - because we had problems. The water issue was one of the biggest. We'd been promised there would be water connected to the boundary of our plot upon our arrival. That had, of course, not been the case. The water pipe ended down in Wushiye, one kilometre from our compound.

In order to get water for the household, we had to hire women, who fetched water from the spring. We transported the drinking water in plastic tanks in our car, from a school at a few kilometres distance.

When our Member of Parliament heard we hadn't got the promised water connection, he ordered our chief to immediately solve the problem. We wouldn't need to pay anything for either the work or the connection. Unfortunately, the chief ignored this order, so we'd been forced to pay a lot of money in order to get a ditch dug for the water pipes. Despite being paid, they'd only pretended to work and cheated us with the digging. We had a hard time trying to get the necessary pipes from the Ministry of Water. Now the ditch was almost finished, but suddenly a farmer living alongside the road had thrown a spanner in the works. He claimed we'd have to pay him for the land close to the road, where the ditch was dug. He wouldn't give in, although landowners, according to Kenyan law and its "Road Reserve" must put space, free of charge, at disposal for water pipes. Not even Chief Weaky could make the man listen to reason.

It was strange the villagers didn't understand that the water would be for the entire village, amongst other things via a water tap on the public land. They looked upon this as something private for the "wazungu" (white people) and therefore we should pay for it. We thought the chief ought to explain this to the villagers, but he didn't seem to care.

Bertil wasn't successful with the Ministry of Water but, as if to compensate for that, we, a few days later, got a wonderful surprise. Our telephone was connected.

"Oh, those were probably the most expensive tears I've shed during my entire life!" I said, having wiped my cheeks. "But it doesn't matter; it was wonderful to hear their voices."

I'd just finished a telephone conversation with my parents. A conversation mostly consisting of noise and crackles and some cut-off words with a long delay. And happy sobbing from both ends. But it didn't matter. I'd heard the voices of both my mother and father. And they'd been able to hear mine. Wonderful!

It was really a bright spot - and such a big one - having our telephone. We'd worked so hard to get this phone. In Kenya, corruption was enormous and no telephone company workers worked other than on Sundays, getting double salary that day. Then they turned out, preferably ten men on a job where only one was needed, and asked for bribes. When they didn't get any, they left without working. It had been like this for a long time.

Nothing happened until we threatened to move from Kakamega. Then the alert was sent from our Member of Parliament to the Minister of Communication. He threatened the men responsible at the Telephone Company in Kakamega with losing their jobs, unless something positive happened before a certain date. When that day arrived, the telephone men excused themselves by saying they hadn't had any car and because of that hadn't been able to connect our telephone. The same day the responsible boss was fired. And only a few days later our telephone was connected. And now it had been inaugurated.

Oh, it was so nice to have a telephone. We weren't as isolated as before any longer. Since communications by phone weren't good and furthermore expensive, we'd certainly not make any long phone calls, but once Bertil had installed email and Internet via a modem, we'd be able to communicate often, writing long epistles to our families and friends in Sweden.

We constantly learned new things about life in Kenya. A phenomenon, new to us, was that people started leaving small printed cards at our gate. They wanted us to write our names on them together with an amount and then send them on to other Europeans. Petrus explained that those were "harambee" cards.

The word "harambee" is a genuine typical Kenyan notion, meaning "pull together," "amass" and "let us work together". Kenya's first president, Jomo Kenyatta, started to use the word as a means of uniting the whole of Kenya and all Kenyans in the work of developing the country as a new free nation. He encouraged the villages to collect money for different local projects. The government would, in certain cases, also contribute with a part of it. Harambees are extremely common today for all kinds of projects – big as well as small – now being the official motto of the country, included on the country's coat of arms.

Petrus advised us to try to avoid harambees. We should limit our participation to harambees for our own village school and different projects in our village. It was important to put a natural limit to our involvement, so that we weren't forced to participate in all harambees, they were so popular.

We really had to learn as much as possible about our new country and the village way of life. We noticed that we, being Swedes, actually had a lot of false ideas about the country and even some prejudices. Development since independence in 1963 hadn't been at a standstill at all but was at a different level than in Sweden.

One example: I had to go to the hospital after spending some troublesome days and sleepless nights because of a toe infection. In Sweden, we'd been warned about the low hygiene level of the hospitals and been told to buy disposable syringes. We now brought one of these and asked the hospital staff to use it. They laughed at me. They were already using syringes like that, by order of President Moi. Doctors and staff seemed competent and worked in a quite modern way – not at all in the way described to us, while we were still in Sweden. They gave me antibiotics, ointments and a tetanus vaccination, so I felt better already after a couple of days.

We'd also expected lots of wild animals in our village, but wildlife wasn't very spectacular. We had, however, some cockroaches, which we were getting used to and to which we no longer reacted. We hadn't seen any snakes and Bertil held his tongue about the spiders he encountered. Hippos were living in a river some five kilometres away but no crocodiles. The last leopard was seen in the rainforest some years earlier and there had been no elephants in this part of the country during the last twenty years.

On the other hand, the number of birds on the compound seemed to be increasing all the time. It would be thrilling to use our bird books and binoculars, once the container had arrived. Daytime some big falcon-like birds were circled high up in the sky and night-time frogs were croaking in competition with the cicadas. In the early mornings, they silenced and were followed by peaceful bird song, after a while crescending into a full symphony. When the bird song had died away, it was time to leave bed, since the sun by that time was on its way over the hill on the other side of the valley.

One evening, our chief came down to the compound, carrying a bag making clinking sounds in his hand. We greeted him respectfully the way we'd been taught. With my left hand I gripped my right forearm while shaking his hand. This is a sign of respect.

The chief offered us lukewarm beer. Sitting outdoors with lighted kerosene lamps, we had a rather friendly talk. We told him about our plans for Riverdale College, a computer centre with dormitories, classrooms and teachers from Sweden. As the distance to the nearest electricity pole was only about 600 metres, we expected to be able to get electricity, so important for that project.

Our chief suggested we start by building a small hotel for all the visitors to the rain forest. We could later add the school buildings we wanted. In that way, we'd get an income quicker. The idea wasn't bad at all.

The atmosphere became much chillier when we brought up the question of the water pipes. Now the chief didn't even try to be nice. He just didn't want to discuss the issue. After a few moments of strained silence, he suggested we give him 5,000 shillings. Favours offered and favours returned… When we abstained from agreeing to his suggestion and instead explained our negative feelings about Kenyan corruption, he understood he'd made a fool of himself. After a chilly goodbye, he got to his feet, disappearing into the darkness, uphill towards the gate.

Bertil and I looked amazed at one another. We'd never have believed any person, in such a direct way, would dare to demand a bribe without shame.

Suddenly the phone in the banda rang and I hurried to answer. It was David, our youngest son, telling us he'd be visiting us within a week. He was curious to see how we were getting on and was missing both of us. Tears of joy ran down my cheeks. It would be so wonderful to see David.

## 13. A wonderful visit

In the afternoon, Bertil and I picked up David at the Akamba bus station in Kakamega. In the evening, David and I sat talking by the light of kerosene lamps outside the banda. Bertil was in the upper part of the compound, giving the night askaris instructions. David looked pale and tired after the trip from Sweden. He'd probably sleep well, although he'd have to be squeezed into the small bed we'd made up in our diminutive kitchen. However, he'd probably not wake up, even if both spiders and cockroaches fell down into the bed.

It was wonderful to have him here. He was the first family member to visit us. My heart was beating at the double from sheer joy. We'd finally be able to share our dreams and ideas. At last, we had a ball plank. You get so blind, when you plan in solitude without influences from the outside. David was studying architecture and that was perfect for our plans. But above all he was our son. A son who needed relaxation, warmth and love and we'd try to give him a lot of that during the short time he'd be staying with us.

"It's so beautiful with all those fireflies," he said after a moment in meditative silence. "And the glow-worms, they look like a thousand small twinkling Christmas candles."

"Yes, it's beautiful" I said. "But don't you see something in the sky that's different from Sweden?"

"Yes," he answered. "I've never seen such a starry sky before. I can see billions and billions of stars. As a matter of fact, I don't recognise some constellations."

Bertil came to join us. He had a burning interest in astronomy and declared, "As soon as the container arrives, we'll get my telescopes out. Then you'll be able to study both the stars and the planets. But, haven't you noticed the way the moon looks?"

David looked once more up towards the moon and started to laugh. "It's lying down. Very strange. But we're almost on the Southern Hemisphere, aren't we? So maybe it's not that strange."

"Yes," Bertil answered, "we actually live only twenty-two kilometres north of the Equator. It crosses the road on this side of Kisumu. If we go to Kisumu while you're here, you'll have to step out of the car and stand on the Equator."

After a while David asked, "When's the container coming?"

Bertil told him about our container trouble: The container had been stuck down in Mombasa for a long time. It had recently arrived in Nairobi, but there it had got stuck with the Kenyan forwarding agent, since they hadn't yet been paid by the Swedish one. The crane that would lift the container off the lorry down onto the ground - without emptying the container first - was the only one of its kind and was on a mission in Uganda. Since we needed somewhere to put the container contents, while the empty container was lifted off the lorry, we'd been forced to quickly build a long building for staff apartments and storerooms.

"Don't worry about the hard work with the container. If it arrives while I'm here, there'll be no problems. I'm strong," David pointed out self-confidently.

We told David about the long caravans of village women, walking from the spring to our compound, carrying water for our building on their heads. The women had also carried mud and cow dung and mixed it all into a sticky sludge, which had been used instead of cement on the walls.

The row of staff apartments, with a mabati roof, had now been finished on the upper part of the compound. It had four small apartments with two spacious rooms in each, separated by a wall almost two metres high. The entrance doors were made of eucalyptus and nicely carved. The furniture in the small apartments would be simple: a bed, a chair and a table. We'd planned that most of our staff would come from our own village, thus being able to live in their own homes. One of the apartments would, daytime, be used as a staff room. Alongside the row, we'd erected another small building with toilet and washroom for the staff.

While the frogs were croaking in the stream at the valley bottom, we discussed our plans for the next few days. David's relationship with the dogs had started as soon as he arrived, when he brought out some liver paste from Sweden for them. Very popular. The consequence was that both the dogs were almost sitting on his lap. Little Merry, still having her puppy teeth, had dedicated several hours to sucking and biting his fingers, so they were now in rather bad shape.

When David finally fell asleep in the middle of a sentence, it was time for all of us to go to bed. Whether it was eight o'clock in the evening or midnight didn't matter to us. Nowadays we didn't need watches.

The following morning we woke with a jolt, hearing, "Breakfast is ready, sleepy heads. Out of bed. We've a lot to do."

David's voice was heard all too well through the small window gap. I almost flew out of bed and of course managed to get both Bertil and myself entangled in the mosquito net. Rufus and Merry howled with joy. The liver paste guy was awake. It was almost as if a bomb had hit our African banda. Oh, my God, what energy. I moved drowsily towards the door in the absolute darkness.

Outside the banda, breakfast had already been set in the shade. The sun was on its way up above the trees and the birds were joining in a jubilant choir. Tender morning hugs were exchanged and with coffee and a sandwich under our safari vests, Bertil and I soon regained energy.

Breakfast finished, we discussed our building plans with David. He made notes, asked questions and made suggestions. Everything in the spirit of a true architect. We looked forward to the evening when he'd present his suggestions.

We spent the rest of the forenoon in the cool rainforest, where Ben, one of our guide friends, led us along a trail, while telling us about the forest birds, plants, snakes and monkeys. The medicinal use of trees and bushes was what fascinated me most. Both Bertil and I had already been lots of times in the forest and heard all the stories, but they were just as interesting as before.

Before dinner, David retired for a while with his sketching block. Within half-an-hour, he was ready to show us his suggestions. We moved around the compound, carrying a number of sharp sticks and a ball of string. We marked the sites as he went on explaining,.

"Here," David showed us, "is where you should put your main building. Up here, above the fence with bougainvillea, here's where it should be. In this way, you'll get a splendid view over the valley from the veranda. Down there, where you yourselves planned to build it, you'd actually only be looking into the opposite valley slope."

He explained his sketches, while we were strolling around. The solution seemed superb.

"If you like my ideas, then I'd like to talk to the carpenter and give him instructions."

When David had marked out the main building, the first three guest huts and a separate building with two showers and two wc's, we started to get a picture of the future rain-forest hotel - Riverdale Gardens - before our eyes. We also marked off an area for the container and took into account probable classrooms and dormitories for the IT-college we dreamt of starting. We felt content and suddenly it didn't feel frustrating any longer to start building.

## 14. The container arrives

A few days later, David had reason to repent his spontaneous remark that unloading and loading the container would be so easy. He almost fell down into one of the chairs beneath the shade, where Bertil and I were already relaxing, saying, "What a day. I'm exhausted."

At the gate, the last of the hired day workers were leaving, carrying a soft drink each and salary for a full day's work. I fetched a lukewarm beer for each of us. The refrigerator was so small it only had space for food and we, as a consequence, usually had to drink the beer tepid.

We could see a light blue monster on the upper part of the compound. Our shipping container. It had arrived the same day. Finally. It would be wonderful to get more clothes, a fax machine, photos, medicines and everything else we'd been missing. Once the first guest hut was finished, we'd move into it with our comfortable beds, furniture and knick-knacks from Sweden. I trembled with satisfaction. Everything we owned had now arrived. Among it were also lots of things for the poor villagers, since we'd asked our community in Sweden to give us all children clothes they were no longer using. We'd used these for wrapping our belongings instead of using paper. This way the container had been packed almost to the point of bursting.

Having pictures on the walls and beautiful things around us would certainly feel very luxurious, but it would probably take a long time before we'd found the things we were most eagerly searching for. Not until now, after a day with caravans of men carrying boxes and furniture for hours, did we realize what tough work we had ahead sorting our belongings out. To avoid thinking about that now, we talked instead happily about the day's events.

These had begun in the early forenoon, when the container lorry had come into the compound, followed by all the villagers. We were lucky the rains were delayed because otherwise the big lorry would probably have slid off the narrow village road down into the tea plantation.

The curious villagers were, in a friendly way, pushed out through the gate but they immediately formed triple lines on the other side of the fence we'd now built on the upper part of the compound.

Bertil quickly organised the unloading of more than three hundred boxes and quite a lot of furniture. The whole container had to be emptied, before it could be lifted off the lorry and a big part of the boxes and furniture must be carried into two of the staff apartments. We'd already hired a number of men, who were ready to start carrying.

I stood in a position everybody must pass on their way to the building, ticking off the box and package numbers on the packing list. It was important to check everything was there. At the same time, I had to check how the men were handling the packages, since there were many breakables. Bertil was standing at the container, directing the men, and David was inside the apartment, pointing out where the things should be put.

After several hours of toil and moil and some breaks to quench thirst, the container was empty. The lorry men wanted to leave with the container still on it.

"No," Bertil objected. "The container in fact belongs to us and should be lifted off the lorry."

In the end, he was forced to get out our documents in order to prove we'd bought the container in Sweden. The lorry driver looked very disappointed and tried to persuade us to sell the container to him, but we refused.

Now the almost impossible work began, to try to get the container down onto the ground in the right spot on top of the wooden frame built by Daniel, our carpenter. We tried to use iron-bar levers, jacks and the Land Rover to heave, drag and lift but it was difficult to make it move. When we put ropes and chains around our biggest eucalyptus tree, the lorry finally succeeded in dragging down the container. After a lot of work and manipulating, it was at last in the right spot.

After that the men started carrying boxes and furniture once again. All the fragile or valuable things had to be back in the burglar-proof container before sunset.

A couple of hours later, we could at last say the day's work was done. We told the hired day-workers we thought they'd done such a great job during the day that they'd be paid in double. They were elated.

So here we were now, relaxing outside our African hut, with a tepid and well-earned beer in our hands.

## 15. The gold mining village

We spent a couple of days poking around and rummaging in the container. Bertil and David found the garden lights and installed them around our banda. It looked unbelievably cosy during the pitch-dark evenings. Ours was the only electric light in our small valley, so our neighbours on the other side of the valley were probably also enjoying it.

"Let's make a full-day excursion, with packed lunch, tomorrow to Sotanini to do some gold-panning," I suggested one afternoon. "Now it's time for some relaxation."

After dinner, David and Bertil hurried up to the container to collect the gold panning equipment we'd need the following day. Then we sat down outdoors with a cup of tea to tell David the story about Sotanini, a small village, which already meant a lot to us. We escaped to that village to relax, when life in our own was too tough.

Bertil and I took turns in talking, because we had so much to tell.

“When we, in May 1996, returned to Kenya and Kakamega District in search of gold panning villages, we found ourselves one day on a small road that seemed to end outside a school. It was time for break at the school and we saw the Swedish colours everywhere. It was the school uniform that was blue and yellow and in exactly the right tones. When we asked for road directions, a teacher directed us onto the village we knew should be relatively close. He seemed very sympathetic and asked us to stop at the school on our way back.

A narrow almost path-like road, which we hadn't earlier noticed, led us via a slanting stony ridge past the school. Branches and leaves swished against the sides of the Volkswagen van and we had great difficulty in advancing. On one occasion, I had to step out of the car to remove a goat grazing in the middle of the road. We advanced slowly and soon had a bunch of happy children running behind the vehicle. They were laughing and smiling. And not even a single one of them shouted, "Give me money." They were only curious and probably not accustomed to seeing white people. It actually felt like our car was the first one that had ever been driven on that road.

Having advanced for a while at snail's pace, admiring the beautiful mountains and the winding river Yala down in the valley, we arrived at some bandas. We parked the car, picked up our blue plastic pans and started walking towards a crowd of people, working with something. We heard a lot of laughter and chatter and wondered what was going on.

Making our way with difficulty between some beautiful deep purple bougainvillea plants, we arrived suddenly at an open air-mine. A crowd of men and women were working there. The men chopped and dug and the women filled baskets with broken-up stones and gravel. They lifted the baskets onto their heads and with majestic posture they disappeared in a long row down towards the river.

One of the men came up to us and said in a friendly voice, while extending his hand for a greeting, "Merembe - my name is Paul."

We answered as we'd been taught, "Merembe mono." Then we explained to Paul that we were looking for a place where we could pan for gold together with the villagers. Paul's English wasn't good and after a short while he shouted to a man, working a little further off, "Kuja hapa!" (Come here!) This man told us in good English his name was Glenn.

Glenn got very excited and declared we'd come to the right village. Here in Sotanini, all the villagers lived on gold prospecting. They'd be most happy, if they could pan for gold together with us, the mzungu.

First of all, however, he wanted to show us the village and how the villagers worked with gold prospecting. He bent down among the rocks and quickly picked up a couple of stones. We examined them carefully and there was certainly gold: yellow dots here and there on both the stones. Glenn showed us a place in the open cut, where they'd recently found a vein containing gold. During our walk, he told us that in the 1930's an English goldmine was still active on the hill beside the school. It was exploited to the extent the mining company even built a small railroad on the hill. He told us the gold in the Sotanini village was discovered at the end of the 1980's, when a man ploughing his field found something yellow in the ground.

After a while, we walked down through the village in the direction of Yala River. At every small banda mothers, grandfathers or grandmothers and children were chopping and grinding stones. Since some bandas only had very little land around them, the family members had to sit on the graves that had been dug close to the banda. Everybody was working hard, while the queue of women was winding down towards the river. They'd now left their cargoes of stones at the bandas and replaced them with baskets full of gravel and stone powder.

We continued slowly down the steep path together with Glenn and Paul. Since it would be easy to slip and slide down the slope, we had to be careful. When we finally, with tired legs, arrived at the riverbank, a fantastic scene welcomed us.

These green and leafy surroundings were crowded. Some villagers were working on the shore, pouring gold dust into rustic sluice boxes but most of them, mostly women and children, were dancing in the river. Yes, it looked like a dance. When one sluice box had been emptied, the contents were poured, together with the linen cloth, which had been on the bottom of the sluice, into a "karaja" (panning basin). The karaja was put on the river bottom and a woman or a child stepped into it and started treading and dancing in it. By this procedure, any possible gold would separate from the sand and the cloth and sink to the bottom of the basin.

It was unbelievably idyllic - or at least, it looked so. We quickly adjusted to the situation. We borrowed some gold dust from a family and started working with our sluice box. People gathered around us and watched us with amazement. The working principle for our sluice box was the same as for theirs, but ours was green and made of plastic. After some time, we emptied the sluice box and started the final wash in a blue pan. The commotion was great and many hands stretched forward in order to correct us. They didn't think we worked in the right way. But, to the enjoyment of the villagers, we got some gold grains, which we returned to the family lending us the dust.

Our equipment was soon passed along among the people. Everybody wanted to test it. The atmosphere was wonderful and we enjoyed life and the fantastically hospitable people around us.

After a couple of hours, we unfortunately had to leave in order to return to civilisation. When passing the "Swedish" school, we stopped, leaving the car. We found the school's headmaster in a small poky hole. We told him about our astonishment on seeing the Swedish colours on the pupils' school uniforms. He told us the school was very poor. Amongst other things they had only two classrooms. The rest of the pupils had to do their lessons outside beneath a tree; that was quite alright during the dry season but not during the rainy seasons.

The school's results in the annual national tests were among the worst in Kenya. According to the headmaster, that was due to the fact they didn't have any schoolbooks. During the lessons, the teacher wrote down the contents of a schoolbook on the blackboard and the pupils then had to copy it into their notebooks. The teachers had no time for revising or explaining what the pupils were copying.

Neither did they have any water connection to the school. Another big problem was that many of the children in this area couldn't go to school, as they didn't have any money for the obligatory school uniform.

After a long talk with the nice headmaster, we had to say farewell but we promised, without any guarantees, to try to find some money in Sweden for this needy school.

When returning to Sweden after that trip to Kenya, we discussed the needs of the Sotanini School with some friends. One of them, working in a fashion shop, suggested they'd organize a fundraising. They were willing to donate the entire amount the store brought in from sewing work done for their clients, to our Kenyan school. We were of course extremely happy about this and when, later on, the result of the fundraising was known, we were overwhelmed: An equivalent to 80,000 Kenya shilling.

We immediately wrote a letter to the school, asking for a list of the schoolbooks most needed. We received the list and, when returning to Kenya in August 1996, we brought the required books, filling many boxes. The day we handed over all the books was a day of joy for the whole area.

To our delight, this was the start of a parent commitment without comparison. Whole families volunteered to build classrooms and desks and organized harambees to get money for a water connection. A parents association was formed which, together with the teachers, led all the work. The best present for all of us was that the school, six months later, was number three in the district in the annual test results.

As a result of all this, we'd become welcome and wanted guests both in the school and the gold mining village."

Now the time had come to introduce David to our friends in Sotanini, at the same time getting a day of relaxation. The weather was beautiful and our packed lunch was already in our rucksacks. The car was loaded with our equipment: pans, sluice box, pump, gold spear, dredge and some small glass flasks for the gold. Bertil looked like an old gold digger from Sofala in Australia in his Australian hat on his curly hair. Our spirits were high driving our creaking old Land Rover towards a day full of thrilling adventure. What if we found a stone with a lot of gold in it?

Outside the Sotanini School, a boy ran up to us and told us the headmaster wanted to talk to us. We got an overwhelming reception. The headmaster informed us he had just planned to send us a messenger with an invitation to a school party. They wanted to organize a real thank-you party for us. We accepted the invitation at once and promised to come all three of us.

Arriving at the village, our friends welcomed us. They had brought a lot of small children who were almost fighting for the privilege of carrying our heavy equipment. Before going down the slope to the river, where we intended to spend the day, we asked Glenn to give David a guided tour. As usual it went via the open-air mine, where the workers once again wanted to test our gold spear. I immediately sank down on the ground checking gravel and stones with a magnifying glass in search of golden specks. With his easy-going manner, David quickly became very popular. He hugged both grown-ups and children and was allowed to crush gravel into dust between two stones. Down at the river, with its colourful life, he soon became a willing pupil to some girls dancing in a karaja out in the water.

Would David, too, be infected with gold fever? I laughed covertly at the thought.

We walked up to some rocks at the river brink to test our pump. There we soon found a couple of water-filled pockets among the cliffs, in the vicinity of a river curve. They looked like what we in Sweden call giant's kettles.

"We'll use the pump here," said Bertil. "There should be gold in these kettles. The location is absolutely right. During the rainy season, when the water level is high, gold has undoubtedly been stored here.

You can see the river curve over there. This is exactly the right spot."

Said and done. The pump soaked up fine-grained sand as well as a lot of black sand. Bertil poured this into a pan, starting the final wash. After a moment, we sure enough saw a yellow shimmer, turning into a yellow string. No big nuggets but still gold. Bertil called Glenn, showed him the result and explained they ought to look for similar places, especially following river curves.

We continued with all our packing to a shallow river part a little further down, where we wanted to test our dredge. Some men were already working there and one of them, an elderly man, was diving in the middle of the river to fetch sand from the bottom. We showed him our equipment and decided to work together.

Bertil took a break and waded over to me, where I was sitting panning on the river shore with a crowd of admirers behind my back.

Suddenly he pointed to the river edge and exclaimed, "But there it is."

He bent down to pick up a white stone of quartz and held it out to me. Yes, you could clearly see a lot of specks of gold. Sun reflecting on the spots had made it possible for Bertil to see the stone at rather a long distance.

After many hours panning, it was time to struggle back up the steep slope. It was nice to have friends, willing to carry our packing.

A few days later, we dressed in the best clothes we could find. Since we hadn't yet been able to locate all our clothes in the container, our wardrobe was still limited. Then we took off to the party in Sotanini Primary School. It seemed as if the whole village had come to greet us upon our arrival at the school. A hectic handshaking started. Everyone was festively dressed and the children were adorable - the girls in tiny swinging skirts and the boys in clean shorts and ironed shirts. David immediately got an admiring crowd of giggling small girls around him and he seemed really touched by how sweet they were.

I felt a bit awkward sitting on the seats of honour on the tribune, built for the festivities of the day, but I was, all the same, thankful for the shade it gave us. It was so hot.

After an introductory speech held by the headmaster, a fantastic dance show was performed by the girls, dressed in African skirts and white T-shirts. The dances and songs illustrated different local tales. After the show, we were invited to lunch in the newly built teachers' room. A very tasty meal. The headmaster told us that more or less all the parents had contributed with food and labour in connection with the party as well as when the additional classrooms and benches were constructed. When they'd thanked us for our contribution, I gave a short speech with greetings from the Swedish shop collecting the money and handed over a folder from the shop's staff with photos and texts, which was greatly appreciated.

Before leaving the school after a wonderful afternoon, we asked the headmaster to select five orphans, who couldn't afford to go to school. We promised to pay school fees and school uniforms for them. We also took the opportunity to hand over a number of sketch blocks to be passed around in the classrooms. Every pupil was to sketch something of her or his own choice. When the sketch blocks were returned to us, we'd look at all the drawings and choose a few of them. The pupils who did the best ones would be given sketching material, so that they could make more. The suggestion was met with exultation.

## 16. The Chief's election

"Finally home. It's incredible how thirsty you get just by a simple shopping trip to Kakamega," said Bertil the following day, driving through the gate.

David looked as if he'd just had a bath.

"An ice-cold beer would have been nice now."

"Welcome," Johannes greeted us in his bad English, with a big smile all over his face.

"Thank you," I answered and then asked him, "What have you been doing, while we've been in town?"

"I've been cleaning and washing up."

In body language, he showed me what he'd been doing. Betty had a day off, so Johannes had had to do some of her chores. It was actually clean and in order around the banda. At the sink, all the plates from the previous day had been put to dry - including our old well-used frying pan, made of cast-iron.

"Johannes, did you wash the frying pan?" I asked with concern.

"Yes, it was dirty, completely black."

He pointed at the big, newly bought, steel-wool packet, which was now completely empty. Then he showed us the old cast-iron frying pan, which used to belong to Bertil´s grandfather. Now, you could almost use it as a mirror. He must have put an awful lot of energy into making it shine like that. It was probably as clean as when it was bought at the beginning of the 20th century.

His intentions had been so good and he really had tried his very best in order to please us. We couldn't rebuke him, so instead we told him it looked nice. Then we carefully explained the pan should be black, otherwise the meat would stick, when fried. We kindly asked him not to wash the pan in the future.

We realized we sometimes took too much for granted. Not many people in Kenya had a frying pan made of cast-iron, so people in general didn't know how to handle it. We felt crestfallen but we had no other alternative but to start all over again, using it the right way. It would probably only take ten-, twenty years to get it back into order.

Later that week, a couple of Timothy´s friends visited us. They told us his father had been the chief of Khasili for many years. Nowadays, the village had no chief and the people, who thought Timothy was a good and wise man, wanted him as their chief. There had been a harambee, resulting in an extremely large sum but still a lot of money was lacking, before Timothy could have a real chief's party with all the pomp and circumstance that should be included. We finished the discussion saying we'd pay for half an ox for the party and lend Timothy money for the other half of the animal.

The day of the chief election arrived. We'd been invited all three of us but David, having an upset stomach, decided to stay at home

The festivities started with a formal gathering close to the chief's future office. Festively dressed people, many of them prominent, convened sitting down under a shade made of parachutes. Timothy was nowhere to be seen. He was kept hidden until the very last moment in order to avoid that another man, who also wanted to be elected as chief, killed him at the last minute. The person telling us this looked as if such a threat was a quite normal thing. We were actually quite upset and got an ugly premonition of future violence. While in Sweden, we'd never ever imagined violence was so common in rural parts of Kenya, and now we were suddenly close to it.

At long last, Timothy appeared in a car and solemn speeches were held, alternating with singing. After this ceremony, the guests scattered since we were to meet again at Timothy´s home for continued festivities. Timothy was carried on the shoulders of Jim, our head askari, for ten whole kilometres all the way to his home. Along the road, more and more people joined the entourage singing, dancing and playing instruments. Extra stops were made at each marketplace and everybody celebrated Timothy. It was a fantastic sight to see how popular he was.

Arriving at Timothy´s home, the exultant entourage was met by the guests having already arrived. We were, in total, two thousand guests invited to the party. Timothy and his wife were seated beneath a canopy and the people's celebration started. Speeches were made and presents handed over. Little by little Timothy was dressed in traditional chief's clothes. Finally he sat, like a chief out of a fairy tale, dressed in leopard skin and a cap made of monkey hides.

The Oscar Gala is a pale thing compared to this function. Everyone was invited to food and drinks. In a special room inside Timothy´s mother's house, all the area chiefs were eating and drinking. It almost seemed to be a competition, when you saw how much they were gulping down - beer as well as liquor. Timothy was a teetotaller but he was obliged to serve everything the rest of the bigwigs might want to drink.

One of David's last mornings with us, he disappeared together with Johannes down to the stream at the lower end of our compound. After a while they suddenly appeared again, carrying a half-full bucket of gravel, sand and clay. The sluice box was put up and buckets of water were fetched. Half a bucket of gravel was poured through the sluice box. Then what was left in the box went through the final wash in the pan. The result was five passable gold grains. And they'd been found less than half a metre from the stream, at a depth of one metre. On our own compound. Even a little gold is still gold. So David now knew that if Bertil and I would depart this life while in Kenya, he and Christian could look for their inheritance by crushing the cement pillars of the future restaurant building. They probably contained gold.

## 17. Back to work

When David had returned to Sweden, we once more had to dedicate ourselves to the long things-to-do list.

Irrigation of the vegetable beds was very important and after a lot of hard work Bertil succeeded in making the new electric pump function. We could now pump water from the stream up the thirty-five metre long slope - approximately twenty metres vertically - to the vegetables, in one step. Consequently we didn't have to sit waiting for the rainy season, which actually seemed to have dried up before even starting.

Bertil daily spent several hours trying to organize our belongings in the container. He was, at the same time, preparing a nice office area in it with telephone, fax and electricity. I could no longer find any excuses for postponing the important paper work we had to do. I had to calculate the capital gain for the sale of our house in Sweden as well as prepare documentation for the Swedish income tax returns. My problem was that it was so unbearably hot in the container. Maybe the tax authorities could grant me tax deductions as compensation for suffering during income tax work? There were probably not many Swedes filling in the forms at a heat of 47 degrees.

In the middle of all this urgent paper work, we had to fire Betty. The reason being that she, on several occasions, had been light-fingered with a difficulty in telling the difference between her things and ours and we'd had enough of it. As a result I had to take care of the household for a while.

One Wednesday morning we went down to Wulushi to buy meat. I had found the food processor in the container and was planning to make minced meat, filling the freezing compartment with it. I missed spaghetti bolognaise so much. So, as said, we went down to the village and bought two kilos of meat in a butcher's shop.

Back at home, I started the generator to get electricity and started mincing meat. Suddenly I noticed a revolting stench. At first, I didn't understand where it came from, then I realised it was coming from the meat. The meat was rotten. All the putrid meat was hidden beneath the nice top layer. I almost exploded with rage. I threw all the meat, minced and not minced, back into the bag and Bertil drove me quickly back to the marketplace, where we met a man and a woman standing talking on a corner. When they'd greeted us, asking why we looked so angry, I explained we'd been cheated with the meat.

"It's so good we've met," the woman said. "I'm the shop inspector for the marketplace. This is Nelson, the village nurse, and he can call in the public health authorities, if necessary."

"Yes," Nelson said, "but I suggest we first talk to the shop owner. We can probably scare him out of his wits without having to drag the authorities all the way out here."

Said and done. We walked up to the shop where both of them gave the owner a severe reprimand. They told him that next time something like this happened - hiding yesterday's meat under meat from today - the shop would be closed for good. We put our bag with stinking meat on the counter and demanded to have it weighed properly and to receive the same weight of fresh meat. The shop owner didn't dare to do anything but obey.

Before we parted, the couple advised us always to check, when buying meat, if someone in the shop was waving a cow's tail to scare away flies. That would reveal if the meat was old.

At six o'clock in the afternoon on March 27th, we had the first pouring rain. I was busy in the kitchen garden, taking care of our tomato plants. The workers were having a soft drink at the building site of our first guest-hut to celebrate they'd just finished the foundation. That work had been going on for ten days instead of one, as promised. Suddenly we heard a roar approaching, together with a cold wind. The shamba boys came running; making signs we should put tarpaulins on the tomatoes. At the same time, the construction workers were running like scared hens, trying to cover the hut foundations. When we were done, I ran as fast as I could to seek shelter in the banda. Then it was as if a blind had been pulled down. Thunder and rain in abundance. It only rained for a quarter of an hour but during those minutes we got 150 millimetres. The hailstones were the size of a golf ball. Our fax machine so important for correspondence with our parents was destroyed by lightning. The pawpaw tree outside the banda was in trouble as the hailstones perforated some of its leaves while others fell to the ground. The eucalyptus up at the "pool" was partly blown down. And the foundations, finished a moment earlier, were of course destroyed.

Standing in the doorway of the banda, I saw how part of the slope came flowing down towards me. Water and mud in steady streams. Bertil dashed off with a spade and started to dig water ditches in order to divert the mass of mud, which otherwise could go over the threshold into the banda. We foresaw a dirty future. How would we, two persons and two dogs, be able to live on our few square metres without being constantly covered with dirt? Our gumboots were indescribable with their extra soles of mud - about ten centimetres thick. Not to speak of what our dogs looked like.

One evening around nine o'clock, we had an invasion of winged ants both outdoors and indoors. Our garden lamps probably attracted them. It was most unpleasant to have all these thousands of obtrusive insects flying around everywhere.

On the horizon, we saw lightning. We'd certainly have a storm also the coming night. Outdoors the vegetation was sprouting. The rain had turned the grass into the lime-green colour of Swedish trees during the leafing period. The dogs were sleeping and the night askari was walking around with his torch.

In the morning, we saw something looking like a white cover, on the ground. The cover was extra thick on our garden lights as well as around them. When looking closer, we noticed it looked like wings.

Later that day, on our way home from Kakamega, we saw a strange sight. Kenyans are walking people. Everywhere you see people walking in long lines along the roads. Maybe they are tired of waiting for the overloaded matatus, which anyhow nearly always break down. It was the same this day too.

Suddenly a man, with briefcase, suit and white shirt, threw himself onto the ground. Then other people started doing the same. What was happening? An air raid? No, after a while I noticed people were actually picking something off the ground with both hands and putting it in their mouths. Other people came running with small tins and buckets and started picking and picking. Everybody looked happy.

What was happening? Well, the termites were swarming. They were known as a protein-rich delicacy and everyone loved them, catching as many as possible.

Now I understood we probably had had swarming termites outside our banda the previous evening and that the wings had fallen off the termites.

We really had a lot to do. When not working physically, we instead had to plan and supervise what others were doing for us. I felt I had no time for household work and, as a result, we employed Milly. She seemed exceptionally competent, was about 35 years old and had four children her mother took care of during the weekdays. We hoped she'd be better than Betty.

When Bertil suddenly got sore toes, like I'd had earlier, Milly checked his foot. She at once knew what had happened and told us it had been infected by a kind of sand flea, a "jiga", which had entered at the nails, building a small nest there, in which it had laid its larvae. The nest had to be removed immediately. I gave Bertil a large whisky, before Milly started sticking into him with her sharp needle but despite that he was grimacing. After this small "operation", we got stern instructions never to walk barefoot in the banda and to come to her as soon as our feet started itching.

## 18. Fiftieth Birthday

"For he's a jolly good fellow, for he's a jolly good fellow..."

Bertil´s and my jarring voices forced their way into the small banda, awakening the hero of the day, my brother Per Erik. He celebrated his fiftieth birthday today and had escaped from possible celebrations in Sweden to be with us in Africa.

Outside the banda, we'd prepared a champagne breakfast for him. The dogs started the kissing party, throwing themselves at him. In honour of the day the weather was nice, so far. Our bronze sunbird was fearlessly sitting in the pawpaw tree, sucking nectar and at intervals burst into jubilant bird song. We had cakes with the champagne. We'd found them in an Indian shop in Kakamega. Oh, the taste was horrible. Without hesitation, they were passed on to the dogs, which devoured them in a flash.

My brother had now spent a little more than a week with us and had already filmed a lot in the neighbourhood. Our parents still didn't know what our home looked like, so Per Erik was making a video to show our relatives at home. I hoped they wouldn't be too shocked.

Per Erik would also be making a TV film about gold prospecting in Kenya. For that purpose we'd decided to go to the Sotanini village, where he could film small-scale local gold mining. On our way there, we told him the story of how we'd found the village and about the school uniform in the Swedish colours. Per Erik was fascinated.

After a lot of jolting and slipping on muddy local roads, we finally arrived and were met by our friend Glenn. He and Per Erik quickly became friendly and the video camera was running hot when the open-air mine and the miners were being filmed. Some short interviews were made before we could leave for the river with a stop on our way at a place where some families were grinding gold ore.

Down at the river Yala, Per Erik, exactly like David, became completely speechless, when he saw the drama. He filmed the beautiful girls dancing in their karajas in the river, and then he suddenly discovered what was going on a bit further away under the trees. Some boys, around twelve years old, were burning mercury in a pan. Mercury steam was rising right into their noses, but being bent over their pans they didn't seem to care. They were trying to purify the gold dust in the pans, using mercury.

I got quite upset when I saw this dangerous process and also Per Erik and Bertil looked quite horrified.

"Don't they understand how dangerous that is?" I asked excitedly. "Their life could be in danger."

We pulled Glenn away from the people and asked him if he understood the danger of using mercury.

"Yes, of course I do, nowadays," he answered. "I've actually persuaded several of the old men in the village to stop. I, myself, don't use it any longer. But you know what it's like with youngsters, they don't listen to the grown-ups."

Per Erik filmed the mercury boys but was careful not to stand in the way of the fumes. Then he started filming Glenn, while interviewing him.

"Where do they buy the mercury?" he asked.

"Well, it varies," Glenn answered. "Sometimes the gold buyers sell it, when they're here to collect gold. Sometimes you can buy it in the kiosk."

"The kiosk? Do you mean special kiosks?"

"No, the normal village kiosk where you buy milk and bread and stuff like that."

"Is the mercury packed in any special way?" my brother asked.

"No, not at all, you buy it by weight just as you buy your milk," Glenn answered.

I felt completely nauseated. Imagine, they bought mercury together with unpackaged milk. I felt like screaming. Didn't they understand what they were doing?

After a short while, one of the boys asked if we wanted to purify our gold with mercury. Bertil, being the calmest of us, turned down the offer in a firm but friendly way. Then he sat down with some of the boys and started to explain how dangerous it was. He described the symptoms of mercury poisoning and said it wasn't only the question of the boys. He informed them the mercury got spread in the water and that fish could eat it; that a lot of innocent people and animals, in fact the whole of nature, in this way were affected by what the boys were doing. A couple of the boys looked rather shocked and declared they'd stop using mercury. They claimed they hadn't understood it was so dangerous.

Next day, Per Erik looked through the video sequences from Sotanini. Seeing that he needed more material, he asked if he could film Bertil and me gold panning. We took some of our things and went down to the river Yala.

Having found a small tributary in a beautiful surrounding, we prepared the equipment and started digging sand out of the river. We poured that into the sluice box. The sun was shining and life was wonderful.

Suddenly I felt something touching my back. We'd been surrounded by a herd of cows on their way to drink water. Crouching down over the sluice box with all the cows around us, we felt rather diminutive. However, they disappeared after a while and then, within a few minutes, we began to see the laughing faces of children behind the rocks.

Eventually a girl plucked up courage and came up to us. She told us no gold could be found at our present location. We had to move further down, to the true River Yala, she explained. The children pointed to a path on the other side of the river. About one kilometre further away, we distinguished the gold panning site. We saw a lot of men digging in the distance and decided to go directly to that place on another day to test our equipment. We made a mental note of the name of the village, which was Nianini. It was close to our home and would probably become one of our most popular excursion destinations.

As we had a guest, we decided to combine business with pleasure. So far, we'd mostly been occupied with necessary tasks, but now we had a legitimate reason to amuse ourselves.

One day, we went to the second highest mountain in Kenya, Mount Elgon, on the border to Uganda. Together with a warden, we drove around the national park, looking for wild animals, but the wildest we encountered was a herd of buffalos taking flight when we arrived.

Another excursion was made to Eldoret. What we thought would be a half-day tour once again took a full day. We brought Petrus, the gardener, since the purpose of this excursion was to buy plants for the garden. He'd earlier worked in Eldoret and knew the owner of the plant shop, so he'd promised to get us good prices.

Oh, what plants. I almost went crazy seeing so many beautiful plants. Thank heavens; we had a big Land Rover which we could load with lots of bushes and trees. It would certainly be thrilling to see all those plants on our compound.

Apart from plants and manure - a quarter of a ton of the latter had been fetched from a man in a neighbouring village - we also needed water. We hadn't yet seen any signs of work with the water ditch, despite the fact many weeks had passed since our Member of Parliament ordered our chief to start the digging immediately. We'd informed him nothing had happened, so maybe the chief would be fired. In that case it would be just as well. He seemed incapable of doing anything right.

As a matter of fact, a large part of the villagers didn't like our chief either. Everybody talked about his corrupt way of handling the issues of the village; how he was just looking after his own or his family's interests not showing any compassion for the really needy ones.

The weather was really strange. We'd believed the rainy season was starting when the first rain came on March 27th, but since then we'd only had very little rain. We were of course thankful for each day without pouring rain, since it became quite crowded inside the banda with three grown-ups and two dogs. So, the more time we could spend outdoors, the better. But at the same time we needed more rain, especially thinking of the vegetables. However, the rains here weren't gentle showers but real rainstorms, against which we had to protect the vegetables. Hence we'd started building a big greenhouse. It would be spacious, approximately eight metres wide and twenty-five metres long, and covered with special polythene which would endure the heat of the sun. Petrus and the boys were busily working on that construction. Hopefully, it would be ready before our vegetables got destroyed.

## 19. In pursuit of grass

When leaving Per Erik at Kisumu Airport a couple of weeks later for his trip back home, Bertil took the opportunity to check his weight on the luggage scales. I already knew he'd lost many kilos but we didn't expect it to be as many as twenty. Since our arrival in Kenya at the end of last year, he'd tightened his belt five notches. And he could now use David's jeans, left behind and too small for him. My chubby husband had become so handsome. He claimed the weight-loss was due to his bad memory. Every time he slid down the slope to the stream at the bottom of the compound, he remembered something left behind up there. Then he had to climb back up and then down again and that could happen several times in one single day

But not only Bertil was working hard. On my part, I tried to remove everything unnecessary on the ground. Bushes, brushwood, old maize stub, twigs and stones. One early morning, when picking stones, I happened to knock over a couple of the poles marking where the guest huts were to be built. The poles fell to the ground and I discovered they were in fact broken. Why? Well, when we looked at them and discovered white marks, we smelled a rat and Petrus and Daniel soon verified our suspicions. Termites.

All other work was immediately stopped. Construction workers and shamba boys started digging the soil in search of the termite nest. It was, of course, not great to have termites under a house. A hole was dug for four days, ten metres wide and about one metre deep, in the hunt for the queen. Finally, we found her. She looked like a thick white worm, approximately ten centimetres long. We'd heard queens could be more than thirty years old. We bought termite poison and poured it down into the termite nests we'd dug out. After that, the ground was restored, something that also took time. We could only hope we'd removed all the termites and that the construction workers were aware the wood in the buildings shouldn't touch the ground.

The polythene sheet roofing on our first guest-hut had now been fastened, so it was time to find grass for the roof. The forester had given us permission to fetch it from the rainforest. It was only a matter of finding it.

One day, out grass hunting, we came to a hill. The forest guard accompanying us, told us grass of the kind that was used for roofs usually grew on the slopes of the hill. So we had to climb it. Arriving, very sweaty, to the hilltop, we discovered all the grass had burnt down.

Having continuing the search for a while, we met a man on a bicycle, loaded with an enormous load of the right kind of grass. We asked him where he'd found it. He climbed into the car and directed us to the place. It was a long and difficult drive and the most part of the distance didn't have any roads. The car bounced along on logs and stone blocks, through bushes and over savannah. Finally we reached the spot and decided we'd come back next morning with people that could cut the grass we needed.

We'd need two thousand kilos of fresh grass for the hut. Bertil drove to the rainforest daily, for almost two weeks. Early every morning, he picked up some hired boys and two forest guards. Then he drove on a small path, really off-road, deep into the rainforest to the opening where this special grass was growing. There, the boys started cutting grass with their "pangas" (machetes). The car was loaded full with grass, which Bertil took home a couple of times a day. On the afternoon trip, it usually rained and since the roof of our car was leaking, he had to wear a raincoat while driving. Even so, he sometimes got soaking wet.

It was a long-winded, time-consuming, dangerous and expensive job to get the grass required. One day when Bertil returned to the forest, a forest cobra had attacked one of the boys. When he pulled back his hand in order not to get bitten, he by mistake cut himself in his left hand so badly the tendon to his index finger was cut off. He nevertheless chopped the snake into three parts. Thank heavens he was able to avoid the snake-bite. The grass and the poor boy were quickly thrown into the car, whereupon Bertil, at express speed, drove over logs and rocks to the missionary hospital. The boy went through long surgery which was successful and after some convalescence with a couple of return-visits to the hospital, he was soon working again, although not allowed to do any heavy work.

As the grass was unloaded, it was put on frames built above the ground in order to be dried and turned. Considering the daily rains, when the grass must be covered, it was indeed amazing it got dry.

## 20. "Your security - my concern"

We certainly didn't only have joy in our lives. We'd become so accustomed to the fact that, as soon as we were happy and content, we'd immediately have set-backs. The behaviour of the staff was now the fly in the ointment.

Having employees wasn't easy. A number of things went up in smoke and quarrels between staff members were common. Milly stubbornly refused to follow orders and continued to dry our clothes on the barbed wire fence thereby causing big rips in them, in spite of us having bought a clothesline and pegs, and Jim had been an uncertainty for quite some time.

At the beginning of May, Jim started going completely astray. We discovered innumerable breaches of duty he'd done, so we gave him a written warning with a list of complaints. He took no notice of the warning.

One Saturday morning, we had a nasty incident with a wild dog running around on our compound, trying to get into our banda. Our dogs went absolutely mad and the noise was unbelievable. Nonetheless, it took a quarter of an hour before Jim came down to us. He'd been asleep in bed, in spite of him being the only askari on duty. He behaved in a cheeky and rude way and furthermore he was wearing our clothes.

When checking the rooms up in staff quarters, where we had some of our belongings from the container, we found Jim had climbed the partition walls and stolen a lot of things, including clothes meant to be given away to poor people. We then gave him his second written caution - getting a third one meant you were fired - and we informed him he could stay at home for 24 hours to think over his deeds. Before we drove him to his village, he nevertheless found time to assault Johannes, threatening his life, as well as doing the same to our second askari. Milly was also crying her eyes out, since he'd cursed her children, telling her the medicine man would kill them.

On our return home, the rest of the staff explained to us that during the time Jim had been working for us, he'd put part of our day workers′ salaries into his own pocket; that he'd been demanding money from people for delivering messages to us and that he'd been threatening the ones refusing to pay. We were furious and decided to return next day to his village, with all his belongings, to give him his third written caution. Timothy, who lived in the same village as Jim, accompanied us to his home in order to be a witness to his notice. It was a really unpleasant experience and we didn't feel any better seeing Jim walking around in clothes stolen from us.

Tired and in low spirits we entered our car, which we'd left on Timothy′s compound, in order to go home. Imagine our surprise when it was impossible to drive the car. It had suddenly broken down. Sabotage?

The only way to reach home was to walk for some kilometres in the heat and then take a local bus to Wageya at the intersection of our local road and the tarmac road. The last six kilometres to Wuasiva would be by boda boda. That was what we'd planned anyway. The fee for the boda boda ride was thirty shillings per person, but since we were white, they asked us for almost seven times that amount each. If we'd been normal tourists we'd probably have paid it, but as we regarded ourselves as permanent villagers – for the moment without income – we thought it unfair.

"No," we said. "Let's walk instead." So we walked and walked, becoming extremely hot on the six kilometres long walk.

Later in the day, we heard rumours, through Johannes, that Jim was furious with us and that he'd threatened to come back and shoot us all. He wouldn't come alone but would bring a lot of criminal friends. We, therefore, asked Timothy for help and he persuaded our own chief, Chief Weaky, to lend us one of the village elders, Luke, as a replacement for Jim for a few days. We really had to be cautious now that we'd been threatened.

And sure enough. The story of Jim wasn't yet over. A Friday, some time later, we heard he'd been seen on the other side of the valley. People said he'd been lying there, watching our property and us. Rumour said he was carrying a rifle. Everybody was convinced this was true and we, of course, got upset.

Bertil sent a messenger to the nearby home of our chief, asking him to come. Nobody opened the door, so the messenger soon returned. Then Bertil went to the chief's home, together with one of the askaris. It took a long time and a lot of knocking at the door, before the chief opened.

On being asked to come to our home, the chief only answered, "It's raining outside."

Bertil kept insisting.

Finally Chief Weaky said, "Your security is my concern. Come to my office on Monday during office hours." And then he closed the door.

That night was long. A torrential storm was raging outside as was customary during the rainy season. A drunken Johannes came, after being summoned, and spent the night guarding. Bertil crawled on his belly in the wet grass, hiding in the hut under construction and later on in the Land Rover. All the time he was on watch, I was sitting trembling in the kitchen part of our banda, holding our two nervous dogs. Thank God, nothing happened. Maybe a false alarm? The chief's phrase "Your security is my concern" on the other hand became something of a family joke.

Since the twenty-year-old mechanic who fixed our car after its breakdown at Timothy´s home, was skilled and was looking for employment, we decided to hire him. The boy, Charlie, would be our driver as soon as he'd received his driver's licence, which we'd promised to pay for. Apart from that, he'd help our shamba boys when not working on the car. He moved into one of the apartments in staff quarters. Martin, who had earlier been working as a professional askari, was also a new employee of ours. And Andreas, Petrus' younger brother, had been hired as shamba boy. Everybody seemed to like each other, so hopefully we wouldn't have any more conflicts like the ones during the employment of Betty and Jim.

Strange things constantly happened. We never got an explanation of how the car broke down. And the telephone line hadn't been working for outgoing traffic for the last week. People could call and send us faxes, but we couldn't even call Kakamega. Nobody knew what was causing the problem. And then suddenly the outgoing line was working again, but then the incoming line was starting to act strangely. Neither was there any explanation for this problem.

## 21. A snake in paradise

One day, Patrick found a big forest cobra in the centre of the compound, near the beautiful old Ficus tree. He was born on the compound and told us the snake had been living in that same place for many years.

Being very afraid of snakes, I'd so far completely repressed the thought of them, in spite of knowing we were living in an area with lots of snakes.

I immediately darted back to the banda with both the dogs in tow, so fast I was almost flying above the grass. I put on gumboots, grabbed a chair and sat down with the dogs on leash in the shade of a tree. I didn't budge until the workers had chased away the snake and cut down all the grass that had grown since the beginning of the rains.

Goodness! Suddenly I realized what a haven for snakes Jim had made for us. I remembered how Jim, on our return from Nairobi in January, proudly told us he'd planted some pumpkin seeds.

"Pumpkin seeds? Why?" I asked.

"Well, all Indians want pumpkins. We can sell them to the Indians and become rich."

"But Jim, how many seeds have you planted?"

"Only four," he answered, "at each banana plant."

"Jim, we've two hundred and fifty banana plants. That will make one thousand pumpkin plants."

"That's good," Jim had then said, shining like a sun. "Then we'll be extremely rich."

Now when everything was growing like mad, we noticed it had perhaps not been such a good idea, after all. The pumpkin is a relative of the cucumber and grows in the same way, with thick foliage covering the ground. The foliage had now spread and should be a cool and nice place for snakes and other horrors to hide under. The plants had already been flowering and the pumpkins were getting big. I decided quickly we'd immediately harvest the pumpkins and clear away the plants.

I very strongly doubted we'd ever get rich on pumpkins. We'd already spoken to quite a number of Indians in town, telling them we'd soon have lots of pumpkins for them. Everyone looked puzzled and said they didn't like pumpkins.

I called Milly. When she arrived, I declared, "Milly, we'll remove the foliage of the pumpkins. I don't like the idea of snakes hiding under it."

"But you can't do that. We love pumpkin leaves. We cook them in milk and it's so tasty."

"Well it's my decision, Milly. If you and the other staff members want to have pumpkin leaves, you'll have to hurry up. Tomorrow we start removing the leaves."

So we were, as a matter of fact, cultivating pumpkins not for the pumpkins but because the staff wanted to eat the pumpkin leaves. We'd have a mountain of pumpkins. Of no use. Why did we always believe what people told us?

It had rained a lot lately, but once in a while, we actually got a couple of relatively sunny days. Then the rain reappeared. The water ditches Bertil had dug to divert the worst water rivers were once more filled with water. How much mud could stick to the soles of a pair of shoes? The mud Bertil scraped off, after a quick rush down to the ready-built greenhouse to empty the water-filled polythene roof, looked as if it weighed many kilos.

As soon as more manure had been delivered, we'd sow and plant inside the greenhouse. Outside we already harvested a lot of cucumbers in the vegetable beds. The tomatoes were big and plentiful and turning red. Some squash plants already had fruits, the cauliflower plants were enormous and the sugar peas were on their way up.

The guest hut was unfortunately still far from being ready. The ceiling was, however, finished. It had been extremely expensive, so we'd probably have to choose another kind in future huts. "Offcuts" (the peeled rounded outer part of a trunk) were put up on the inside as well as the outside of the hut. After that, some painting, mounting of windows and doors and thatching remained. Since Daniel had been working on one hut for two months, we'd now persuaded him to bring one more fundi in order to make work progress quicker. As soon as that hut was finished, the workers would continue with the restaurant building.

One afternoon, I heard a lot of commotion echoing on the compound. I ran up to the building site and discovered Bertil demonstrating to the workers how to hammer a Swedish nail. It didn't bend. It was straight and nice. The workers cheered. Everyone wanted to try hammering a nail like that. In Kenya they used mostly Chinese nails and those could bend just by looking at them.

Before thatching, all the dry grass had to be bundled and cut into the right lengths. Our shamba boys had been busy doing that for the last few days. You had to be prepared before the arrival of the thatcher. The thatch was, according to local traditions, most important and had to be made in the right way by a specialist. He could have come from far and had to be treated with kid gloves and the utmost respect and when he'd finished the roof, he should be rewarded with a cock.

## 22. Hospitality

We noticed, especially when visiting Timothy, that showing respect and hospitality was essential among the luhya people. In Timothy´s home, we always met several old men sitting in the best chairs drinking tea or eating food. Regardless of the hurry we were in, it was important we sit down, take part in the meal or the tea drinking and listen. We understood we were neither allowed to turn down food nor drink, nor allowed to press our mission.

During our walks in Wuasiva, the villagers often wanted us to visit their homes. When we entered a banda, they invited us to tea with milk and sugar and often also hard-boiled eggs. If it, in addition, was our first visit in a home, we received a live hen as a gift – regardless of if it was the family's only hen or not – and we weren't allowed to refuse to accept it. All that was expensive, even by our standards, and it didn't feel right to force the people to such extra expense, which we knew hit hard on their economy. Subsequently we determined to try, with a few kind words, to avoid entering people's homes. It was better to have a talk on the village road.

The hospitality shown by our villagers had already at an early stage resulted in us having a large flock of hens plus a couple of cocks; the latter were given to David during his visit. Jim unfortunately, after some time, managed to kill the cocks and two of the hens by giving the animals an overdose of the medicine they should have. I'd instructed him several times on how big the dose should be. He didn't listen and I found him giving them two spoonfuls of medicine to one decilitre of water. The dose should have been mixed in ten litres of water. Ten chickens and the rest of the hens fortunately rejected the medicine and survived.

Timothy once gave us two beautiful geese - worth fifteen hundred shillings each - when we visited him. We had to accept the gift in spite of him being a poor man with eight children. So we brought them home and there the geese had, for a long time, been pestering my life. As soon as I left the house, they came running, emitting a horrible hissing sound, and tried to bite me. Ever since being a child spending a summer in Skanör with my cousins, I'd been scared to death of geese. They probably felt that, because they only attacked me. When I one day couldn't take any more pursuit, we asked our shamba boys to take care of the monsters at their homes.

## 23. Moving in

Mid-May, we'd still not been able to move into the new hut. Our fundi, who in his own African way was very skilled, had made a mess of the windows and doors. They were slanting and askew, which made it impossible to fit the windows ordered; the doors looked nice only on the outside and they were too big. Bertil rejected all the doors, so they had to be re-done.

On May 20th it was finally D-Day. Finally, finally we'd be moving into our first new hut and could feel like normal human beings. At last, we'd be surrounded by our furniture and be able to hang up our clothes.

Ever since the construction of the hut began, I'd been feeling depressed and impatient. Being in bed with malaria in total darkness inside the banda hadn't made me feel any better. I was completely content with the situation as long as construction work hadn't been started, but since then, waiting had been difficult. And now that special day had arrived.

All the workers were happy. Laughing, they helped us carry down the furniture and boxes from the container. We had two big rooms and a small entrance to furnish. The hut was round, something that would make it a little tricky, but it was also a challenge to make our home nice and homely.

One room, the one facing the upper part of our compound, would be a combined bedroom and office, and the other room - with even more windows - facing the valley, would be the living room. We put up bookcases, comfortable chairs and coffee tables in the living room. I had a tiring job unpacking books, photos and ornaments, rolling out carpets on the red cement floor and hanging pictures.

We hadn't finished furnishing the bedroom until late in the afternoon, but then we celebrated with a luxurious dinner and a good wine, which we ate in our living room, chatting happily.

Imagine having a pine ceiling, thus being spared the rain of spiders, dirt and old grass onto floor and bed. What luxury. And windowpanes and curtains, furniture and shelves for all our clothes. And being able night time, when I felt like it, to leave bed and sit down comfortably in the living room, lighting a kerosene lamp and read a book.

It didn't matter that we, for some time yet, would have to cross the compound to the old shower and toilet. At night, I'd have to ask Bertil to accompany me if I felt scared. The kitchen would remain in the old banda until the restaurant building was finished. It would, of course, be a nuisance to run across the plot with food on rainy days, but when the weather was nice we could have our meals outside the banda, as we'd been doing until now. And showers, WC's and a kitchen would soon be ready. If I'd been coping with a Spartan life for such a long time, I could certainly wait a little longer for the ultimate luxury. I felt completely content, happy and strong. We were finally well on the road to our new future, I thought while falling asleep under the mosquito net.

Suddenly I woke up, feeling a bit confused. Where was I? I lit the torch. What was that thing up there, above me? A ceiling? Then I remembered and decided to go into the living room, light a candle and snuggle up for a while. I sneaked out of bed in order not to wake Bertil and padded into the next room, followed by the dogs. Oh, it was so cosy. Even the wedding photos were in the right place; there were carpets on the floor and flowers on the table. Finally a real home.

## 24. The thefts

At Riverdale Gardens we were, as usual, having problems with the staff. Andreas, one of our shamba boys, had proven to be a thief. We'd been lucky finding the expensive stolen goods - 35 CDs with computer software - before he'd had time to move them away. He'd hidden them under a heap of leaves he'd raked together outside the gate on the public plot. Johannes and Fred, a temporary shamba boy, came and tittle-tattled. When checking the heap, we found our things, stolen from the belongings we were still keeping in an inner locked room in staff quarters.

We took Andreas to Police Headquarters. The other two boys came along as witnesses. While they were being heard, Andreas escaped from the chair in the corridor where he was waiting. Now the police were chasing him and we could only hope they wouldn't catch him because in that case he'd probably get shot during the police chase. He'd really been stupid to escape, because as a result he'd have to stay away, whether guilty or not.

"Do you know what?" Bertil said upon our arrival home from the police station. "I wonder if it was Andreas who stole our small TV. While we were unpacking some of the boxes after the arrival of the container, everybody kept asking if they could take home empty boxes to use for insulation in their bandas. I remember reacting, on seeing Andreas walking with an unfolded box on his shoulder. Why hadn't he folded it? It seemed heavy. It's not improbable at all he had stolen goods in it, maybe our TV."

We'd been such idiots. We'd given all those helping us with our household articles a splendid tool to use for carrying stolen items out of the compound without being seen. Lots of our things were missing. We hadn't thought of telling them to fold the boxes, before taking them away.

Since Andreas no longer worked for us, we employed Fred instead. He came from the other side of the valley, spoke good English, was hard-working and seemed to work well together with Johannes. It was those two, who had told us about Andreas' theft. Maybe they were honest?

A few days later, it was Sunday and we could have a lie in. The sun was shining through the panorama windows in our hut and shone all the way into our bedroom. We heard a knock at the door. Who on earth could it be? I decided to stay in bed. Bertil was anyhow on his way up to make some coffee in the old banda, so he could just as well open.

Martin, our day-askari stood outside the door. He said, "There's a hole in the fence."

It took a moment for Bertil to grasp what Martin meant. He asked, "What?"

"There." Martin pointed towards the generator shed below the banda.

"Wait a second, let me finish dressing," said Bertil, putting on his trousers and a T-shirt and jumping into his gumboots.

Martin led the way down towards the shed and pointed at the fence. Yes, indeed, Bertil saw a hole immediately behind the generator shed. It was exactly the right size for a person to step through it. He studied the fence wire and could see it had been evenly cut with a wire cutter, a tool most people didn't have.

"Let's look in the shed," suggested Bertil and tried to open the hasp on the inside. It hadn't been hooked. "It's not locked," he pointed out in an irritated voice.

"No, it was open when I came, so I closed the door."

Bertil could see through the open door that someone had been rummaging about inside, looking for something. The main generator was still there anyway. Bertil went up to the Land Rover and fairly soon he discovered that the water pump for the dredge was missing. Footprints were still visible in the grass.

"OK, we'll have to call the chief before reporting this to the police. Meantime you can check the whole fence to see if there are any more holes in it."

Bertil was rather angry with Martin. It was almost 11.30 in the morning and the thief could be far off by now. If Martin had performed his duties as day askari, we'd have known about the hole already around six o'clock in the morning.

I had by now reached our shade outside the old banda and Bertil had briefly told me what had happened. Sitting down to a late breakfast, I looked at the fence behind the shower. Was it really that hole Martin had been talking about? Since Bertil was sitting with his back towards the fence, he didn't see what I saw: a hole in the fence. Another one. We immediately went up to the hole and could quickly establish the thief had cut another similar hole, just behind the washing-up place at the shower building.

"Don't tell Martin," suggested Bertil and returned to our breakfast.

After a few more minutes, Martin came back and reported, "There are no more holes in the fence."

Bertil and I looked at each other and Bertil said, "Martin, please check once more - from here to down there."

He made a sweeping gesture with his hand from the left and down towards the generator.

"Check carefully."

Suddenly Martin stiffened and exclaimed, "There's another hole in the fence."

"Yes, Martin, there's another hole in the fence you didn't see. You told us a moment ago, there were no more holes," said Bertil

Seeing Bertil′s cold eyes and firm mouth, I was happy I wasn't Martin.

"Do you think you did a good job checking the fence? I wonder if you always do a very bad job like now, when guarding our belongings."

Martin was sweating.

"Martin, do you think you did a good job checking the fences? Don't you think, like I do, you deserve a warning now?"

Martin went almost pale and answered, "Yes, I suppose so."

We gave him a written warning soon afterwards, suspecting he wouldn't be working for us very much longer.

Later that day, our chief and Timothy visited us and we reported what had happened. They both agreed the thief by now, so many hours after the theft, was probably far away and that we probably would never regain the stolen goods.

I was so tired of all the thefts and all the disruption. Sometimes I wondered if there were any honest people at all around us. We'd really checked all our staff before hiring them, either through our own chief or through Chief Timothy in order to have their clearance, and we'd only heard the best about the people we wanted to employ. And still things like that happened all the time.

And now it was Midsummer Eve. Oh, how I missed the rest of my family and a quiet normal Midsummer. To be sitting on the terrace at our summer house in Tyresö on a wonderful evening, looking out on the lake and seeing some brightly coloured balloons soaring above the Nacka forests. Of course always after having eaten something superbly delicious - for example salmon followed by strawberries and cream. And drinking a good wine too.

If it weren't for our new hut, I'd give up. We felt happy in it, in spite of some building mistakes.

## 25. Pickled herring and schnaps

"Oh, what a wonderful scent," said Bertil, putting his head into the banda.

I was standing at the stove preparing a big saucepan with a delicious meat casserole. It really smelled heavenly. For once, I'd found nice fillet steak, carrots, onions and tomatoes. Some claret was left in a bottle and that also went down into the saucepan.

We were expecting day guests. A Swedish-Kenyan family, who knew one of Bertil´s brothers, was coming to spend some hours with us. They'd be our first guests in the new hut and I felt very proud at the thought of showing it to them.

Food was ready and several hours passed. No guests were seen. At lunchtime, Milly came to ask if the staff could have a little of the stew for lunch, since the guests hadn't yet arrived. I answered that it was OK.

At around four in the afternoon, we heard a car higher up on the compound and Bertil hastened to meet it. Our guests were arriving. I was inwardly thinking they'd apparently decided to make a quick visit instead of spending many hours here, something I'd been looking forward to.

We walked around on the compound, showing all our projects. Everybody was in high spirits but I started wondering if they wouldn't soon be leaving as it would not be long before it was dark. Maybe they were hungry? I had better heat up the stew and cook some rice to go with it. As rain clouds were gathering, we had perhaps better eat indoors in the new hut.

"Milly," I shouted, "would you be kind enough to light the stove and put the casserole on. I'll soon be there to boil the rice."

She came up to me slowly, looking a little strange.

"There's no stew left. You told us we could have it for lunch. It's finished."

I completely lost my composure.

"You asked whether you could have some of the stew and I answered yes to that. The three of you have finished a stew with **three** kilos of fillet steak and I don't know how many vegetables. What am I supposed to do now?"

I noticed my blood pressure was getting high. Looking at Milly, I felt the beginning of a throbbing headache. She'd turned so fat, since she started working for us, she could no longer close the zip of her skirt.

I told the others what had happened and that we unfortunately didn't have any more food at home. They merely laughed and told us they'd brought a lot of delicacies such as Swedish caviar, pickled herring, potatoes, crisp bread and schnaps. They'd bring it out as soon as they'd fetched their bedding in the car.

Bedding? Aha, they intended to spend the night here? But where would they sleep?

Suddenly I remembered what my mother had written to me when she and my father were living in Sri Lanka, "In the tropics you don't make such a big fuss about order and tidiness. You just put mattresses anywhere. The main thing is socialising." We'd have to do the same.

Now a real gale was blowing and together we quickly emptied the guests' car, carrying everything into the hut. Then I ran, in the storm, to the banda and cooked the only things with which we could contribute - one egg and some potatoes. We also had a couple of beers. Glasses, plates and cutlery were thrown into a basket and, soaking wet, I returned to the new banda. I hoped nobody would need to go to the bathroom in the middle of the night, because then they'd have to cross the compound.

We spent a superb evening together with lots of laughter and good food. When the guests had left in the morning, I tried to talk some sense into our employees. I was still upset about their having eaten all the food, but maybe I was the one to blame. I should have given them their share of the food myself.

## 26. Construction work

It was incredibly exciting with everything now happening on the compound. The speed of construction work had, to our amazement, increased a lot since we hired yet another fundi with extra workers. Everywhere were men doing carpentry work, sawing or hammering. A steady stream of people with wheelbarrows or bicycles, loaded high with goods, was coming through the gate.

Poor Bertil, he was working so hard trying to solve the transport issue. Thousands of things had to be fetched or delivered: timber, cement, off-cuts, concrete, paint and nails. Everything should somehow be transported to our compound. There was a constant juggling of different means of transport: our car, other people's cars, bicycles, carrying… When it was all planned, heavy rain would often make it impossible to go where Bertil had intended. Then the supplier would wonder why nobody came, the construction workers why they weren't getting the timber and so on. Apart from this time-consuming work, he had to arrange transportation to and from the rainforest for the grass for hut number two's roof and for the fifteen boys cutting the grass there. Since a lot of grass could be found in the forest at this time of year, we'd decided the boys would continue cutting even for hut number three while they were still at it.

The car almost never had time enough to cool down between its different missions. It was working better than ever, but fuel consumption was high. The roads could hardly be called roads any longer and it was often better to drive at the side of them. Swedish roads full of ice damage were smooth as living-room floors in comparison, and that was why most cars got shaken apart. When it was raining, the cars slipped around like butter in a hot frying pan, ending stuck or tilted to one side in a ditch.

In the toilet/shower building the pipes had been laid and the WCs and showers would soon be installed. One day, we discovered the ceiling height in that building was too low, which meant we'd have a rather large, unused area behind the showers. Tearing down and rebuilding wasn't an option, so we'd instead have to look upon this as a piquant detail. The septic tank had taken a lot of time and money to build, but it was now ready and the plumber said we could have guests for twenty years without having to empty it.

As soon as the chimney in the restaurant was finished, we immediately asked the bricklayer to put on a big fire, so that we could enjoy the heat for a while in the cold and rainy weather. We sat down on the floor beams in front of a blazing fire. What a nice and luxurious feeling.

I've always loved external chimneys, covered with climbing plants, and suddenly I was getting one myself. Petrus had promised to find me fast-growing climbers to plant at its foot.

The wall beams had been finished in the restaurant building, so now we could actually see what it would look like. The view was magnificent from the three-metre wide veranda running outside the lounge and the dining room. If everything continued as planned, we could soon have a celebration party for that building. In other words, not very much was missing, before we finally would have our big house ready.

While Bertil was working awfully hard, we were both stricken with health problems. Bertil continued to struggle on with work, while I had to give up and take to my bed. In spite of taking lots of medicine, my ears and throat and a stubborn cough were giving me trouble. The humid weather was probably the cause. Hopefully the fact the weather would soon be warmer would cure me. It still rained almost every afternoon or evening, but the fireflies were back and the sun rose farther and farther to the right of the eucalyptus trees on the opposite hill, so the dry season would probably soon be here.

The new solar panels had proven a big step forward. On evenings after sunny days, we were able to watch a video or read by electric light for a couple of hours, without having to start the generator. What a wonderful feeling.

I tottered out of bed, feeling the need to get some fresh air. I decided to have a look at the small kiosk we'd built immediately inside our entrance gates. It had just been finished and was probably the finest village kiosk in the whole province, made of beautiful timber and with a tin roof. Two tiny rooms, one of them with a customer opening through the fence to the public plot. Furthermore a roofed space for our askaris. Njombo, the son of our neighbour, who had earlier had his kiosk in his father's house, would rent it from us. It was big enough for him to live in, something we were happy about, since his father had threatened to kill him. It was, of course, also convenient for us to have the kiosk this close. Maybe we could even sell fruit and vegetables in it.

On my way down from the kiosk, I saw a lot of people coming from our neighbour's compound. They looked content and were carrying parcels wrapped in newspapers. What had happened?

Daniel, our fundi, told us the neighbour's cow had hung herself. It had been grazing on the slope on the other side of the valley, with a rope trailing behind. Suddenly the cow slipped and slid down the slope with the rope stuck in a tree. The cow couldn't breathe and died.

Now the cow had been cut up and the meat was sold at a bargain price, so all the villagers were there to buy meat. A long caravan of people, hungry for meat, came flocking from the other side of the valley, crossed the stream and climbed the slope on our side. Everyone carried big pieces of meat.

The staff was so tiresome. Why couldn't they behave like grown-ups? They constantly quarrelled. They accused each other of misbehaviour. They had pacts between them. They spread rumours. The last one was that Milly had stolen timber which our neighbours were trying to sell on to third parties.

The situation became so serious that the assistant chief appeared, one day when we were in town. He started an investigation together with Timothy, some neighbours and a couple of our staff members in order to find out if any timber really had been stolen. We doubted it, since the timber was always checked carefully. But while we thought Milly was innocent to that, she told a lot of lies about Johannes. She didn't dare to eat, because she feared he'd poison her lunch in revenge. We didn't know what to believe. And Milly had unfortunately deteriorated as a house girl. She was completely incapable of obeying our wish as far as cooking was concerned. Hence we now had to prepare all our food ourselves, if we were to get any at all. She ruined our clothes, washing them too harshly and broke plates and glasses when dish-washing. All this was done in a nonchalant and almost rude way, as if wanting to show us she was against anything not common in an African village.

It was actually a relief to have only one askari on the compound at weekends. No quarrels, no attempts at mediation. We could then be our own masters instead of playing parents, mediating in disputes.

## 27. Peace Corps volunteers

We now had one less forest cobra on the compound. Our fundi killed one, almost two metres long, and got a reward of two hundred shillings from us.

I couldn't help being terrified of snakes. In the centre of the compound, I could walk without checking the ground at every step but everywhere outside, I felt uneasy and preferred to wear gumboots. I wondered how my mother had managed to get rid of her snake phobia, when she and my father moved to Sri Lanka at the end of the 60's. She found snakes even inside the storeroom.

Early on, we told our employees we didn't want any snakes on the plot. We even offered a reward for each snake killed. It wasn't until recently we understood we'd been cheated out of a rather large amount of money. The staff used the same snake skin several times over. So now we gave the order that the offending reptile must be chopped into pieces in Bertil´s presence before we'd pay any more rewards.

One day, a man came from far away, carrying a big jute bag. He opened it and pulled out an enormous snake, which he placed on the ground just in front of my feet. I hardly had time to get over the shock before the man demanded money for it. I nearly went berserk. He didn't get anything from us as we were only interested in removing snakes from our own compound.

We became preoccupied with our financial situation, when being stopped in a random car inspection. The police found a lot of faults on the Land Rover and told us to have them repaired within twenty-five days. The repairs would cost a fortune though the amount would also include paintwork and re-covered seats. Charlie was fantastic and worked almost twenty-four hours a day on the car, so we set our hopes on getting the green sticker (which showed the police had approved the car's condition), which had become obligatory since July 1st.

Life without a car was hard. As a consequence, we lived mostly on avocado, boiled eggs or our own vegetables. We didn't want to go by matatu – unless we absolutely had to.

The International Monetary Fund had withdrawn its support to Kenya and all prices had risen enormously. The talk was of forty percent in one year alone. The exchange rate was 8.50 instead of around 6.50 to the krona. It was our normal bad luck we had to repair the car and buy building material for the restaurant and hut number two - just when everything had gone up in price.

We were expecting a couple of Swedish gold prospectors as guests in September, approximately at the same time as my brother Per Erik would come down on his second visit. By that time, construction work had to be finished. The carpenters were now working almost 24 hours on end, with only a few hours rest on the floor beams. We were really in a hurry. It was so important to have the buildings ready before our guests' arrival.

Since we'd run out of drinking water, we had to fetch more. This time we decided to fetch it in a bar up at the tarmac road. That way we could, at the same time, have a beer and relax for a while. On our way home, we passed a European man walking towards the rainforest. Since it was hot and we were in no hurry, we stopped and offered him a lift to the forest, which he gratefully accepted. After a while, we passed two white girls walking in the same direction, so we gave them a lift too. The man, an Israeli ornithologist, found a spare room at the forest so he remained there in the guest-house. The girls had planned to visit a friend for the day, but since she was away we invited them to lunch at our home. They happily accepted the invitation so we spent the day together and had a really good time. The girls were American Peace Corps volunteers, stationed further north. One of them was assigned to teach villagers to bake bread in a basket, that is to say without oven or fire. The other one was teaching agriculture.

By now, we'd met quite a number of Peace Corps youth on different occasions. Bright and brave young people. They were stationed mostly in the villages, where they were meant to teach better work methods. A girl we'd met earlier on our way home from Mount Elgon, told us that after having attended a three week long course in Swahili, she was dropped off in the village assigned to her without any other white persons in the neighbourhood. Quite a challenge.

## 28. The gold panners

When I woke up, I was still full after the inauguration of our new brick grill the previous evening. An imposing thing with a fireplace of 1.5 x 1 metre. Bertil had barbecued a couple of big steaks and at the same time we'd tried to bake cooking bananas, unpeeled and wrapped in foil. They tasted like baked potatoes. Next time, we'd try to wrap them in banana leaves. The dinner was truly spectacular, even though Bertil′s béarnaise sauce could have been better.

Our gold panners would arrive in a couple of days and before that we had to test some more dishes. We'd, as a matter of fact, not yet tried all the different kinds of vegetable we were cultivating. It was time for that now.

"Milly, could you please make sure we get sweet potatoes for dinner today. And you can also pick some casava. We want to see what it looks like."

Milly walked slowly down towards the kitchen garden. As usual, she looked sullen. We'd lent her money, so that one of our carpenters could make a solid entrance door for her house. We'd also driven her and the new door to her house; yet she never seemed content.

After a while, she was back, declaring, straight out, "There are neither sweet potatoes nor any casava." And then she just walked away.

What on earth was this? We'd most certainly planted both sweet potatoes and casava on the slope leading to the stream.

Bertil and I discussed the matter and then we asked Petrus what he thought. Could the whole harvest have been destroyed?

"No," he replied, "it hasn't. Last time I was down looking, there were a lot of both kinds. I think the girl from the other side of the valley, who worked extra here during the maize harvest, has stolen both the sweet potatoes and the casava. During lunch break, she used to go home to breast-feed her baby. Then she always went down the slope and crossed the stream. She probably carried an armful of vegetables every day."

We were completely dumb-struck. Were people out of their minds? We gave them work and they stole from us. I wanted to scream out in anger.

I was frantic also for another reason. Last week, we'd had our telephone repaired after having waited ten weeks. A couple of days later, it went dead again, during one of the most powerful thunderstorms we'd had during the past few months. Typical. What if the guests we expected needed to contact us by phone? I could only hope they'd been in contact with Per Erik, who would come the following day, and told him where and when they wanted to be met.

The last few hours before the arrival of the guests, the atmosphere among the construction workers in the restaurant verged on hysteria; such was the sense of panic. They were still putting up inner walls and adjusting doors. When Bertil left to meet the guests, I reminded him that on his way back he'd have to fetch the windows we'd ordered. Two minutes before Bertil returned, the hammering stopped. The workers then quickly put in the windows Bertil had brought back and the restaurant was finally ready. Some fittings and decorations were missing, but the house was fit for use. It didn't matter that the rails on the lovely veranda were absent. You could at least sit on it.

We installed the gold panners in the new hut and showed Per Erik into the living room in ours. Both my brother and the guests thought Riverdale Gardens, the name we'd given our place, was five-star and that was also our feeling. We'd never imagined it would be this good. It was no longer a camp, it was a home.

And it was exactly that homelike feeling and the fact that our house was on a beautiful valley slope that had made us choose the name Riverdale. We'd been inspired by the book "The Hobbit" by J R R Tolkien. In the book Rivendell is described as a beautiful and peaceful place, where you can meet your friends and find answers to your questions. That was precisely how we wanted our home to be so we gave it an almost similar name.

## 29. Liburi village

At nine o'clock in the morning, we were walking along the narrow, winding, dusty road behind the church in Wushiye. We were on our way to Liburi Village; Bertil, Per Erik, our two guests Micky and Kenneth and I. George, our door carpenter, had invited us to his home to see what life was like in a typical African village in Western Kenya. This early in the morning, it wasn't yet too hot so we'd decided to walk instead of going by car. Charlie would come in the afternoon with the Land Rover to fetch us.

We turned right from the main road into a small side road. It was as narrow as a path but was still used by cars. We already had the inevitable escort, a small group of children, curious to know where we were heading. It wasn't often they saw white people. Questions were showered down on us. "Where are you going? Why don't you go by car? Will you visit us?"

When we arrived at a small turning place, located in Liburi, we'd become quite a big group. George came out of his house and laughingly wondered whether also all the children were our guests. We explained they were our temporary guides.

George directed us into the village, which was enclosed by a simple wooden fence. Leading the way he showed us into a thatched banda that was the kitchen. It was dark in there. The stifling smell of an old fireplace, made of three stones on the floor, was sticking in our noses. You light a fire between the stones, put your kettle on them and cook your ugali. You don't need a chimney, since the smoke exits through the grass on the roof. That way, at the same time, you expel insects and other small bugs, which would otherwise stay in the grass. I realized we'd never made a fire indoors, while living in our banda. That was, without any doubt, the reason why we got uninvited guests like cockroaches, crickets and small house snakes. George also showed us the banda in which he and his family lived. They slept together with their cattle; in that way they were able to have them under supervision night time.

A little later, we gathered in the village centre, where a lot of villagers had already assembled. We could obviously expect more than just a tour of the village. A clay pot was placed on the ground and a woman poured hot water into it. George told us we could find "busa", a home-brewed corn beer, in the pot. Only men were allowed to carry the busa-pot. The women's assignment was to pour the hot water.

A lot of people were sitting on logs around the busa-pot. Everyone was holding a long straw, between one and a half and two metres long. It had a filter in the end, which was put into the pot. They sucked up the greyish slush, while laughing and joking. George had put jars with busa and soft drinks and also some bottles with a transparent liquid on a table and told us we were welcome to serve ourselves. Micky was courageous enough to test some busa in a glass, but the rest of us chose Coca-Cola.

The transparent liquid was homemade liquor, produced out of distilled busa. Bertil became curious so he carefully smelled one of the bottles. Instead of the expected strong nasty smell you often find in home-brewed spirits, he got something similar to that of tequila.

"We make the spirits with an appliance we've made ourselves," George told us and disappeared into a banda.

He soon returned together with his wife. They lugged a big earthenware jar, approximately one metre high. The jar was placed on the ground and a smaller container, made of aluminium, was put on top of it.

"And then we seal the joint here," George continued and showed with a piece of cloth how they sealed the join between the jar and the container.

An even smaller container was placed on top of a hole in the aluminium container and on top of that yet another container, with a curved bottom. It seemed to be a simple gadget but it obviously produced rather clean alcohol.

The busa-drinkers were now so tipsy they started singing and dancing. Micky joined the frenzy, wanting to show off. He took out a small signal rocket to which he'd added fins. He poured a black powder onto the ground from a jar and put a rocket in the middle of it. Then he took out a small bottle and poured a liquid from it into the heap of powder. A borrowed spear in his hand, he started to dance around this spectacle. Soon smoke was coming from the heap. A flame flared up lighting the rocket, which with a hissing sound went off into the treetops where it exploded with a red flash. The people around him went completely silent and seemed completely dumb-struck, watching the white sorcerer. Understanding he must calm the villagers down, Micky showed them a signal gun. It was usually used to fire emergency rockets. He loaded it with a signal shot, aimed it upwards and discharged it. With a hissing sound, like the one earlier, the signal rockets took off making the same crack and flash as during the previous performance. All the children were amused and Micky grabbed the opportunity to hand out sweets he had in a bag.

A local group of musicians joined us. The instruments were mostly percussion, like "sukuti", a drum made of a tree trunk, and metallic parts from cars. Everything that could make a noise was used. With these simple instruments, the group produced a magnificent rhythmic sound, which was accompanied by song in the local language. Everybody was in high spirits.

George came to inform us lunch was served. What an unexpected surprise. With George leading the way, we entered his house. In the darkness inside, they'd laid a long table quite informally and George and his wife served food and drinks. The meal consisted of pork, ugali and rice, the beverages, as usual, soft drinks or beer. Very tasty and good.

When we came out of the banda after lunch, Charlie was standing outside. He looked preoccupied.

"What's the matter, Charlie?" Bertil asked.

"I must have hit a nail or something like that. Now we've got a flat front tyre."

"But you can just change it, can't you? We've got a spare tyre."

"Yes, but the jack is at home. It was used to lift the container."

All the villagers gathered round our Land Rover. It didn't take those many seconds to understand the problem. They approached the car and with united efforts they managed to lift it up, so that Charlie, without any trouble, could change the front tyre. After this impressive display of strength, we thanked them and returned home eagerly, cheered on by all the Liburi villagers.

In the evening, Per Erik took out his video and showed us a film of the day's events. Fantastic scenes of women and men smoking pipes, drinking through long straws and dancing. What a party.

One day, we took Micky and Kenneth to Nianini to pan for gold. When we fetched them again in the afternoon, they were delighted but tired. They'd found quite a lot of gold and had really enjoyed panning with the locals.

Our guests invited us to a different farewell dinner - with a dish Micky had learnt from the aborigines in Australia: steamed lamb. He'd found the perfect place to cook it - at the bottom of our future swimming pool.

This is how it's done: you dig a hole in the ground. Then you put firewood in and a lot of sticks across the top of the hole. On the sticks, you place a good number of stones. When you've lit the firewood, the sticks start burning. The heated stones tumble into the hole and the fire is extinguished. You put pieces of meat, wrapped in banana leaves or foil, on the hot stones and the hole is covered with timber. Finally, you put soil on top so that it becomes airtight. After two to four hours, you remove the soil and the timber, lifting up the meat parcels. The meat is then fantastically tender and delicious.

## 30. At last a butler

It was tough work having guests, so when the gold panners had left, the three of us - Bertil, Per Erik and I - spent a mostly lazy time on our fabulous veranda. Once in a while, we went in to light a fire - just because the fireplace was so cosy. With the heat, of course, it was quite unnecessary.

I couldn't refrain from walking around admiring how homely and nice everything was. We now had a functioning kitchen with two big stores with locks. The dining room was big and airy. And the lounge was really homely with its fireplace, its group of armchairs and, of course, my rocking chair.

The restaurant building was painted white on the outside and bamboo rails were put up round the veranda. The tin 'mabati' roof would be red. New climbing plants were clinging on to the chimney and a row of kerosene lamps hung along the veranda.

We had flower arrangements on the tables. The brown bookshelves had been placed in the lounge with our various ornaments displayed. The cupboards had been filled with glasses and plates for eight persons. The rest had been packed in boxes for the time being.

We built shades for the barbecue area and the panning area with its cement pool for gold panning beginners. We'd also dig a hole in the ground near the barbecue area for cooking meat and chicken in the Australian way Micky had shown us.

The first four guest beds had been delivered and soon some dining tables and chairs would arrive, initially for eight guests. A lot of details were still to be sorted and put right, but it was still a fantastic feeling seeing it.

Adam, who was like a silent shadow - a real butler - had infused our house with his creativity and service. He was the gifted and thoughtful houseboy cum cook I'd always wanted. He pottered about the house, swept, prepared food and cleaned. As he'd earlier worked for Europeans in Eldoret, he knew how we wanted things done.

In the mornings, we were welcomed by the sight of a breakfast buffet with fresh cucumbers and tomatoes, different fruits beautifully cut, tea and coffee, cereals and milk and eggs prepared in every possible way. Adam's father was a chef and Adam seemed to have learnt from him.

Adam took such good care of us we no longer risked dying of starvation. This was indeed a luxurious lifestyle after all those months more or less camping.

One day, we went north on a full day's safari with Per Erik. When we returned in the evening, around half past eight, a wonderful dinner, beautiful table setting, lit kerosene lamps and candles were awaiting us. Once again Adam was showing his talents.

Yes, Adam was really great but I wanted him to be perfect. Hence, I spent a lot of time drilling him. Under my supervision, he learnt to make dishes like potato gratin, pies and soups. He wasn't quick in mind or in hand, but he had a feel for cooking. He was absolutely perfect in plating a dull salad so it looked nice and tasty and he was clever at seasoning. He wasn't, like most Africans close to us, afraid to taste foreign food but was happy to test it and actually seemed to like it.

Then Adam suddenly became terribly ill with malaria and we were extremely worried. He was unconscious for several days while we drove about like mad between his home and the pharmacy in Kakamega to get medicine and syringes. After a few more days of anxiety, the medicine started taking effect and, thank God, Adam was back on his feet.

It was very difficult to concentrate on work when it was hot. This dry season felt much hotter than previously. At night, out on the veranda with the light of the kerosene lamps, we were literally dripping with sweat. At such times, it was a bonus to have decent showers. Since four persons had to work for a couple of hours every day to fill the water tank for the showers and toilets, this was a bit extravagant: we were living like millionaires. We needed to get the water connected as soon as possible.

In fact, we really wondered if the water would ever be connected. The laying of the water pipes from the big road in Wushiye down to the public plot outside our gates was almost finished at the end of the previous month. We'd been told the pipes would reach all the way. But the water engineer had, of course, once again miscalculated the number of pipes needed, so now the pipes ended three hundred metres short of the compound. And, as usual, it would probably take forever to get the missing pipes.

## 31. No IKEA

Swedes take so much for granted, I thought while sitting on the veranda waiting for the carpenter. I'd give anything for an IKEA store in Kisumu.

We'd never have guessed it would be so problematic to find simple dining tables and chairs for our restaurant. Swedes are practically weaned on IKEA from birth - or 'OBS Interior'. In Kenya such stores exist only in the big cities and then only with a rather more exclusive and very expensive selection.

We'd visited several carpenter workshops in search of ready-made dining room furniture but they either hadn't anything suitable or the price had been an unreasonable 'mzungu' price. One carpenter, however, offered to make a free sample for us: a table and four chairs for 1,700 shillings. It was quite obvious the furniture was hand-made but then that was actually rather charming, so we accepted his sample and ordered more of the tables and chairs.

There was a lot to think about - lots of small details. I had a tough job sewing tablecloths for the tables and curtains for the huts. We'd found nice "kangas" – a material women use as skirts - in Kakamega. They'd be nice, both on the tables and in the windows, giving it all an African atmosphere.

The reception in the main building was now ready. The front counter had been decorated with vertical varnished bamboo and on top we'd glued black shining PersPex - the outer very thin layer of a Perstorp-laminate. It looked exclusive but hadn't cost much.

We found groups of armchairs, made of papyrus and wood, both for the veranda and the huts, in Busia close to the Uganda border. Though they were also sold in Kakamega marketplace, they were several times more expensive there so Bertil made a trip to Busia and loaded the car full of furniture.

In the guest huts, we put up hooks for different purposes: mirrors, mosquito nets, clothes and kerosene lamps and also furnished them with shelves, vases, mats and pictures. When the carpenter delivered the last guest beds, I could finally start making the beds with new blankets and sheets - from IKEA. We'd been wise enough to buy a large pile of duvet covers, pillows and quilts before leaving Sweden.

We wanted to prevent our dogs from annoying future guests, so we built a dog fence around our hut as well as around the banda. This way the dogs could have a big area for themselves without interfering with anybody.

Since the light-blue container at the centre of the compound was really ugly, we painted it white and planted passion fruit on three sides. Hopefully these would one day hide the hideous thing.

In order to lure guests to our establishment - and get business going - we had to put up signs on the bigger roads in the area. We certainly repented our meanness when ordering the signs. The sign-maker was intoxicated most of the time so when he painted the signs, he misspelled or forgot words. When he didn't do that, he forgot to plan the location of the text. The result was that he started with big, flashy letters after which he had to squeeze the rest together in order to make it all fit. Bertil had, on innumerable occasions, asked him to remake the signs. We'd now given up and accepted them as they were. We'd later let a professional redo them. Strangely enough, our signs were the only ones in the area which mentioned the famous Kakamega rainforest. Not even Kenya Wildlife Service had put a sign or an arrow on the main road, showing the direction of the rainforest.

No hotel works well without good staff. Therefore we employed, on probation, a young girl - Veronica. She lived in a banda not far from us and had had a three-year long computer education in Nairobi. We wanted to test if she'd be a good reception clerk and hostess, when we started having guests. She was alert and pretty and seemed intelligent. I gave her as an assignment, when she had time, to write down for a future folder the basics about manners and customs among the Luhya people in our village.

In a similar manner, we'd test Ben, one of the rainforest guides. He'd list all birds, trees and plants at Riverdale Gardens and go round marketing us. Both these young persons were showing a go-ahead spirit, had studied and would probably be able to help us quite a lot.

Milly, on the other hand, alas, had been fired. She'd proven to be dishonest, negligent and lazy. We knew, from earlier, she'd stolen clothes from us and on several occasions had been lying. As a result, she'd already received two written cautions. Our patience with her came to an end when we discovered she'd stolen a bag with 80 kilos of maize, meant for staff lunches.

As a replacement for Milly, we employed Maria from the other side of the valley. She'd worked for a Swiss family in Nairobi, so we hoped she'd be better.

There was obviously a lot of talk going around about our hotel. All week, visitors had come to look at it. Missionaries and doctors, guides from the rainforest, teachers from local schools and catholic nuns. Everyone was curious and everyone seemed impressed.

They came to see what we had to offer. The mouth-to-mouth method apparently worked well, since they often referred to friends who had earlier visited us. It was rather time consuming showing the visitors around, but we believed it was important to be nice to everybody. Also our competitors from other hotels in the area appeared and wanted to be shown around. We'd of course already visited them.

One afternoon, the forester and a friend of his came on a visit. They were dumbstruck by the restaurant, the presentable and detailed guest folder, excursion programme and price-lists and they were completely taken aback on seeing the rooms. And they'd never have believed we had a telephone.

Finally, the moment arrived for our first non-Swedish night guests. A man called from Eldoret, saying he'd received our marketing leaflet with a map from someone at Eldoret Hospital. He would come with his wife and three children and they wanted to visit the rainforest. They never showed up and we'd forgotten to ask for their telephone number. This no-show turned out to be a good dress rehearsal.

## 32. Cinnamon buns

The weather changed and the period of the short rains was approaching. We had a rain shower almost every day and it was somewhat chilly, although probably not very cold since we were still wearing shorts and T-shirts. One day, it rained for six hours on end and, after only twenty minutes, our one-thousand-litre tank was full of rainwater and started overflowing.

The water issue had of course not yet been solved. We kept hearing we'd get the remaining water pipes delivered the following week but they never showed up. At the moment it was actually not that important, since the daily rain fed water into the tanks via the gutters.

The last weekend in October was really busy. On the Friday, three people came, amongst them the managing director of a new luxurious hotel in Kakamega, not yet inaugurated. Two of the visitors wanted dinner and an overnight stay. When the director saw the menu, he also wanted dinner. We served tomato soup, Chicken Riverdale with potato gratin and, as dessert, a fruit salad. In spite of their background within the hotel and restaurant industry, neither of them had ever eaten potato gratin before. They loved it and exclaimed, "Imagine you can make this out of potatoes."

Saturday evening, some nice Indians had a family dinner at Riverdale. Candles, kerosene lamps and a crackling fire in the fireplace provided an intimate feeling. An excellent three-course dinner with good wines and coffee with home-baked biscuits ensured the guests were overwhelmed. They promised to return on many more occasions.

"Kanelbullar!" someone exclaimed. "I can see cinnamon buns."

A young man, around twenty-five years old, pointed at the table in the dining room.

"I love kanelbullar."

We'd put coffee, tea and a mountain of cinnamon buns on the table. Seven American medical students crowded around it. They'd just climbed down from the roof of the matatu, which had brought them from Eldoret, a distance of around one hundred kilometres. The young people tucked right into the delicacies of the table and the "cinnamon boy" informed me he was partly of Swedish origin and that his mother sometimes baked "Kanelbullar".

Having settled in their rooms, the students packed themselves into the Land Rover. Charlie drove them to the rainforest, where the guide Ben met up. Everybody was interested in the forest so Ben would probably have to tell them a lot about the medicinal values of the forest plants.

The excursion had obviously been a success. They were all in a good mood when returning and spent some time on the veranda drinking beer before dinner.

We'd been working hard preparing this. On booking, I'd been told there would be meat-eaters, vegetarians and vegans in the group so we had to watch our step. Bertil had made small signs that we put on the serving dishes, showing which kind of food there was on each plate.

In the evening, the students played party games and when the stars came out, Bertil brought out his big telescopes. A storm of cheering burst forth. Everyone wanted to have a look and Bertil spent a large part of the night outdoors with some of them, insatiable to watch the spectacle.

The following morning, the matatu returned to pick up the guests. I asked one of the girls if they'd like some pumpkins. We had a pumpkin mountain lying under one of the eucalyptus trees and Americans ate pumpkins, didn't they?

The girl's face split into a wide smile and she said, "Yes, yes, pumpkin pie."

She called her friends over and together they started loading a lot of pumpkins into the car. As we waved goodbye, the medical students promised to write about us in the suggestion book in their lodgings.

## 33. Parental visit

"They're standing over there," Bertil said, pointing towards the pavement at the entrance to Kisumu International Airport. "Park here, Charlie."

Flying out of the car and criss-crossing between the cars at the parking lot - closely followed by Bertil - I came up to them in a second. Tears streamed down my cheeks. I hugged them both. My parents had at last come to visit us. It was really wonderful.

Oh my goodness, how old and tired they looked. But maybe it wasn't so strange. My father was actually eighty years old and my mother only two years younger.

After all the hugging, we went to the car. Bertil and I carried their luggage. We'd in advance asked Charlie to come with us to take care of that, but as usual he'd defied us, staying in the Land Rover. Damned boy! Bertil took out the special stairs we'd made to help them climb into the Land Rover. They weren't needed. Unaided, they hopped in without a murmur. They'd probably been practising during their years in the tropics.

"Now, we'll go to Hotel Imperial so you can get some breakfast and relax for a while," I said. "What on earth happened? You should have arrived yesterday and spent the night at the Imperial."

My parents told us the aircraft had been delayed for twenty-four hours in Cairo, due to engine trouble. After a several hours long wait at the airport, they were driven to the Sheraton for a short rest. Arriving in Nairobi at 5.20 in the morning, they'd decided it was best to proceed directly to Kisumu. They were feeling well but very tired.

After resting for a couple of hours at the Imperial, we needed to do some shopping at Nakumatt, a relatively new shop in Kisumu, where you could find everything you might wish for. It was heavenly to shop there, since all the things you couldn't find in Kakamega were there. Even salmon - but at an exorbitant price. It was, of course, dangerous to shop at Nakumatt because once you entered, you "happened" to buy things for several thousand shillings.

Shopping done, we were finally on our way to the Northern Hemisphere together with my parents, so eager to see our paradise.

During the trip home, we talked constantly. We had so much to tell each other and were happy Charlie was driving and that he didn't understand Swedish.

We told my parents about our problems with the staff. Milly had been fired and as a consequence had contacted the Labour Office, making demands on us. One meeting during which Timothy was present to help us, with a rude representative of the authorities, had already taken place and the next one would be in a few days. We'd sent extensive explanatory letters to chiefs and assistant chiefs, both at our location and at Milly´s, giving details about what she'd done. Milly had also something going on with Tomas, one of our night askaris. He'd been keeping the maize she stole from us at his home and consequently we didn't dare keep Tomas either. Bertil had been forced to sleep on the floor of the restaurant, with the car parked outside, in order to keep an eye on both the house and the car, while Luke had been keeping watch at the lower part of the compound.

The man from the Labour Office claimed we'd broken the law, having lent money to our employees. It was forbidden to lend more than one month's salary. It didn't matter that we helped those in need by lending them more money. He also said it was illegal to employ people without going through Labour Office. We were guilty of a lot of criminal acts, according to this man. It seemed irrelevant that no other employees in the district were treated as well as ours. We paid them the double minimum wage and they had lots of benefits.

My parents were full of compassion. We didn't want to scare them by divulging that the man from the Labour Office appeared to be one of Milly's relatives. Timothy had warned us her relatives apparently were rather murderous people and that we therefore might get unexpected visits from them at night. My parents didn't need to know that.

We also told them Charlie was messing around, complaining about most things. He was using the shamba boys as servants, didn't tolerate any criticism and told everybody he was working too much without getting paid enough.

By now, my parents were looking rather worn out, so we let them relax for a while in the car - as far as possible, notwithstanding all the bumps and large potholes on the road.

At long last, we reached home and, as always when we had visitors, immediately took them out onto the veranda to show them the wonderful scenery. We served them a cold beer while the shamba boys carried their luggage down into Hut Number One. After that, a rest and later in the afternoon a small tour around Riverdale Gardens.

"Oh, how wonderful!" my mother exclaimed several times. "We've been a little worried to tell the truth, since Per Erik showed us the video he filmed in April. What progress."

A drink before dinner and then a really delicious meal, after which I put my eighty-year old parents to bed. It was wonderful having them with us.

A few minutes later, I too sneaked off to bed, although not yet bedtime. Once again, I had malaria, though I was beginning to feel better. My last attack started during the fierce quarrel with the Labour Office, when I suddenly became ill with a high fever and terrible headache. I didn't want my parents to see how weak I was, so I'd put on a bit of an act, pulling myself together with all my strength. But now I had to rest.

It was really fun having Mother and Father with us when we had guests. My parents were very easy-going and good at making contacts, far better than Bertil and I. The visitors must have found us a rather exotic family, thinking of all the stories we could tell from so many different corners of the world. My father, though, was number one. I really wished he'd write a book about all he'd experienced during his many visits to far-off countries.

We very seldom met Europeans. Living in isolation in the countryside, it was impossible for us to visit others. We didn't dare spend the night away and we couldn't return home after sunset, since it was dangerous to be out on the roads in the dark. Starved as we were of a social life, it was nice that a lot of spontaneous guests had arrived of late. European doctors from the missionary hospital came for lunch. An old American lady, studying the monkeys in the rainforest, wanted to use our telephone. A Brit from Kitale, born in Kenya, had heard about us and paid us a visit…

We spent evenings without guests planning and discussing our future in Kenya. My parents had wells of knowledge we could drink from. They'd spent so many years in the tropics and could easily and quickly understand our problems and, in many cases, find the solutions for them. They'd lived, like we were doing in Kenya, far away from civilization in Sri Lanka, without anybody else to rely on. So they knew how to encourage us and make us roll up our sleeves, when things got frustrating.

It was nice for Bertil having Father to discuss technical solutions with. They were going through the construction of the first and second huts in detail in order to avoid possible mistakes with the next one. The problems that you sometimes meet when constructing in the tropics were the subject of long and often humorous discussions. Father had profound experience, both from Sri Lanka and Ethiopia, where he, amongst other things, had worked on school construction. And, as far as Bertil was concerned, he'd already gained quite a lot of experience the hard way.

One example was that timber didn't always have the dimensions you'd ordered - not even when buying from a saw-mill in town. We didn't notice that until the floor was being laid in the restaurant. All possible and impossible widths on the floor planks had the consequence that the beautiful floor we'd had in mind never became reality. Furthermore, we had to make the construction workers understand what quality and finish meant. Now Daniel knew what we wanted, but that had taken a lot of time and discussion.

Another problem, when getting local timber, was that transport took such a long time due to the fact that the timber was sawed where the tree was felled, which wasn't always close to a road. The planks would then have to be carried and, since hard wood was rather heavy, it often took two men to carry one plank. It could take several days to get the ordered timber to our compound and that kind of timber had had no time to dry. We got a big surprise when we suddenly had wide gaps between each floor plank - the timber had shrunk.

Mother and I had long talks and she helped me organize the unpacking of the remaining boxes in the container. A lot of different exciting things were taken out. Suddenly, for example, I had a whole rack full of evening and dinner dresses hanging for airing. Where on earth would I be using them here? After airing, they were packed again while both of us were amazed over how slender I used to be.

November was, if possible, rainier than October. The torrential rains lasted for hours on end and our water tanks overflowed daily. We didn't have sunshine every day; a contrast to the rainy season in spring. Everything was damp. Umbrellas, gumboots and raincoats were always within reach. In spite of having already bought more than a dozen big golf umbrellas, they kept disappearing. Once again, we had to buy several more as well as boots for my parents. And it was maddening how cunning the umbrella thieves were. One day, my father was standing at the gate talking to Daniel. He'd put his umbrella, standing in the soil about fifty centimetres behind him. It suddenly just vanished into thin air.

Anyway, we saw a big difference in comparison with our first rainy season: much less mud. The grass had survived the drought and as a result, the mud no longer streamed down the slope. The growth absorbed the water. Trees, bushes and flowers were shooting up and the garden was getting more and more beautiful.

During the rains, we noticed rather soon that our greenhouse was a real mistake - and an expensive one. It was completely falling apart. The polythene had split almost everywhere and we'd probably have to tear it down, before the weather and the wind had scattered polythene bits all over the neighbourhood. We'd made an enormous constructional error, building the green house far too big: two hundred square metres. The slope of the roof had, as a consequence, become far too small. Water stayed on the roof during the rains, weighing it down so that the polythene sheets split. Furthermore the greenhouse had been placed in a location where storms could hit it, pushing the polythene walls inwards. All the tomatoes in it now had mildew and had to be thrown away. That was the end of our beautiful plan - but this time we could only blame ourselves.

## 34. Christmas in the village

It was now December, which meant that almost exactly a year had passed since we left Sweden. So much had happened during that year; many positive things but also many more negative ones than we'd imagined.

One of the latest negative events was that our generator had broken down. We used the oven a lot and it was electric. How would we now be able to cook for our guests? When Bertil and I were in Kakamega, the day after the generator crash, we went into the Indian hardware store and told the owner about our problem. The nice Indian immediately offered to lend us his generator, something we'd actually hoped he'd do. What a relief.

The weeks passed quickly and soon it was time to drive my parents to Kisumu for their return by air to Stockholm. It felt bleak without them. It had been so wonderful to have them as guests at Riverdale Gardens. They'd been alert and well during their entire stay and helped us with decorating, cleaning, planning and much more. As a farewell present, they gave us another six solar panels and a transformer. Since we now had ten solar panels in total, we'd hopefully be able to run the freezer on solar power as soon as the sun started showing itself more regularly.

Suddenly, it was the 13$^{th}$ of December, Lucia Day which Swedish people celebrate. We had to do without mulled wine during the celebrations but instead we had saffron buns and gingerbread biscuits. In the evening, we relaxed over a glass of whisky and shrimp chips with lit candles standing on Christmas tablecloths. Perfect moonlight made the banana plants look as if they were covered in snow. Bertil was busy on the veranda watching the star-speckled night sky. Planet Earth would soon pass through a meteorite swarm and he didn't want to miss that.

We were, as usual, having a lot of problems with our staff. Charlie made a mess of things and the Labour Office sent us letters. These were probably about large damage claims from Milly but we weren't sure since we'd put off opening the envelopes. Luke, one of our night askaris, who was also one of the village elders, had been attacked one night by his brother and hit on the head with a wooden club, while mediating in a quarrel between his brother and sister-in-law. At first, nobody knew if he had a brain injury or not. This lack of respect for human life was terrible.

Our friend Karin had been with us for a little more than a week. When she arrived, she was suffering badly from stress, so she spent the whole first week sleeping, relaxing and eating. Now she was feeling well again. The two of us took small walks and tested different vegetable dyes by boiling flowers and leaves in water. We also wanted to see if we could make our own Earl Grey tea, using bergamott oil, bought expensively in Nairobi. The leaves came from our tea plantation neighbours. If we were successful in making Earl Grey, we'd also experiment making hibiscus and cinnamon teas. It would be so nice to have different kinds to drink and to serve others. In spite of Kenya being an important tea producer, you could only find one kind of tea in the local shops and unfortunately the taste was poor.

Apart from Karin, we enjoyed a lengthy visit by Ann, a friend from Nairobi, with her one-year old son and his nanny. They occupied the old banda and seemed to enjoy living there.

George delivered a three-kilo ham and spare ribs, two days before Christmas. We salted the ham, using a syringe. After that, we made "Janssons temptation" (sliced herring, potatoes and onions baked in cream) and some other Christmas food, using all the delicacies my parents and Karin had brought. Of course, we also had mulled wine and ginger biscuits. We decorated the house but declared we wouldn't exchange Christmas presents.

All the construction work stopped a couple of days before Christmas. Our staff members were organizing parties for their relatives, often as many as 40-50 persons, and had to have some time off for preparations. We gave them Christmas presents before they went on leave: money, a couple of kilos of meat and some vegetables. Even Kabeji, the old wilful and corrupt water man in Wushiye, got a Christmas gift and a warm blanket.

Christmas Eve started with a nice buffet breakfast. During the meal, we listened to Christmas carols sung by Bing Crosby. Only snow was lacking for a true Christmas spirit. In the afternoon, we had our Christmas buffet on the veranda, dressed in shorts and tank tops. We had almost everything that should be on a Swedish Christmas table: pickled herring, Jansson, barbecued spare ribs and ham. Schnaps, white wine, mulled wine and Swedish punch. As Bertil was loading herring onto his plate and the schnaps had been poured, a car appeared with our generator now repaired. What a welcome present!

A heavy rain and thunderstorm drove us from the veranda. Carrying full plates and glasses, we moved into the lounge and continued our meal in front of a blazing fire. We lit kerosene lamps and candles. My little family Santa Claus, carved in wood, was on the table. As a Christmas tree, we were using a cypress, which actually looked like a spruce fir.

On Christmas morning, Karin and I went to early service in the Catholic Church. Afterwards, we continued to Wulushi, where we went into a couple of other churches and listened to singing contests or watched dance shows on the streets. It was fantastic to see how musical the villagers were.

On Boxing Day, Bertil and I walked down to the village to watch family contests in a nearby school. As soon as people saw us, they told us to sit down on the honorary seats at the side of the parish priest. Guess who was chosen as prize-giver? Bertil, of course. He handed out cups, plaquettes, soaps, toothpastes and matchboxes to at least one hundred persons, shaking hands with all of them. The prizes were for the contests of tug-of-war, sack race, running with a water-filled Fanta bottle on your head, picking oranges out of a water bowl with your mouth and so on. It could have been a Swedish Midsummer party.

One day between Christmas and New Year, Bertil and I felt we needed a moment to ourselves for relaxation. We decided to go to Lirhanda Hill, a mountain inside the rainforest. Not much could compete with the forest, when you wanted to rest your head. We went there by boda boda, which is a normal bicycle with a padded carrier for transporting people - rather comfortable. You just sit; keeping a flexible position round bends. Your bottom actually gets rather sore from negotiating all those big stones on the road.

We strolled around on the hill in search of interesting stones. Rumour said a man, many years earlier, had found quite a lot of gold there. So why wouldn't we? The boda boda boys would pick us up at three o'clock. By half past two, it looked as if we'd soon have a heavy rain which might stop the boys from coming, so we decided to start walking homewards. It was only a little less than a ten kilometre walk, at worst. We hadn't reached far, when the rain commenced. It wasn't a drizzle, it was a tropical downpour. Within minutes, we looked like drowned rats but since we knew, from experience, that after rain we'd have sunshine, we continued walking. Thirty minutes later the sunshine, sure enough, was warming us up. Soon afterwards, we met the much delayed boda boda boys and then the speed dried us out as we sat jolting, with sore bottoms, on the carriers.

## 35. Kenyan elections

The Swedish Embassy had cautioned all the Swedes in Kenya there could be riots in connection with the Kenyan elections. Consequently, we stayed at home as much as possible.

We'd had some guests, who'd now moved on. Otherwise no guests in sight - in spite of our intensive marketing efforts. The weather didn't encourage travel, particularly on these local roads. The election campaigns were probably a contributing factor too, but we were hoping for a better future.

The elections had been preceded by party propaganda, just as in Sweden: cars with loudspeakers, posters and TV commercials. In the papers, we read about fights and riots in other places but in Western Province we hadn't seen much of that. Not until the election of the KANU party parliamentary candidate for Wulushi took place. Then it became known that the winner had embezzled astronomical amounts from the party funds to buy votes. The President intervened, declaring the other candidate, our earlier Member of Parliament, victor.

This resulted in riots and vandalizing of the victor's cars in Wulushi. Riot police intervened. From our veranda, we could hear the police firing lots of warning shots. Next day, it was calmer but people said several persons had been injured and killed. Happily enough, it was a false rumour.

The presidential election took place on December 29th. Since there were problems with the ballot papers and, in certain places, also with the weather, the elections were prolonged until December 30th. Everything was closed and our staff got the day off to vote.

Wulushi, earlier a stable KANU-area, converted to Ford Kenya. The elections, fortunately enough, surpassed all expectations as regards peace and order. A couple of opposition leaders, however, didn't accept the outcome, but certain well-known persons in high positions in society officially asked the troublemakers to respect the result, which was to be regarded as proof of the Kenyans′ will.

On Election Day, Karin fell ill with violent diarrhoea and vomiting. Since there was cholera in the vicinity, we took her to hospital. The doctor could see she was getting dehydrated and diagnosed either cholera or an amoeba. As a precautionary measure, he wanted to keep her in hospital for a couple of days. Poor Karin, alone in an African hospital where she couldn't even talk to anyone. That couldn't be easy and, to make matters worse, she'd be there over New Year.

While Karin was in hospital and Ann was trying to cheer her up, a family from Kakamega visited us. They were very nice people. The wife was Spanish and the husband Kenyan. Elena, the wife, told us about her main interest: plants. We seemed to have many interests in common and it would be nice to have some friends in the area. We were delighted, when she suggested we visit them next time we came to town.

New Year's Eve was spent in a listless mood. We toasted Karin, hoping we'd be able to fetch her soon from hospital. None of us were in a festive mood and being tired, we went to bed well before twelve without any fireworks. People here were far too poor to buy such luxurious things.

Hopefully 1998 would be a better year for us, as well as for the villagers.

## 36. El Niño

The sun had for a long time been conspicuous by its absence, though we should be in the dry season by now. In consequence, our solar panels hadn't yet been of much use. El Niño had hit Kenya extremely hard with torrential rains and floods. Roads were collapsing, bridges falling down and water pipes leaking, in different parts of the country. According to the newspapers, it would take three years to rebuild the destroyed infrastructure. Huge areas were destroyed and people were homeless and ill. Bad harvests, another famine and more malaria carrying mosquitoes were expected. The situation was so bad Kenya asked for emergency aid from abroad.

Up in the mountains, we were probably much better off. The water drained away very fast, but the roads to Kakamega were from time to time almost impassable.

But right after New Year, the sun shone and the weather was beautiful. The grass was sprouting as well as the flowers and the trees. We'd sown a lot of new seeds and had already an abundance of vegetables so if the predicted crop failure came, we'd never starve.

Karin had by now left the hospital. Her amoeba was diminishing and she'd soon have recovered completely. Luckily, she didn't have cholera which even the doctors had feared to begin with.

Bertil was constantly working on improving our security. For that purpose, he designed a computer program, which would generate random patrol lists for our night askaris. It was important they didn't walk the same route every night. People who wanted to harm us could be lying outside the fence, watching what was happening and noting all our routines. To make sure the askaris really checked all the places they'd been told to watch, we'd use an 'askari-supervisor'. This was a computer box, which registered when the askaris were at a certain checkpoint. By reading the patrol list Bertil printed every evening, they'd know which route to take. Via the askari-supervisor, we'd also be able to check if the askaris were sleeping instead of watching. As it was, every day we found places with traces of their having been used for sleep: flattened grass in a corner, the back seat of the car looking different...

The askari-supervisor worked well but for one small problem. Our askaris couldn't read; something we'd taken for granted.

We received a letter from Mother and Father with an offer to lend us money for an extension to the restaurant building. A small apartment for ourselves. They'd seen how we had to move around with all our bits and pieces, depending on where the guests were staying. This would now come to an end. It would be so wonderful to have a place of our own to retreat to. David promised to help us with a plan for the apartment but we wouldn't start the construction work until we'd gathered all the building materials, so we were little by little buying them and storing them away.

My parents also lent us money to buy a smaller car to be used as an everyday car. The Land Rover was expensive to drive and to maintain, something we discovered with horror when it returned from the workshop, after a long and extensive repair.

All this help from my wonderful parents made us quite lyrical.

One Monday afternoon, the telephone suddenly stopped working. The possibilities were many. Disconnected due to an unpaid bill? A tree felled onto the line...?

We sent a messenger to a telephone booth to check if we had any unpaid bill - but no. A boy checked the telephone wires and noticed someone had felled a tree without taking into consideration the wires. Bertil quickly made a temporary repair with leads, ladders and soldering tools. It worked. We made some urgent telephone calls and sent some emails.

It was almost evening and darkness was falling. At around seven, it was time to check our evening email. What now? The damned telephone had stopped working again. Out with the measuring instruments. It looked like the wire had been cut again. Maybe Bertil had made a bad connection but that was unlikely. He found a night askari, took the tools and walked into the black night to check the connection. It looked perfect.

On the way back, he measured along the entire cable. After a while, he found, in amongst the bushes, another tree cut down by someone. A couple of kids pointed into the darkness and told him the old man felling the tree across the telephone wires lived there. Bertil started rejoining the wire. It was important to get the wires up into the trees, so that nobody ran into them.

Yet back home, he found out the telephone still didn't work. After a break, he went out again. This time, he used his measuring-instrument at different locations along the whole cable and found a suspect connection just outside our compound at the top of a pole. By now, he was tired and gave up for the evening.

In the morning, after several hours of fruitless work, Bertil finally discovered that the fault was in the connection box down at the banda. After he'd exchanged some faulty screws, we could at least be certain that future faults wouldn't come from that box.

This was only one of Bertil's innumerable "mend-the-telephone-wire" expeditions. We'd come to realize we couldn't expect help from the Kenyan telephone company. You might have to wait for them for weeks or even months. "The best place to find a helping hand is at the end of your own arm," as a Swedish proverb says. And since our neighbours deliberately sabotaged the telephone wire by cutting it and also by felling trees over it, our telephone was often out of order - sometimes several times a week. Subsequently, the only solution was Bertil himself.

## 37. A lunch - a life

Carpenter Daniel and his wife were terribly ill with malaria and also Veronica's one-year old son. We contributed as much as we could with money for medicine. At the same time, we knew, sadly, that in most of the bandas around us, other people were in bed as ill as they were or even worse. But unfortunately we couldn't help everyone.

Furthermore, there were now positive cases of cholera on the other side of Wulushi, towards the rainforest. One person had died so far. Nowadays, it was possible, with the right treatment, to save most cholera cases in hospitals, provided the ill were quickly submitted to treatment. According to the doctors at the Missionary Hospital, we didn't belong to the risk category, but we were still vigilant on the cleanliness and health of our staff. You could, however, not yet talk about a cholera epidemic, since there were only stray cases. Malaria was probably worse.

The villagers' situation was very difficult. It was probably as bad - or maybe worse - in other places in the country, but it was in Kakamega District we saw the misery. People weren't dying in heaps on the streets. They suffered quietly in their homes. The biggest problem was transporting the people, who were ill, to the existing clinics. They either had to walk or to be transported in a wheelbarrow - if they could find one.

A large quantity of malaria medicine was required. Some people could only afford the cheapest kind of chloroquinine pills. These were sold in the local kiosk. A lot of people couldn't afford to buy the entire dose needed, so they bought only one or two pills. As a consequence, they didn't get better and the parasites became resistant to chloroquinine. Drips were also necessary to prevent dehydration in connection with diarrhoea. The need was quite obviously enormous.

We were feeling downhearted as we were sitting in the darkness on the veranda with a cup of tea. We couldn't do enough. We could do so much if only we had money. We could take "the mountain to Mohammed" - build a clinic where it was needed, decentralizing the health care. Build a simple clinic amongst the people living out in the bush. It wouldn't be such a big project. Just a simple brick building of around 20-30 square metres with some equipment. It would cost less than 300,000 shillings.

The problem with official aid channels was, alas, all the leakage along the way. Corruption was endemic at all levels within the administration. We fervently hoped the new daily television feature from the Anti-Corruption Committee - informing people it was both immoral and illegal to bribe - would have a positive impact. As the situation was now, you needed big amounts of money to begin with if you wanted something to be left at the end. That was if you were doing things the official way.

"Gunilla, I think I'll send an email to my friends in Norrland and maybe to my old office, telling them how people here are suffering. Who knows, perhaps they can help" said Bertil suddenly.

"Yes, do that," I answered. "Think of how people in Sweden every day go to a restaurant to have lunch. Suppose they could abstain from one lunch each and send the money down here. Imagine what a lot of money that would amount to."

We decided to send the email. If we got a positive response from our friends in Sweden, we'd contact

Nelson, the local male nursing officer, to discuss the issue with him.

## 38. Threats and sabotage

Our existence had suddenly become chaotic. Someone had stolen the padlock to the garden gate, so outsiders could easily get into the compound. The car had been subjected to sabotage, Adam had been threatened with death and we could also be in danger.

We sent Mark, one of our night askaris, to our chief's home with a letter. In it, we asked the chief to come as we had a crisis. In Sweden you call someone by phone, in Kenya you send a messenger with a letter.

The chief's answer was, "I'm tired - maybe I'll come next week." That was the answer we got from the man, who, when we purchased our piece of land, had told us, "Your security is my concern."

The chief's reply felt devastating. Bertil left immediately, together with Mark, for the chief's home in order to persuade him to come. We had to talk to him. Tired. Who wasn't tired? Bertil is a very calm person, but now he was angry.

And the chief still refused. If that was the way he wanted it, we might have to contact our new Member of Parliament as well as the District Officer - the chief's nearest boss - in Wulushi.

But it all came to nothing; the situation reverted to normal: Bertil, creeping around the compound with the night watchmen, checking.

"Do you want us to give Charlie a public beating, before the criminal police officers come?" Corporal Wekesa asked us a couple of days later in Wulushi, outside the District Officer's office.

"No," I answered. "That's against our principles. Swedes can't accept a thing like that."

"We do that to all Kenyans who break the law. This morning, for example, we beat a house girl, who'd stolen from her Kenyan employer. She'll be sentenced to at least seven years in prison, on top of that. Nobody will blame you, if we beat him a little." The corporal smiled at us.

This kind man, who had visited us on several occasions at Riverdale Gardens, didn't at all seem capable of beating anyone in public.

While standing outside the D.O.´s office waiting for the C.I.D., we saw prisoner transports arriving and leaving and some beatings being executed. The beating was physically not worth mentioning. One of the soldiers would quickly strike an arm or a leg with a branch with its leaves still on. It probably didn't even hurt. But as far as we understood, the psychological punishment was very harsh. Being publicly beaten was degrading. Our Swedish education was causing problems. Regardless of how much money Charlie had been cheating us, we couldn't permit them to give him a beating. That was over the limit for us.

"Well, we've at least put handcuffs on him. He looks dangerous and we don't want a fight with him, so you'll have to accept that at least," the corporal continued. "He's sitting in there, waiting for his stepfather. Let's go inside together."

In the office, Charlie averted his eyes when we greeted him. As a matter of fact, he looked quite hateful.

We'd hired him as he was known to be a clever mechanic, above all on Land Rovers. We'd been paying for his driving school tuition as well as his driver's licence, as we sometimes could be in need of a driver.

He had board and lodging at our place, as well as a high salary.

Strangely enough, he'd always had things to do on our Land Rover. One thing after the other and everything had cost an awful lot of money. In total, we'd paid a couple of hundred thousand shilling for car repairs. Unnecessarily, it now appeared.

On occasions when Charlie hadn't been working on the car, we'd asked him, in accordance with the employment contract, to help the rest of the staff with gardening chores. On such occasions, Charlie had been quite impossible. He'd been supercilious towards the others and many times refused to work. He'd also often answered us rudely. All this had resulted in us becoming more and more irritated with him and his haughtiness.

The event that was the final straw was the following: Charlie explained to us he had to go to Nairobi for a one-week vacation. When he'd left, Bertil and I needed the Land Rover. Bertil started the engine, the car advanced one metre and then it stopped. We couldn't move it and were forced to leave it immediately inside our gates.

When our night askari Moses turned up, we told him why the car stood there. He then told us something interesting. The previous evening he had, on duty in the darkness at the upper fence, overheard Charlie boasting to a girl on the public land that he'd sabotaged our car, by removing something from the gearbox. According to him, Charlie didn't want us to use our car, without him being present. He said he wanted to be the one to decide when we were allowed to leave the compound.

Hearing this, we asked a mechanic to check the car. He gave us a written testimonial that it was sabotaged.

Thereafter we asked the mechanic to repair the car. Charlie called us from Nairobi a couple of times, wondering if everything was OK with the car. Bertil answered we had so much to do at home that we hadn't used it at all.

When Charlie, not knowing his sabotage had been discovered, returned from Nairobi, we stopped him from removing from his rooms the maize bags he'd bought on speculation. In his absence, we'd put an extra padlock on the door, handing over one of the keys to the District Officer. The other key we'd kept ourselves. We'd notified both the D.O. and the Police Headquarters in Kakamega about the crime and had agreed with them Charlie wasn't to fetch his maize, until a police investigation had been made. Charlie immediately contacted a lawyer and then the police arrested him. And now he was sitting inside the D.O.´s building.

After a long discussion with Charlie's stepfather, we and the police made him realize he had to persuade his stepson to stop his actions against us. Finally, Charlie signed a paper stating how much he should pay us for the repair of the gearbox and for the loans he'd still not repaid. He also withdrew his case from the lawyer and declared he had no further claims on us. After that, we felt sorry for him and tempered justice with mercy. We decided not to bother bringing the issue to court and permitted him, as usual against our better judgement, to fetch his maize.

However, more unpleasant facts were discovered. When tidying Charlie's apartment next morning, we found empty receipt blocks, complete with the workshop's stamp. We went to the workshop to check with the owner Edgar. Charlie, who had worked there previously, had obviously stolen the receipt blocks and stamped them. After that, he'd filled in the sums we should pay for all the faked car repairs. That way he'd cheated us out of a large amount of money. We were fed up with the hassle with Charlie. As we'd never be able to prove exactly how much money he'd embezzled from us, we decided not to notify the police about the new development.

But like so many times before, we were surprised at how blue-eyed we actually were.

Returning home one afternoon and wanting a glass of sherry, we discovered someone had stolen the recently opened sherry bottle from the cocktail cabinet. The following morning, we discovered the newly bought seed potatoes had disappeared. We brought in our staff and handed out new written instructions and rules. We'd no longer be tolerant. Of course, that was what we always said but, within short, we'd forget how little we could trust them and alas soon be cheated again.

The staff was also quarrelling among themselves. Accusations were made about attempts at poisoning each other and about witchcraft. We tried to mediate and once in a while we had to yell. They were like teenagers.

Adam, who in fact was a nice old man, was deteriorating. We were quite convinced that the missing sherry had gone down his dry throat. He was stinking of liquor almost daily, staggering about with a happy smile.

One day, we wanted to test opening-up for the locals and for that purpose we made a nice small marketing folder. We sent Adam with a stack of folders to Wageya. He was fired with enthusiasm and returned proudly, having handed out all the folders. When we asked him what kind of people he'd given them to, he told us he'd been very clever and got on the bus to Nairobi. He'd handed out all of them on the bus. He didn't understand, when we tried to explain, that the travellers would be in Nairobi when Riverdale Gardens was open to the public. Everything had been wasted. We might as well have burnt the folders.

I saw the gentle Adam angry, on only one occasion. That was when Petrus had put big pots with green plants on the veranda and planted some wild bananas at some distance from the house. Adam went mad. According to him, all the flowers had to be removed at once and the banana plants dug up. We thought Petrus had done a nice job and didn't understand the problem. Adam told us those were witchcraft plants and that Petrus was trying to get us into his power, using them. The whole discussion ended with us taking away one of the pots and that only in order to calm Adam down.

## 39. Cholera

The cholera situation was getting serious. It was approaching. One person had died some three hundred metres from us, which felt a little too close. Together with a health team, the village nursing officer, Nelson, visited the home of the deceased and forced the villagers to immediately bury the dead person. They destroyed all the funeral food and buried it and all the guests were dispersed.

As popular entertainment, the local funeral customs contributed to the spread of epidemics. Everybody gathered around the deceased, quite untroubled by the possibility of getting contaminated. You socialized, cried and drank together, digging the grave on the compound. This could go on for many days and nights.

"Gunilla, my sister has died. Can I have some time off to go to the funeral?" Veronica wondered, on arrival one morning.

"Oh, I'm sorry to hear that. Which one of your sisters? What was the cause of death?"

"It's the married one, who lives just on the other side of Khasili. She died of cholera. I need to borrow some money for travel expenses," Veronica answered, looking worried.

Since she mentioned a rather large amount of money for her travel costs, I objected that Khasili was actually quite close. On the other hand, I understood completely her need to borrow money in order to help with the funeral expenses, but giving travel as the reason seemed strange.

Veronica's explanation was news to me and added more information about the traditions of the Luhya people. She told me that if a husband hadn't yet paid the dowry when his wife died, he had no right to bury her. The wife would instead be buried in the home of her parents. In Veronica's case, that was far away. In such a case, people claimed he hadn't loved his wife enough and as a punishment the man was expected to live a miserable life, not being able to remarry.

If the wife's death, as in the case of Veronica's sister, was furthermore caused by a contagious disease, making it necessary to bury the dead immediately at her husband's home, soil from that grave must be carried by her relatives to her parents' home. A small coffin was made and the soil, wrapped in a white cloth, was put into the coffin and the complete burial ceremonies commenced. Veronica would consequently first have to go her brother-in-law's house together with her parents and siblings, to collect some soil from the grave and then carry it to the parental home, where the funeral would go on for a week.

Our employees were given new orders regarding illness and hygiene. From now on, we'd probably be walking with our hands in our pockets to avoid handshakes, not buying milk or meat and picking and cooking vegetables ourselves.

Quite astonished, we said to each other, "Could you imagine we'd be sitting in Africa in the autumn of our lives, devoting ourselves to charity and having cholera at our very doorstep?"

The strange thing is that we weren't at all afraid but felt fatalistic. Whatever happened happened. I suppose this was because of our age.

We had a very positive clinic meeting with Nelson. We declared we couldn't promise anything, but that we'd try to find money in Sweden for a clinic in the Wuasiva area. In this way, people from a very large area without any health care within reach would be helped. Nelson thought it was a splendid idea but warned us we shouldn't involve the church in the project. Corruption was apparently also widespread in the churches and the money would only disappear. Neither should the local administration be involved, because in that case a hundred percent of the money would go up in smoke. He therefore suggested we start a Village Health Committee. To begin with, we should keep silent about the fact that money might come from Sweden.

In order to get Government aid later on, family counselling, maternity welfare and health care counselling should be included in the plans. Nelson visualized a clinic with many rooms for different purposes, but we stopped him, telling him that to begin with, something small should be built that could cover the primary needs - provided we could find any money at all. More rooms could be added later.

A big health problem in our village was that such a high percentage of the villagers had AIDS. On one side of our fence, where the poorest people lived, 35 percent of all grown-ups and a very high percentage of the children were infected and had developed AIDS. This was something nobody talked about. When someone died of it, they just said that person had been submitted to witchcraft.

When our meeting had come to an end and Nelson was about to leave, I saw Johannes sitting on the ground looking ill. I asked Nelson to examine him. The diagnosis was malaria. Nelson pointed out that Johannes was also part of the group, which risked getting cholera. As a result, Veronica was sent down to Wulushi to get the necessary medicines, including tetracycline that was given as a cholera prophylaxis. Veronica, too, needed tetracycline, since she was going to her sister's funeral. Once more, money we couldn't afford to give away but what else could we do?

That same evening, another neighbour died, quite close to one of our fences. You noticed that someone had died when you saw people running from every direction, crying as loud as possible. These were professional mourners. A little later, the night askari informed us that these women were also heard from close to Maria's home, on the other side of the valley. Maria worked for us. We hoped nothing had happened to her children. We'd recently helped her to get out of hospital, where she'd been given a drip for a few days, by paying her hospital bill.

After a few more meetings with Nelson, we asked him one day if we could accompany him on one of his rounds in the area. We'd need photos for the clinic project.

We started the walk with a visit to a family living very much off the beaten track and far from our home. A group of completely apathetic family members were sitting in ragged and dirty clothes outside a small broken banda with big gaps in the thatched roof. Three grown-ups and five children; all family members had developed AIDS. They also had pneumonia and serious malaria. The oldest woman, grandmother, had caries on one hand, which was impossible to cure as the cost was far too high. The mother was, according to Nelson, only eighteen years old but already had five children.

Since the family had no money, they hadn't sought medical assistance.

Nelson had heard, by reputation, about the family and therefore had visited them. Their malaria was serious and the most expensive malaria medicine must be used. He'd already bought it, having himself paid 2,400 shilling for it. Tears came to my eyes. The family members probably didn't have a long time left to live, but we couldn't just let them die. Having taken a number of photos of the poor ill people, we gave Nelson a considerable sum of money as a contribution to the family's medicine.

Malaria was constantly claiming new victims in our village. A couple of days earlier, a two-year old girl had died of it. According to Nelson, her parents regarded her illness as witchcraft, so they contacted the village medicine man instead of giving her medicine. Nelson was angry when he told us this. He couldn't stand children dying unnecessarily. He felt powerless against witchcraft and black magic, so common among the villagers.

We passed the village school on the walk and were invited in. The headmaster showed us the entire school and we visited all the classrooms. The children greeted us in chorus saying, "Good evening, visitors." The teachers asked us to tell the pupils about Riverdale, what we were doing there, which vegetables we were growing, etc. The school seemed well cared for, but poor.

After the visit, we spent some time discussing the school we'd just left. As in the Sotanini School, many of the girls wouldn't complete primary school because of pregnancy. The government had recently decided that all pregnant girls less than fifteen years old had to have a caesarean. That way, they could avoid the babies getting injured during delivery. It was very common with twelve-year old girls giving birth. They didn't know how to care for a baby and consequently there were many unnecessary cases of infant mortality. That was why Nelson wanted child/mother care and family planning mentioned in our clinic project.

We'd always believed that all the small girls carrying around infants were taking care of their smaller siblings but now we understood that in many cases it was actually their own babies.

As the last item on the day's programme, we wanted to take some photos of water being fetched from the stream. It was starting to get hot. After a long walk on small curving paths, we reached a small dirty-looking stream. At the side of it, someone had dug a small hole, where water was pouring only to form a stagnant puddle. A woman soon approached to fetch water. She took water for laundry from the stream, drinking water from the puddle. Clearly inappropriate. Having taken the photos we needed, we climbed the steep riverbank. It was a long and tiring climb the women had to make, several times a day, carrying water basins on their heads.

On our way home, Nelson talked about the water problem. People didn't boil the water they fetched from dirty streams or springs. They couldn't collect rainwater, since most of them had thatched bandas. Strangely enough, the ones having a tin roof never put up gutters to lead the rainwater in. Gutters would save them a lot of water carrying, especially during the rainy seasons.

Cattle were often grazing quite close to the water hole and that caused contamination. A consequence of dirty water was the spreading of many diseases: typhoid, amoebas and cholera. Already, several villagers had died of typhoid in this area in January and many had amoebas, giardia or other parasites.

Before leaving, we told Nelson about our earlier whip-round for the Sotanini School and the success the school had had since then. Now, we were thinking of a begging letter with the headline, "A lunch - a life" to send to some friends in Sweden. That way, we might collect some money for the clinic project. Nelson informed us he'd been in contact with the small parish, sponsoring the village school, and that they seemed interested in contributing with a piece of land for the project.

## 40. Few and far between laughs

We tried to save the few shillings we had left, using them only for survival - our own and that of others. Hence, we seldom used our car now and instead went by matatu when we needed to go to Kakamega. Bertil had gone there twice during the last week to fetch one of our title-deeds. It had taken us more than a year to get it.

Every matatu trip to Kakamega was a nuisance. First we had to walk for a couple of kilometres and then we'd have to wait for up to an hour for the minibus. When that arrived, the driver squeezed us in with twenty other individuals. The bus jolted away and, with luck, arrived about forty-five minutes later or else broke down during the journey, never reaching town.

But maybe we ought not to complain. So many people could only dream of affording a trip by matatu. For example, Glenn, the foreman in the Sotanini mine, who one day came walking all the way from Sotanini, a walk that had probably taken him several hours. He gave us a stone as a present. A stone with a lot of gold in it, taken from their gold mine.

He told us they were now working in a different way. They'd formed a mining cooperative and had got a mining licence and changed to underground mining. The main shaft was approximately thirty metres deep with tunnels going out in different directions. According to Glenn, gold could be found everywhere, evenly spread. A rock the size of a football could give gold worth up to 2,000 shillings.

Their problem was that they could only work for five to ten minutes before the oxygen came to an end. They offered us a partnership in the cooperative in exchange for our coming up with a solution to the air problem. Bertil had seen this problem on the opal fields in Australia and promised to start working on a solution.

After only a few days, we went to Sotanini and presented sketches of a large air pump which looked like a bellows. It was important to use material and methods the villagers themselves could maintain and repair. Hence, we intended to build the large bellows out of planks and PVC-coated fabrics and we'd use ten centimetre plastic pipes as ventilation pipes. The construction was simple and cheap. Bertil pointed out it was important that a couple of cooperative members were present during the construction work, so that they could see how it was made and that way be able to teach other cooperatives. Our suggestion was received jubilantly. The bellows would be built the coming week and paid for by the mining cooperative, apart from a small sum we contributed as a gift. As thanks, we became members of the cooperative and would now have a part in any profit. However, it wasn't for the money we'd help them, but because we wanted to teach them how to help themselves.

Once again, it was Bertil's birthday. Per Erik, who had arrived a few days earlier, and I aroused Bertil with an off-tune "For he's a jolly good fellow". Breakfast, with a home-baked sponge cake, was served on the veranda.

Bertil had celebrated his last birthday, his 50th, running around at the ministries in Nairobi. Looking at my dear husband, I couldn't help but notice his condition, the best he'd been in for a long time. In a year, he'd lost twenty kilos and he was in good shape. Having spent one year at an altitude of almost 1,800 metres, our lungs were as strong as those of young people.

A little later in the day, we got some real entertainment (it must have been to celebrate Bertil). It was exactly like a Donald Duck cartoon. Isn't there a film in which Donald is working on a golf course? I laughed, as we stood watching the garden that overnight had suddenly acquired a lot of small mounds of earth here and there. I noticed a small head in a new mound that was being made close to the hibiscus plantations.

"Over there! Hurry up!" I shouted to the shamba boys, who were cutting the grass.

They immediately ran to the new mound but arrived too late to get the marauder. Yet another heap was being formed, this time some fifteen metres further off. I pointed again and the boys ran again, but again in vain.

We'd been going on like this all morning: I pointed and they ran. As new holes were being dug, the boys put out traps and empty bottles in the old ones. The marauder had to be stopped, before it would bite off the roots of our newly planted shrubs.

And the guilty digger? A small mole. But by the number of heaps, it could have been a whole colony of them. Exactly like Donald Duck at the golf course, we tried to stop the small rascal. It wasn't until Bertil put a couple of fireworks into a hole and lit them that we managed to finally put a stop to it, persuading the mole to flee to quieter hunting grounds.

Later in the week, we finally saw one of our hen thieves. An Egyptian mongoose, approximately one and a half metre long. The askaris told us it usually crossed the compound diagonally passing the container at night, but we'd never seen it before. Oh, so that was the scoundrel that loved eating hens. We hoped it would also catch snakes like Rikitikitavi in Rudyard Kipling's story.

Another animal that seemed to have taken a liking to us was Elvis - a magnificent long-crested eagle. We called him Elvis because the crest on his head fell forwards like on the rock star. Elvis had actually been keeping us company ever since our arrival in the village. He usually sat on the fence pole, close to the first hut. Sometimes he circled high above us and then we heard his very special cry. He didn't seem to scare easily and the dogs had stopped bothering about him. It was really nice having him so close.

It was evening and Bertil was in the kitchen making evening tea.

We heard a knock on the kitchen door. The night askari, Mark, stood outside in the darkness.

"I need batteries for my torch, sir," he said.

"Mark, as a matter of fact the torch is mine and you're only allowed to use it when you're working. Didn't you get new batteries a couple of days ago?" Bertil asked irritably, since he'd just spilt the tea.

"Yes," Mark answered, "but they're almost empty. Look how faint the torch light is."

He lit the torch and - very true - it hardly gave any light at all.

"OK, Mark. Here are two new batteries. But don't light the torch unnecessarily. You'll destroy your twilight vision."

"Yes, bwana, I'll be careful with the light," Mark answered, turned around and disappeared into the night.

I'd overheard the whole conversation from reception.

"I think the batteries are failing too fast. We're always buying new ones, aren't we?"

"Yes," Bertil agreed, "I'll make a note to see how long their batteries last."

We usually bought torch batteries at least twenty a time and they went like hot cakes.

Next evening, it was the same old story. Mark came to show us the torch was hardly giving any light. Bertil, now becoming suspicious, asked Mark to lend him the torch for a while. He wanted to check if something was wrong with the torch itself. While Mark was waiting in the darkness out on the veranda, Bertil entered and removed the batteries from the torch. He discovered they were of a completely different brand than those he'd put into the lamp the previous evening.

So that was how it was done. Before arriving in the evening, the night askaris put a couple of old batteries in the torch. When they later complained of the weak batteries, they got new ones from Bertil. When returning home in the morning, they took out the new batteries and put them in their small radio at home. A clever way to get free energy.

This had to be stopped. Bertil started marking the batteries with signature and date, when they'd been put into the torch. Furthermore he made a note on a list when he exchanged batteries. This simple measure reduced the battery consumption considerably. Why had we not thought of that earlier? All our night askaris had undoubtedly done the same. Bertil remembered that Jim had a small transistor radio, operated by a torch with cables instead of a light bulb. The cables were connected to the radio. A simple but effective way, especially with us paying for the batteries.

If we'd thought of this before leaving Sweden, we'd have bought several more rechargeable torches, not only the one we ourselves had. It was really good. We used it every night and charged it from the solar battery. No matter how little electricity we got from the panels, it was still enough to charge the torch. It's so easy to be wise after the event.

It was really sad that we continuously had to fire staff members because of dishonesty. This time, Adam was the unfortunate one. We had to give him his third warning, since he was once again drunk at work after a visit to our cocktail cabinet. Now we had to sack him. We, however, parted as good friends, honestly hoping we'd soon meet again. We'd miss his fantastic meat stews and salads as well as his calm and friendly way.

Maria, who was working extra in the garden, was temporarily moved to work in the kitchen. She was used to a European household and was also the only person we'd met in the area, who knew something about different cuts of meat, thus being able to buy really good meat.

I still didn't fully understand these beautiful, hospitable and cheerful people. I could understand if they stole because they were poor and hungry. But stealing as a hobby was incomprehensible to me. They didn't even seem to be embarrassed when they were shown up. We were generous to others and, when necessary, were happy to give away blankets, food or sometimes money. But they still stole. Why? Was it only because we were white?

But the violence was even worse. People were killing each other everywhere in the country. Wasn't it enough that so many persons died of illness and in accidents? Why also murder? Our district, Wulushi, was according to the police, number one in Kenya when it came to robbery and violence.

A couple of days earlier, a massacre had taken place near Nakuru. In the newspapers, survivors reported that members of the Kikuyu tribe had been transported there by car and, emitting battle cries, had stormed the villages, killing everyone with poisoned arrows and jungle knives.

A few days later, there was a funeral in Wageya some few kilometres from us. Suddenly two robbers appeared. They were going to attack the funeral guests but got more than they bargained for: it was the mourners' turn to get angry and they turned on the robbers and butchered them. Rumour said only scraps were left of one of them.

One night, we thought that there was a massacre in our village too. At half past two at night, we were aroused by a lot of vehicles driving along our small road. It was an extremely bad dead-end road and normally only our Land Rover used it. A little later, people started shouting and we heard women screaming at the top of their voices. It sounded like yodelling war cries. We groped for the panga, the sword-like jungle knife with a broad blade we normally kept under our bed in case of invaders. The number of people screaming was far above the number of people living in this part of the valley. The cars seemed to go back and forth along the road. When fully awake, we understood what had happened.

One of the chief's brothers had died in a car accident in Nairobi. During the night, the corpse had been transported home to our valley. It arrived at half past two at night. By then, big groups of people had gathered to receive the dead body, among them also professional mourners.

The party was still going on twenty-four hours later. Some funeral guests came to our gate wanting a drink, after having started with home-brewed alcohol, but they were denied entrance. We were a little worried as one of our night watchmen was himself at the party. The other one usually slept tight. Hearing cars just outside the gates made us nervous. Maybe the drivers would force the gates? We'd probably have a problem with our chief, having rejected his friends. That couldn't be helped. We certainly didn't want a lot of unknown drunk people on our compound at night.

Some days later, I woke up long before dawn to the sound of blows behind the hut. A stick was lashing the air, time after time hitting a body with hard blows. Swearing and short commands, moaning but no cries. When I looked out of the hut a little later, I saw that it was our neighbour. He'd borrowed four oxen and was trying to plough his land. It was the oxen that were being beaten.

Per Erik and I were sitting on the veranda having morning coffee, when our Land Rover entered through the gates. How strange! Bertil had left a few moments earlier to spend several hours with the car at the workshop. Perhaps he'd forgotten something?

When Bertil got out of the car, I saw something serious had happened. He was grey in the face and had been weeping. I silently grabbed his hand and together we went into the restaurant, without saying a word. There, the tears started again. My poor husband, what had happened?

After a moment, he pulled himself together and tried to tell me. His voice cracked now and then.

"Driving along the village road, I passed a mother carrying a small wrapped-up child in her arms, only a couple of hundred metres from here. She waved to me asking me to stop, so I did. I wondered what she wanted. She said that her daughter was ill and that she needed to go to the clinic very quickly. I understood the child was seriously ill, so I told her to jump into the car. I drove at express speed to the clinic down in Wulushi. It only took a couple of minutes, at high speed. When I opened the car door, I saw the child's head and arms hanging limply. The eyes were wide open and the expression was empty. The baby had died inside our car. It was so terrible."

At night, we heard the death drums again. This time we knew for whom they sounded. Probable cause: malaria and the delay reaching the clinic.

## 41. Water hyacinths

Per Erik wanted to film the water hyacinths on Lake Victoria and, as we hadn't seen them either, we decided to go for an excursion there. Full of expectations, we got into the car and drove off towards Kisumu.

We'd also been in Kisumu the previous Saturday to shop for things we were in desperate need of. In Kenya, Saturday is a normal working day. When we came to the store, we discovered that everything was closed, in spite of it being Saturday. It was frustrating, as we'd driven so far. We had lunch in the city before returning home. When we asked the waiter why everything was closed he told us the President, the evening before, had declared this Saturday was to become a national holiday. The public was not informed until on the news the same day, so a lot of people on their way to work had to return home again. Since we didn't have any radio, we, of course, didn't know about it either.

On arrival in Kisumu, we turned off towards Lake Victoria and found a nice guide who took us out to the waterfront.

The water hyacinths are really beautiful, when flowering. Tall blue flowers looking like hyacinths. You could understand they were a nuisance to the fishermen, when you saw the enormous, floating, green mass of plants completely covering the lake. A lot of large boats crowded the harbour. They should actually have been in traffic on the lake but were shut in and would remain so until a wind could move the hyacinths away.

Research was going on into alternative methods to get rid of the scourge. Sizeable rewards were on offer. You couldn't just cut them, since they'd multiply extremely quickly. Furthermore, cobras lived out on the floats and that made people unwilling to come too close. The guide told us he had been bitten by cobras on a couple of occasions, but that he'd rapidly managed to burn the wounds, thus being able to survive.

We told Per Erik about KICK (Kisumu Innovation Centre-Kenya), which was an alliance of different local village projects, involving hundreds of people in the small villages on the shores of Lake Victoria. Many of the fishing families in these villages had become out of work, owing to the water hyacinth invasion. KICK was leading the work of utilising the water hyacinths in the production of a lot of different objects. Paper and books, souvenirs, lampshades, carpets, office articles and a lot of other things were now made of the plant. And last but not least, wonderful, beautiful furniture.

While at the lake, we took the opportunity to visit the fish market. What fish we saw. Enormous Nile perch, tilapia, lung fish and several other kinds we hadn't seen before. Small fishing boats with one sail managed to reach the shore, cruising among the banks of water hyacinths. Those weren't as close to each other in this place as in the main harbour. Lots of beautiful seabirds were tripping around among the fish entrails. The sun was shining, the water glittering and the bird song was mixed with happy laughter. It was really incredibly idyllic.

On our way back, we made a quick detour into the small animal park, Impala Park, on the shore of the lake to see the impalas and a leopard sitting in a small cage. This very leopard had been caught in our area, in Wulushi, some years earlier. It ought to be living free in the rainforest.

Fred, who had come with us in the car, suddenly stiffened while walking around on the shore. He pointed excitedly to big heaps of animal droppings on the ground.

"Can I take that?" he asked our guide.

The guide laughed and said it was OK. Fred immediately spread a polythene sheet at the back of the car and started to scoop up the droppings into the car with his hands.

We asked Fred if he'd be using the droppings as manure. No, he wouldn't. He looked somewhat embarrassed. Finally, he told us they came from hippos coming out of the lake night time to graze. The droppings were very sought-after and Fred hoped he'd be able to sell them for a lot of money. When asked what they were used for, he was rather vague but in the end he proclaimed people said it stimulated their sex life. Whether you should put them under your pillow or eat them, we'd never know. In any case, we wished Fred good luck with his business.

Our full-day excursion seemed to have pumped fresh blood into our veins. We worked from morning until late in the evening to ensure a wonderful time for our guests. Thank heavens also hut number three was now ready. We certainly needed the capacity as we suddenly had an influx of visitors. The guest stream was still not at an end, since many more were on their way. Although tired, we enjoyed it. Since the Swedish Embassy in a circular letter had advised all Swedes against going to our area, due to the malaria risk, there were none among the guests. But it was so nice to see how everybody, regardless of nationality, felt at home. Although feeling exhausted, we felt quite encouraged hearing the guests praise the establishment, our food and our hospitality.

We had to do all the cooking ourselves. Maria had been fired, with a crash. It was obviously impossible to trust anybody at all. Maria's dishonesty was actually discovered by Veronica, who one day asked me to step out onto the veranda, since she had something to tell me. She informed me she'd walked into the reception exactly when Maria was going through the pockets of Bertil´s waistcoat which was hanging on a chair. The following day, we set up a trap for Maria and could catch her red-handed, stealing some notes out of the waistcoat.

About a week later, when checking the fence, we found a plastic bag with some of my medicines lying between the toilet building and the fence. It was so close to the fence that someone could pick it up from the outside. It was probably Maria, who had intended to fetch it on her way home after work. Evidently she ran out of time. What on earth was she going to use a lot of unknown medicines for?

My astonishment increased as we continued discovering new proofs of how light-fingered Maria had been. How had she been able to remove so many things from our compound? All my dresses - including the evening and dinner dresses I, for nostalgic reasons, had brought to Kenya - my underwear, some of my shoes, outdoor clothes and lots of other stuff. She'd probably thrown them all over the fence or done as per the medicines. Her children and relatives had probably come daytime, fetching whatever she'd stolen. Why were we so stupid? Why did we never question the honesty of our staff?

In spite of it still being only the beginning of March, the rains seemed to have already stopped. We had a couple of weeks without rain and suddenly it was 38 degrees Celsius on the veranda. It was actually a lot easier to have guests when it wasn't raining. But the heat, at the same time, made it awfully hot in the kitchen, where we retreated while the guests were eating. We hoped we, one day, would have a small private space to which we could withdraw when we felt that the guests wanted to be alone in the dining room or in the lounge.

Now that so many guests were visiting us, it was a great relief that the cholera had diminished in our closest neighbourhood. The nearest village market had earlier been number one in Kenya, when counting cholera cases. We hoped that the sudden very dry and hot weather didn't mean we'd have a drought. In which case famine would undoubtedly return, as all the newly planted maize had been washed away. People were still dying like mosquitoes and we heard the death drums almost every night.

One starry night, we heard muffled drums in the darkness. It was the father of our friend Nelson, who had died of AIDS. The funeral would take place next morning and tonight the grave was being dug.

Rift Valley fever had also caused the death of a veterinary surgeon in the vicinity.

When we unexpectedly had fewer guests and consequently some spare time, Bertil sent an information letter - "A lunch - A life" - to his former employer. We got an overwhelming response both from the employees and from a school class in Gothenburg, which sent us all the surplus money they got when organizing a disco. What nice children.

Now we could start the clinic project and Nelson would soon be able to go to Kisumu to get the most essential medicines for the project. They were needed immediately.

## 42. The mob

I was so tired I was shaking. I had difficulty staying on my feet and had a burning headache and back ache. Bertil and Per Erik were sitting on the veranda, having a drink. When I tottered out to them, they looked questioningly at me.

"What's the matter?" asked Bertil. "Aren't you feeling well?"

I felt like throwing something at him. How insensitive and uncomprehending men could be. I felt quite cross.

"As a matter of fact, I'm exhausted. I've been on my feet the whole day and haven't been lucky enough like some other people, to sit down during lunch," I spat out.

"There, there, Sis, take it easy. Sit down and have a glass of whisky. I'll serve you."

Per Erik gave me a glass, drew out a chair and put my feet on it. In spite of everything he was actually rather kind.

"You've done a fantastic job today, Gunilla," my dear Bertil said. "The food was delicious and beautifully presented. You were fantastic, managing all that by yourself."

We'd had a press luncheon. Veronica was supposed to help me in the kitchen, but when she arrived in the morning, she was ill with malaria so I had to send her home.

So, suddenly, I was all alone, preparing food and also waiting on twenty-seven persons. We served roasted sliced roast beef with rice and mushroom sauce on slices of eggplant. As dessert we had flambéed bananas. Soft drinks and beer and, as was customary, whisky for the District Officer.

It was fortunate the kitchen floor had recently been scrubbed. Since we hadn't yet installed any kitchen counters or shelves, I was forced to spread clean sheets on the floor. I put the plates on those as soon as they were ready. I had to shuttle between the kitchen and the dining room, serving. At the same time, I had to remember in which order to serve the guests. People here were sensitive to that. The food was nonetheless appreciated, apart from the sauce: in Kenya you eat your meat without it. And they seemed to have no idea what eggplant was. Per Erik sneaked out into the kitchen to take care of the flambéing of the bananas.

Bertil and Per Erik sat with the others at table during lunch in order to take care of the guests: chiefs, clinic committee, reporters from four newspapers, people from the national TV (KBC) and representatives from a private TV-channel (KTN). On top of that, Bertil made a speech, handing over a cheque for the money we'd managed to collect among kind Swedes. The money was to be used for construction of the clinic in our village.

The press luncheon had been organised to celebrate the fund-raising and to show off Riverdale Gardens, which was now also an Internet café.

After lunch, Bertil demonstrated the much-discussed Internet. Everyone was impressed and for many of the people present it was the very first time they saw a computer. One of the journalists was very happy when he, with enthusiastic cheering from the rest and Bertil′s help, managed to send his story by email to the editing office.

Thereafter, we arranged a guided tour around Riverdale Gardens and the huts and facilities. Our toilets aroused enthusiasm and admiration, as well as our big vegetable patches. The filming teams worked hard, so we hoped to see our property on TV soon.

Next day, I stood outdoors between nine a.m. and half past two p.m., washing up after the press luncheon. When I was done, I decided I'd spend the rest of the day just being lazy. I sat down on the veranda in my rocking chair, put my feet on the veranda rail and started reading a book. The men were in town doing some errands and filming.

Suddenly, I heard the Land Rover come chugging down the compound. Bertil and Per Erik came out onto the veranda and sat down. They were silent, looking thoughtful and pale. Something seemed to be wrong. Per Erik was usually never this silent.

Bertil broke the silence. "Gunilla, we were almost lynched in town. It was horrible. A crowd of I'm sure a hundred persons wanted to lynch us - especially Per Erik."

Shuddering, I got up and fetched them a drink. What had happened?

They'd gone to the matatu station, where Per Erik wanted to film some matatus. One of the Kakamega matatus had recently been involved in an accident and scores of passengers had died.

When Per Erik started filming, the mob thought he was trying to film to get evidence of cars working illegally. People surrounded him and were very threatening. Bertil saw what was going on and quickly came with the Land Rover, with an open door, so that Per Erik could jump into the car. Bertil rammed the car into gear and tore away. The now agitated mob pursued them, trying to stop the car, but somehow Bertil and Per Erik finally managed to escape. And strangest of all was that two policemen in a police car quite close were just watching and smiling. They obviously didn't care at all if a couple of white people were lynched.

A few days later, we met one of the TV guys from KBC in town. He told us that a few days after the press luncheon while in Nairobi; he saw a news feature from Riverdale Gardens. A couple of minutes long and at the peak news time. They showed Bertil´s speech, the handing over of the cheque, the interior of huts numbers two and three and also the shower/toilet building. What publicity. And typically enough, television in our district didn't work that day so we never had the chance to see the feature and neither had our poor chief. He'd been most anxious to stay in front of the TV-cameras at the luncheon.

The clinic money was still in the bank. Before starting construction work, the title deeds for the land had to be issued. The money raised would be insufficient for the whole construction as some of it had to be used for medicines; the need for these was urgent. The clinic project was, however, now official and the villagers would have to start coming with their own contributions: a tree for timber, three days work without pay, a thousand bricks and so forth. All contributions would be published on the project website.

## 43. Dreams of gold

The following week, we went to the Sotanini mine to shoot some film. Bertil wanted to make a feature about it for the video he wanted to send to his father as a gift for his 80$^{th}$ birthday and Per Erik, as usual, was shooting his film about gold.

You entered the mine through an ordinary hole in the ground, with a primitive winder at the top of it. It required two men at each crank, made of wooden poles fastened with nails at the main axis of the winder. The shaft was as deep as a modern eight-story building: around 30 metres.

Per Erik was lowered first, with his feet in a bucket and one arm around the rope. He was using his free arm to avoid hitting the soft clay walls, which could easily loosen. He had all the filming equipment on his back. It was pressing outwards, towards the walls. When only ten metres were left, he was convinced he'd fall, without the protection of the bucket, down to the bottom of the shaft. My brother is no lightweight, so the sight of him standing in a bucket on his way down to the centre of the earth really made me nervous. When the call came up from below, my husband also disappeared down into the hole. I was left all alone, wondering whether I'd ever see my beloved husband or Per Erik again.

While filming, Per Erik forced his way into a narrow mine drift, supported with beams. It led steeply down along the gold vein, which could be seen as a broad band a twenty centimetres wide, along one of the walls. The only light, apart from the torches and the camera light, was a burning candle at the start of the drift. The burning candle was a sure sign there was enough clean air.

Bertil and the mining team's supervisor, Glenn, crawled further down the main shaft to try to reach the mining site at its end. They were, almost at once, forced back up again due to lack of oxygen. Per Erik had slithered down a drift. At the bottom, two men, each of them with a candle, sledge and crowbar, were filling a bag with gold ore. It was slow work and the candles burnt with an alarmingly small flame. However, the following week the bellows and the pipes would be installed and then the miners would no longer be blue in the face from lack of oxygen, when they came up after their shift.

"What'll we do with all the gold we find?" asked Bertil, while sipping his morning tea. "According to Philip, you can find all the gold you might ever want in the rainforest."

"Well," I answered. "Don't you remember the investment plans we had, when we thought we'd found enormous quantities of gold up north, near Boliden? Oh, how rich we felt at the time. At least until someone told us it was only finely grinded arsenic pyrites. Anyhow, it's forbidden to pan for gold in the rainforest, isn't it?"

"We'll check, of course, that the panners have a valid permit. Anyhow, we're just coming along to show them our equipment. You can always hope, can't you?" Bertil added, full of yearning.

"Don't be such a pessimist," Per Erik objected. "Of course we'll become filthy rich."

Philip, one of the forest guards, had told us about a week earlier that he'd met some gold panners who had obtained a licence to pan for gold in the rainforest. He'd briefed them about us and our gold panning both in Sweden and in Kenya, describing the equipment he'd seen at our home. The gold panners had become extremely enthusiastic, so now we were going to make a joint rainforest expedition.

We fetched Philip at the guide office and continued on bad roads to a sentry post far out in the forest where the two gold panners were awaiting us. Together, we continued by foot down the hills and through some small villages.

Finally arriving at the edge of the rainforest, I was so exhausted by the heat I felt almost like turning back, but after a short break we continued on into the forest. The path was very narrow. Mostly we had to walk in line, so that there would be room for the panning equipment. It was much cooler here, since the tall trees were protecting us.

After a couple of hours, we reached a steep slope and Philip declared; "Now, we have only twenty metres down to the river."

We grabbed lianas, hanging from the trees. Carefully - almost sitting on our behinds - we slid down the precipice.

It was marvellous coming down to the small Ikuywa River, which was curving in a lush green glade. Being hot, we grabbed the opportunity to cool off in the water.

"I've found a lot of gold here. The biggest nugget weighed forty grams and I got quite a lot of money for it," one of the gold panners told us.

Then he and Philip talked to each other in Swahili. Philip explained to us that we were to follow the river downstream a couple of kilometres to a good place for test panning. The vegetation at the side of the river was so dense that we had to wade in the river, the water reaching above our knees. We kept our shoes on, in order not to damage our feet on the stones on the river-bed.

"Bertil, is anything wrong?"

Bertil was standing in the middle of the river, sniff-ing the air.

"I'm having a déja vue-experience, as if I were on a wooden jetty in the archipelago of Stockholm on a sunny summer day," he observed. "I feel a distinct smell of tar in the air. Smell it, Gunilla. Can you feel it?"

"What do you mean?" I answered, not understand-ing at all.

"Can't you feel the smell of tar?" Bertil asked.

I sniffed and suddenly I understood what he meant.

"Yes, you're right," I answered.

Philip, who was standing close to us, came forward, looking inquisitive.

"Do you have a problem?" he wondered.

Bertil, somewhat astonished, declared he sensed a smell of tar in the air. But how was that possible: we were actually in the middle of the rainforest, far from any tar.

"Yes, you're right!" Philip added, "From what direc-tion is the wind blowing?"

Surprised, Bertil wet his forefinger, held it up and said, "From there!" He pointed diagonally to the left.

"Stay here, I'll be back soon!" Philip looked resolute and rather grim.

Per Erik joined our sniffing group, wondering whether he could join Philip to film a little.

"No, that's too dangerous," answered Philip and trudged away across the river and into the bush. He was soon swallowed up by the mass of green vegetation.

"I'm going to bathe," Per Erik decided, leaning the tripod against a stone. He handed over the camera to Bertil with the words, "Use it!"

Soon we saw a glimpse of something white in the shadow of an enormous Benjamin Ficus. It was Per Erik, who was lying splashing in the water, enjoying the coolness.

Sitting on a stone in the shadow of another tree, Bertil and I shared a beer. Philip came wading through the water. He didn't look happy.

"What was it?" I asked Philip.

"Exactly, what I suspected. Some criminals have cut down a couple of big trees in order to make charcoal. That's illegal logging. They destroy the balance of the forest. And they don't hesitate to murder those who discover their deeds."

"What'll you do with them?" asked Per Erik, who had finished bathing.

"I'll write a report tonight and tomorrow a patrol will come and arrest them," Philip answered, looking really grim.

"What'll happen to them when you've caught them?" I wondered.

Philip answered with a contented smile, "First, we'll beat them really hard and for a long time. After that, we'll hand them over to the police and hope they'll never be released."

"But let's continue now. The clock and the river don't stop, just because we do," he continued.

We kept on wading. Sometimes we passed the most fantastic places, where we had to crawl under low trees forming tunnels over the water. Once in a while, we waded through beautiful small waterfalls, where Per Erik couldn't refrain from throwing himself flat into the clear water. On one occasion, we saw some Colobus monkeys jumping from a 20-30 metre high tree across the river to a tree on the other side. Unfortunately we also watched how one of them missed and heard the thud, when it fell onto the ground.

Benjamin, the rainforest guide, was quite lyrical. He, who worked every day in the forest showing tourists the flora and fauna, was overwhelmed. He could never have imagined though that you, from the riverbed, could get such a wonderful view over the canopy, where many colourful and unusual birds had their habitat.

After a small break, Bertil dug out some sand from the river edge. I washed it in my pan. Soon, we saw a couple of big gold flakes in it – enormous joy! These were the biggest gold flakes we'd found in Africa up till now. We set up the sluice box on the other side of the river. One of the boys poured sand into it, while I poured bucketfuls of water from the other side. Bertil at the same time removed all the big stones. After twenty minutes, I couldn't wait any longer. We emptied the sluice box into a pan and washed the remains properly in it. A fantastically good result, considering the small amount of sand we'd examined. We had 20-30 middle size gold grains and some nice-looking nuggets. On our gold panning expeditions in the north of Scandinavia, we'd never even come close to a result like this.

Now, it was time to start thinking about the home journey. I was full of misgivings about it, since I was hungry and very tired and hot. While we packed our equipment, the gold panners hid theirs among the bushes as they'd return the following day.

The walk back to the car was tiresome. We had to walk several kilometres through, at times thick jungle, at times open areas, in boiling sun. Several times, I was afraid that Per Erik, who wasn't exactly a slim figure, would collapse.

We drove the men to their homes in different parts of the rainforest, agreeing to meet again within a week. We'd bring our heavy artillery, which was actually a dream for a gold panner: a dredge (a joint sand sucker and sluice box, operated by a petrol driven water pump), petrol cans, pickaxes and spades.

Once at home, we relaxed out on the veranda with a cool drink in our hands. What a day. A sudden rainstorm made us move quickly indoors and light a fire. Per Erik wanted another drink, but the bottle was down in the hut. He was forced to undress almost completely and run in the rain to get it. It was dark outside, but he didn't need any torch as the lightning came so often it was almost as light as daytime.

We didn't understand the weather. We'd thought the rainy season had already come to its end - being extremely short this year, but this was obviously not the case. The water from the roof was streaming down into our tanks. Continuous thunderclaps and rain hitting the tin roof with a deafening noise. Rainfall was near horizontal. Our big veranda was three metres wide but the rain still hammered against the wall and the windows - so hard we feared the windows might one day shatter.

A week had now passed and Bertil, Per Erik and I were up at dawn, as we planned to spend many hours in the rainforest. After a quick breakfast, we prepared bottles of water and some simple food for the excursion and then left along with Johannes and Mark. Johannes would help us carry our heavy equipment and Mark would watch the car.

The drive through the forest to the gold panners´ houses took about three quarters of an hour. After greeting them, we told them we wanted to reach the panning site by wading in the river. Philip had assured us it was only four kilometres by water, which was considerably shorter than our walk last time. However, he'd forgotten to tell us he meant as the crow flies. The gold panners looked surprised, but after a little hesitation they answered it would be possible.

We left the car at a small bridge, crossing Ikuywa River. Mark had brought a heap of magazines to read and stayed in the car. He promised to wait for us, regardless of what time we returned. With rucksacks on our backs, we put the dredge in the water and entered the river. Then the walk started or, with a better description, the wading. It was a fantastic experience to follow the curving river beneath the green canopy of the rainforest. At the first rapids, Bertil had to carry the dredge past the stones. When the river ran quieter, the dredge could float on its own - navigated only by the rope in Bertil´s hand.

After a couple of hours, I'd lost count of all rapids, water falls and river curves, not to mention all the trees lying across the river bed. When we encountered these, we had to carry our packing or, in Bertil´s case, the dredge, while balancing on slippery trunks and other matter until we saw the water again. It was tough work for all of us but once in a while Per Erik, pretending to be a blue whale where the water was somewhat deeper, livened up the atmosphere. Time passed and we understood we'd have to test the dredge at the next possible spot as we might not have time to reach the fantastic place from the week before.

Bertil found a place worth trying, behind a river curve. The gold panners seemed happy. Now, they'd finally see the European's gold digging device at work. The dredge was mounted and the engine started. Water and sand streamed into the sluice box, just as it should. After another thirty minutes, we emptied the box in the gold pan. One of the gold panners gave it the final wash. Three tiny grains of gold were found. We threw them back into the water.

Several hours had passed since we started at the little bridge crossing Ikuywa River and we'd got rather accustomed to having wet shoes. Johannes was holding the rope to the dredge, so that Bertil could have his hands free for filming. He was fascinated by the scenery around us and looked for something to film. Unfortunately he didn't have the right equipment for filming birds, so he had to be satisfied with looking at all the beautiful and unusual birds we saw.

We arrived at a passage, where the river was flowing more gently. To the left, in front of us, we saw a small opening in the rainforest. I stepped out of the water to look at a dead snake that Philip had discovered a moment earlier. I had to get accustomed to snakes, at least dead ones. I felt so brave.

Bertil moved to the right side of the riverbed. The vegetation hung over the edge, like a thick green curtain. After a while, I found it strange that he was standing quite immobile in the same spot.

I called to him, "Bertil, what's happened? Have you been hurt?"

"No," he replied in a calm voice. "Right now, I'm filming a snake that caught a frog a second ago."

"Are you mad, get away from there – now," I almost howled, being terrified of snakes.

Bertil waded back to me, sat down on a stone and explained, "Over there I saw a snake, right at the water surface. Since Philip has warned us about snakes, I proceeded cautiously towards it. It was an emerald green snake, with a light-green undulating pattern, approximately 20-30 centimetres long. It'd just obtained its lunch in the shape of a small frog. I actually had time to take several pictures before the snake, with the frog in his mouth, decided to find a quieter restaurant. I think I might've just taken the all-time best nature picture: a green snake in the rainforest with a frog in its mouth."

Philip who had seen the last centimetre of the snake disappearing into the vegetation said, "That's a small tree snake. They're not dangerous, unless you're a frog or something of the same size."

The three of us laughed, somewhat relieved, and continued around the next river curve. Every time we asked the gold panners how much farther we had to walk, they answered, "Only three more river bends."

It was getting close to four o'clock. Darkness might fall, before we got back home, so we decided to test the dredge right where we were. Result: zero grains after one-hour's intensive work with our machine.

We gave up, feeling we needed to return home. Staying in the rainforest overnight didn't feel like a good idea. I thought of all the snakes and shuddered.

Philip told us he knew a short cut to the car. "It's only three kilometres of light trekking."

We had to believe him, since finding his way in the forest was part of his occupation. Yes, he was right in saying the trekking was easy, at least the first three hundred metres. After that, we suddenly had a wall of vegetation in front of us. Philip took out his panga and chopped off some branches. At first, we thought he was only removing a bush or two in our way. But one hour and five hundred metres later, both the gold panners and Philip were chopping so hard that sweat was dripping off them. For long periods, we waited in a queue for the two men in front to make a passage through the vegetation. The rucksacks got caught every ten metres. Thank heavens; we had Johannes at the rear. He could help free the rucksacks when we couldn't manage ourselves. Sometimes the only smart thing to do, in this thick tangle, was to crawl on all fours past the most difficult parts. We went through some thorny patches and I thought of Johannes, last in line, and how his poor bare feet would manage all the thorns the men in the lead were cutting down.

We continued like this for a couple of hours. It was beginning to get dark. On one occasion, we saw a steep, almost vertical slope in front of us. It led down to a small river, hardly half a metre wide. An old tree trunk crossed it a couple of metres above the surface. Everything was embedded in steaming green. We had to cross the river balancing on the slippery tree trunk. The gold panners, Philip and Johannes, had already disappeared to continue making a passage for us in the forest. They didn't notice our dilemma. Bertil volunteered and slithered down into the river. Using Per Erik's tripod and holding it against his breast, he managed to support Per Erik and me as we crossed. When it was Bertil´s turn, he had no support and had to act like a tightrope dancer balancing with the tripod.

Now we were going uphill. It was unbelievably steep, but we dragged ourselves up the slope, by grabbing the vegetation. Once up on the level again, we found a little clearing with long grass – or so we thought. Alas, we were so wrong. It wasn't firm ground but a network of branches and roots half a metre above the ground. Everything bounced when you moved, and our feet were constantly stuck down among the roots. It was also pitch dark by now. We started to talk seriously about spending the night in the forest.

Johannes and Philip argued about which direction we should take. Finally, we decided to trust Philip, as he worked in the forest. We passed bush after bush. I asked Johannes to walk in front of me, as his white T-shirt was the only thing I could see in the darkness. After three hours, we'd advanced a little more than one kilometre and arrived at a path. It branched to the right as well as to the left. Philip decided we should walk to the right. The path was now rather wide. In spite of only seeing the T-shirt in front of me, I managed to keep up the boy's rapid pace. After another twenty minutes, we came onto a bigger forest road and, after a descent we were suddenly at our car. Our faithful Mark was asleep in the front seat. He hadn't been in the least worried in spite of having waited for so many hours.

We drove the gold panners to their homes and then headed for Riverdale Gardens. Entering through the gates, we saw our whole house illuminated by kerosene lamps. It looked so wonderfully welcoming. Fred had stayed behind with our house girl, Linda, so that she wouldn't feel lonely waiting for us. She'd made us a delicious dinner and a fire was burning in the fireplace. I was very moved by their thoughtfulness.

Before dinner, we sat down in front of the fire for a while to remove different seeds and thorns from our clothes and hair. It had been an unforgettable day.

Bertil´s last sentence, before falling asleep, was, "I had a torch in the car, why didn’t we bring it into the forest?"

## 44. My poor dogs

Since the kitchen was very important in our work, we decided to dedicate some time and money to improvements in it. We added practical shelves and white laminates beside the sink and the result was very nice and hygienic. Happily enough, our freezer was now in service in Petrus' small shop in Wulushi. We'd, little by little, started putting food in as well as a buffer supply of our own vegetables. Hence, we no longer needed to go to town every day on shopping expeditions.

The carpentry work also included a gate leading into reception, so that the dogs could lie there. People in the neighbourhood were afraid of dogs, especially black and brown ones like ours. We felt safer having them close in the event of unwanted visitors. The dogs had learnt to stay still on their blankets beneath the counter, keeping completely silent, so our visitors didn't, for the most part, even notice their presence and even we almost forgot they were there.

We were so used to Rufus and Merry not making any sounds that, to begin with, we didn't notice that they suddenly fell very ill. They just lay asleep on their blankets; stopped eating and playing and, later, drinking. We injected water into the corners of their mouths, using the big syringe we'd bought for the Christmas ham. In this heat, it was extremely dangerous that they'd stopped drinking. After a couple of days, we realised something was seriously wrong and called the nearest veterinary surgeon.

A vet came from Wulushi, looked at the dogs - almost without touching them - and prescribed a certain brand of deworming medicine. After a lot of searching in town, we found the specific brand but it didn't help at all. The dogs were getting much worse.

Then we found another vet in Kakamega. He examined the dogs thoroughly and told us that both of them had tick fever - a tick-borne disease - and on top of that pneumonia. He didn't think they'd survive but anyhow gave them antibiotics and vitamin injections. Two horrible days and nights followed with us staying close to them on the floor, dripping meat broth and water in their mouths every third hour.

We felt enormously relieved when Rufus and Merry, for the first time, wanted more broth and then, twenty-four hours later, some minced meat in the broth. Thereafter, their recovery was quick and only a couple of days later they were out playing again. Everything was back to normal.

Maybe the anxiety for my dogs had lowered my resistance. Once again, I was ill with malaria. I almost fell off the chair with fatigue. My arms as well as my legs weighed tons. As usual, it took time to regain strength and I doubted I'd ever feel strong again. How would I be able to cope with the French guests arriving the following day?

It was cool in the rainforest: I might feel better there. We quickly packed a lunch basket and drove off to Ikuywa River in the forest. A couple of hours in the shade on the riverbank worked miracles. I felt as if I'd had a vitamin injection and as my strength returned, my spirits rose. I no longer doubted I could take good care of our guests. They were really important to us, as our economy was reaching rock bottom.

We somehow managed to get along day by day, hoping for more paying guests. The booking situation had been bad for about a month and a half, but it had suddenly turned better with several reservations for the latter half of April. This was such a nice feeling. Could it be the beginning of a steady flow? All the same, it was most important to take good care of each and every guest, so that the news of our existence spread. And water was absolutely necessary, if we wanted satisfied guests.

The abnormal hot weather and the stagnant air made every breath an effort. We should have daily rain now, but several days could pass between the showers. Without a change of weather in a near future, the risk of crop failure was imminent. The maize needed a lot of rain at the beginning of the growth period and the few drops coming down once in a while were far from enough for both the maize and our household. We measured rainwater used for hand washing, toilet flushing and showers. Our tanks were empty so we urgently needed water.

One morning, Assistant Chief Nixon turned up with some wardens and prisoners. They had come to dig down the forty water pipes that had been lying on our compound for two months. On our way to Kakamega, we made a stop to talk to Nixon. I brought a big plastic bag with at least four kilos of passion fruit to give to the prisoners. Nixon suggested that he'd hand out the fruit to the men, but no way. I gave them the passion fruit myself; otherwise they'd probably not have seen a trace of them. The prisoners really brightened up, as they didn't see fruit very often in jail.

On our return from town, we asked what had happened with the pipes. Assistant Chief Nixon told us that they hadn't been able to finish their work since they'd run out of pipes: not the first time this happened. This time only thirty metres of pipes were missing up to our boundary.

Bertil grabbed the measuring stick and went out to check how many metres the prisoners had dug. He quickly calculated that some of the pipes we'd had resting on our compound had been stolen during today's work. And that must have happened in the presence of the assistant chief. I could have exploded.

The whole pipe laying had, up until now, taken sixteen months. The distance was a little less than a kilometre. The biggest part of the time, we'd been waiting for the chief to decide one thing or another. This had been a deliberate way for him to sabotage us. The whole mess was probably due to the fact that we'd refused to pay him the usual bribes.

Time was really passing at express speed. Suddenly, it was Easter again. And we wanted Easter food, even if only a little. We had to improvise. We had a tin of pickled herring, brought by Per Erik on his last visit, and instead of salmon we used Nile perch. A small perch weighed twenty kilos, so we'd only bought a tiny piece of it. We had also "schnaps" since Per Erik had given us some small bottles from Ålborg.

We also needed eggs for Easter. We'd actually believed we'd be self-supporting on eggs. What a mistake. Our ten hens had already become food for cobras, neighbours, birds of prey and mongooses. The last two hens didn't produce any eggs for three months and as a result turned into lunch for unexpected guests.

Our plumber, who should have come to build the new hot water device a long time ago, sent a messenger to inform us he was ill.

When he finally turned up, he looked awful. Full of bruises and with one arm in a sling. He'd been knocked down by a motorcyclist, when out cycling. The police arriving on the scene of the accident took the plumber's bike, although he was innocent of the accident and told him that it would cost him a lot of money to get his bike back. For the police.

The plumber worked well, so now we had hot water in the showers almost twenty-four hours a day. A small fire for a couple of hours under a big oil drum which rested in a fireplace down at the showers provided us with hot water. The night askari lit the fire around six in the morning and it continued burning until around nine or ten in the forenoon. That way we had hot water all day long, often halfway through the night.

A few days after Easter, Bertil installed the ventilation system in the Sotanini mine. Everyone was enormously happy, when the bellows worked. Pumping only a few times, the men could stay down in the 30 metre deep shaft for approximately an hour. Now they felt motivated to work hard with the gold mine to get money to pay for school fees.

When we left for home, the rain started. Uphill it was like driving a car in a river. On the somewhat bigger road, half-metre deep water furrows developed. Slippery mud made the car slide down into the deepest furrows. On a couple of occasions, we were indeed afraid the car would tip over, but it didn't get stuck and faithfully continued all the way. But of course - it was a Land Rover. When we arrived at the public plot, outside our main gate, it was already late afternoon and the rain was literally hanging in the air.

"Gunilla, can you feel the smell?" wondered Bertil.

"Yes, there's definitely something familiar about it. What is it?"

"I think it is ozone. We're driving through a thundercloud, I think. Can't you feel your body tingling?"

"Yes, but I thought it was the speed wind of the car," I joked.

The air was loaded with electricity in an unpleasant way. More or less, the same as when you're at the Technical Museum of Stockholm, where you can stand on an insulated glass stool holding a generator and feel the charge.

We'd just finished unloading all the things we'd bought, when the storm broke. Simultaneous thunder and lightning. The dogs ran like lightning itself onto the veranda, where we joined them to watch the fury of the elements.

"What luck we don't have any guests today," I said, when we'd settled on the veranda.

"It's a good thing we had enough time to disconnect the telephone and everything else," answered Bertil.

He shouldn't have spoken.

At exactly that moment, the private intercom whistled like a madman.

"So now the intercom is broken," I said.

"Let's hope, it can be repaired." Bertil looked gloomy.

The intercom had more or less exploded, both up at staff quarters and down at the banda. Bertil managed to repair three out of the five telephones. With electronics and long cables you fare badly against the forces of nature.

## 45. A group of ornithologists

During the past few weeks, we'd had a tough job with lots of guests from embassies as well as from UN organizations. People who lived in Nairobi and Mombasa. It was much more rewarding with guests residing in-country than with tourists. For one thing, they didn't expect everything to be working; when it did, they were happy. Many of them were also used to a somewhat lower standard, from camping in the national parks and similar adventures. In such places, standards weren't taken so seriously. Having a good time was the important thing.

On booking, I always informed potential guests that our standard was rather basic and that Riverdale Gardens was located off the beaten track. At the same time, I always checked if the guests had any preferences regarding food or if there were any vegetarians in the group.

Bertil and I were standing on the entrance veranda, waiting for a group of ornithologists from England. The telephone line had been bad at the time of reservation, so I hadn't received any answers to my usual questions. It wasn't great knowing that.

"Here they come," said Bertil. "I can hear a car up at the gate."

A moment later, the minibus came down and parked on the lawn in front of the house. Seven persons stepped out. The atmosphere in the group seemed gloomy and I felt nervous. I just wanted to go back to bed.

"Bertil," I declared. "This is going to be a disaster. They're far too old for a place like this. What shall we do?"

"Just take it easy. We'll manage," answered Bertil, cool as a cucumber. He left and walked up to the car to receive the group. He spoke to them for a few minutes and soon afterwards, he was back at my side.

"They want to start bird watching immediately," he told me. "I suggested they should stand on the septic tank. I'll show them the way."

The group disappeared down the garden where they remained standing on the tank with binoculars to their eyes for I'm sure over an hour. I wanted them to check into their rooms before sunset, but no way. It was almost pitch dark, when they returned. The luggage was sorted out and our boys helped carry it. I walked around making sure everyone had received his or her luggage, showed them the sanitary facilities and informed them at what time dinner would be served. Everyone was silent and reserved.

We offered them a glass of sherry before dinner - they were after all Englishmen. I thought it would soften up the atmosphere a little. During the conversation, we understood that they were deeply shocked at being out in the middle of nowhere. Furthermore, their rooms weren't even en suite. So far, during their trip, they'd only been staying at golf hotels and lodges, so the difference was of course rather huge for the poor things.

We noticed that the group leader wasn't popular and a moaner in the group immediately complained he didn't have a toilet close to the room; there might be lions and leopards outdoors; of course nobody would know how to wash clothes and it was impossible to lock the door. Bertil immediately changed the lock in torchlight. I pacified the moaner by promising him his clothes would be washed and assured him there were no wild animals in the neighbourhood. The delicious food we served was hardly touched.

After dinner, the Englishmen sat in the lounge, ticking off on their lists all the birds they'd seen during the day. Bertil disappeared outside to check that the water tank for showers and toilets was full.

At around nine in the evening, we heard a knock at the kitchen door. It was the night askari Mark. He pointed at a rope-like object quite close to the solar panels. He'd just killed a green snake. Thank heavens; it wasn't a bush viper but a snake similar to the one Bertil had shot a close-up picture of in the forest. And what luck our scared guests hadn't seen it.

All night through, the kerosene lamps were lit in all the rooms. A pity that our guests didn't believe our protestations that there were neither lions nor leopards in the vicinity. Now they'd be even more tired the following morning. We slept in the half-ready third hut, something we told the guests, in case they needed us to hold their hands.

We'd promised to have a light breakfast ready, so that the guests could be in the rainforest by 6.30 in the morning. I was up at around four. Going to the toilet, I discovered to my horror that we were out of water. How on earth could that have happened? I ran in panic to Bertil and told him the horrible news. He flew out of bed and pulled on his clothes as fast as he was able. We ran together up to the main building. The important thing was to fix the water before our guests woke up.

A quarter of an hour later, I was splitting my sides with laughter. It looked so funny. Bertil was standing with only his underpants on, down in the one thousand-litre tank. His head was about all that was showing. With a plastic bowl, he was scooping up what little water was left at the bottom. The night askaris crossed the lawn, ran up to the toilet tank, climbed the ladder and added the water into that tank. It all looked like the fun games we play in Sweden on Midsummer Eve. Finally, we had enough water for the guests' visits to the toilet before breakfast. We hoped they'd wait with their showers until returning from the rainforest.

As soon as the minibus disappeared through the gate, Bertil asked the shamba boys to start digging up the ground on both sides of the water pipes. Surely, there must be a leakage somewhere. No guests had ever managed to finish 400 litres of water in a few night hours. No leakage was found. It was a total mystery. When the guests returned to have a second, fuller breakfast, we'd had enough time to fill the tank. They never noticed what had happened.

After breakfast, I prepared a big picnic basket for the group, with a wonderful chicken salad and all kinds of accompaniments. The Englishmen would spend the rest of the day in the rainforest. A couple of the ladies came into the kitchen and told me the lunch looked really nice. It looked as if their spirits were rising.

It was already late afternoon, when the minibus returned. Seeing the guests stepping out of it, I immediately understood something unpleasant had happened. The tour conductor was walking separately and the others seemed very agitated.

According to the moaner, who had turned into a nice man once he got his ironed laundry nicely folded and delivered by Veronica, the tour leader had made a fool of himself. He'd left the group together with a guide in the forest and driven off with the minibus to Kakamega to have its silencer repaired. He'd been gone for six hours and had taken their lunch with him, in the bus.

The bus had been standing in the sun in Kakamega the whole day, so our starving guests dared not eat when the minibus returned. They'd had nothing to eat or to drink during the whole day in the forest.

I made an effort, out of the ordinary, with dinner. It was important to get delicious food quickly on the table. But the guests still only pecked at their food. Didn't they like my food?

Next morning, I heard that all of them had been suffering from a stomach bug for several days before arriving at our hotel. My blood pressure rose. When I saw the tour leader, I asked him why he hadn't told us about the upset stomachs. We could have sent for a doctor and medicine in no time at all. He looked most astonished, as if it was no concern of his. Some tour leader. But we'd at least got an explanation as to why we'd run out of water in the toilet tank. The poor guests had probably been sitting there all night long.

When the bird watchers had left, it wasn't long before new guests arrived, and it continued like that for several weeks. Only now and then, a night without guests. The dogs and we were moving around between different huts, depending on the number of guests. Sometimes, we slept on mattresses in front of the fireplace in the lounge. On such occasions, we hoped the guests weren't night owls, since we couldn't go to bed until they'd retired to their huts. The dogs seemed a little lost, not quite understanding what was going on.

We had a new talent working in the kitchen. Free of charge. Western Hotel College needed trainee jobs for its pupils for three months and we'd accepted a boy learning to be a chef. His name was Max and he was very ambitious. On his first working day, he prepared a lot of delicacies for our guests. He lived in one of our staff apartments and seemed to be getting along well with the other staff members. We kept our fingers crossed he'd turn out okay. What we'd seen so far was extremely good.

We were really fortunate to have Max in the kitchen and Veronica helping in the reception and doing the washing-up. The rest of our employees also behaved well. Washing-up, cleaning, grass cutting - everything went like clockwork and everyone behaved in a polite and pleasant way towards the guests.

Our staff had been informed that, at the least sign of theft from the guests, the guilty one would be severely punished and reported to the police. They were, furthermore, told we had a moneybox on the counter in the reception. All tipping was put into that to be divided later in equal parts among all the employees. This way, they also learned that carrying luggage was worthwhile. The villagers seemed to like the fact we had a lot of guests. They laughed, waved their hands and smiled, seeming proud of "their" hotel.

Our village walks were a well-liked feature in the guests' stay. We found out the guests' interests and then one of our staff members took them on a walk down into the village. They visited huts, talked to the villagers and heard explanations about local customs. Some guests, for example doctors, wanted to meet the medicine man together with Nelson, the nursing officer. Teachers often wanted to visit the village school. Our guests found this intriguing. We even had a friend, an Englishman from up-country, who brought his guests down to us so that they could do a village walk in our village.

It was unbelievable so many guests were vegetarians. We tried out more and more vegetarian dishes. The last one had really been a great success. My mother had sent me a recipe, cut out of a magazine, for banana flower burgers. We now had a couple of thousand banana plants and they kept increasing in number so we didn't have to let all the banana flowers develop into bunches of bananas. The lilac coloured flower was cut into pieces and parboiled. Chopped into smaller pieces, it could be used in the same way as minced meat, for example to be made into hamburgers. Very tasty.

Maybe we were making things difficult for ourselves, serving so much and such tasty food for lunch and such big buffet breakfasts. Everyone found the food superb but the guests often said they couldn't manage another meal the same day. Maybe we should cut down on food? But, at the same time, it was actually nice to hear that the guests thought our food among the best they'd eaten in Kenya. So why economize?

One of our bigger and most expensive problems was that the grass grew so desperately fast and long. Almost constantly, we had to hire extra workers to cut it. Our compound was 20,000 square metres and at least three quarters of it was covered by grass. If you had long grass, you couldn't see forest cobras and other dangers hiding in it. So you had to keep the grass low. It wasn't just because I was scared to death of snakes, but for the sake of our guests.

Some time ago, we'd consequently started planting another kind of grass. The villagers knew that, so they came with wheelbarrows full of that kind to sell to us. This grass grew along the ground, not upwards. A small tuft grew quickly in size, so we planted such tufts here and there. They were gradually spreading: one day in the future they might take over control from the long grass.

The water issue was still a permanent source of worry. We'd been subjected to cheating and string-pulling. When the remaining pipes up to our boundary were to be dug down, once again pipes were missing. Now we bought the missing pipes ourselves and let our shamba boys dig the rest of the ditch. Finally, everything was ready so that the waterman could connect the water. What a change it would be to have running water.

## 46. Blue-eyed

Like on so many other occasions, things didn't, however, turn out as we'd expected. On a Thursday, we finally got the water pipe connected. Kabeji, the old man responsible for the water in the village at the big road, wanted a bribe of 250 shillings for turning on the water at the main tank. Bertil wasn't at home, so I paid the sum. Of course, we got no water.

That Friday, Kabeji returned with two helpers in order to search for leaks. He wanted two of our shamba boys to dig. The old man's two helpers just stood watching. In the evening, some water slowly came out of the tap. We were content and invited the men to lemonade and bread in the garden. Bertil went to bed, since he had malaria.

Half an hour later, I called Bertil and told him the watermen refused to leave until they got another bribe of 1,000 shillings. Bertil got angry, jumped out of bed and got the small tape recorder. With the recorder in his pocket and brandishing paper and pencil, he strode up to the men and asked them to write their names on the paper. Thereafter, he asked them what they were waiting for.

"We want a bribe," they explained, "one thousand shillings."

They didn't understand it was illegal to ask for bribes, but after a lot of discussion, they finally left. Since there was no longer any water coming from our tap, the men obviously closed the connection on their way back to the village. But the tap was beautiful anyway, standing on the upper part of the compound.

Rumour said the old man quite simply turned off the water and claimed he must have money for the diesel needed for the water pump.

We planned to dig a well of our own, later on. That way, we could avoid having any contact with the corrupt old man.

We'd also been cheated regarding the title deeds when we bought our land. Copies of the title deeds for our two adjoining plots were sent to us by fax before we left Sweden but, later, we found out that they'd never been stamped. Ever since then, we'd been nagging and quarrelling about it with the authorities. They'd answered that the laws had been changed since our purchase, so that foreigners no longer could own agricultural land. The reason was that Kenya wanted to stop foreigners from speculating in Kenyan land. In order to get our title deeds, we'd hence been forced (for a very large sum of money) to let an architect and town planner help us write an official request with a description of our investment plans. This request showed that we hadn't bought the land for speculation purposes.

On the way to town, one day at the beginning of May, we bumped into Timothy. He told us that our last title deed was ready for us to fetch. We at once changed our plans and after four hours of waiting at the Lands Office, we finally had our title deed number two. At last, we had legal documents on what we owned in Kenya.

On our way home, we stopped at the Post Office to check our post box. In it, we found our next lovely surprise: the logbook for our Land Rover. It had disappeared somewhere in Nairobi, when a new stamp was to be added. Now it had suddenly arrived in an envelope from the Tax Authorities. Not even an accompanying letter was enclosed.

Although we still didn't have any water, we felt we had reason to celebrate with a glass of wine on the veranda.

Now, it had happened again. We'd been cheated with the meat we'd bought. For two consecutive days, we had to improvise the meals at the last minute. Max was completely superb and in no time at all managed to put other tasty dishes on the table. Our guests never noticed what was going on in the kitchen.

On the second of the two days, lots of people, including seven children of different ages, arrived from Kisumu for lunch. They were served an improvised and much-liked oven pizza.

After the meal, our grown-up guests had coffee on the veranda. The house was surging with all the sounds happy and playful children can emit. Some children were panning for gold at the panning pool, together with Petrus. Fred was sitting on the floor in the lounge with other children, feeding our small rabbit babies, who were running loose: one rabbit escaped. Other kids were playing with stuffed animals and cars or whirling around in the revolving chair. The parents were having a wonderful time on the veranda, while the rest of us were running around with their children. A formidable success. We expected to have every European family with children coming here, sooner or later. Just think of the parental vacation they got.

When, once again, it was a little quieter with fewer guests, we took the opportunity to do some maintenance work. A plasterer started cementing the outer walls of staff quarters. We were ashamed of the way that building looked, because the rains had washed off quite a lot of the mud on the walls.

One day, when our staff members had lunch up at staff quarters, Fred felt something on his arm. It was a sweet little wriggling snake. Its life ended quickly. That same evening, Bertil had to turn out to kill a snake in Max's apartment. Max was from a city and hated snakes. He became hysterical and refused to stay in his room. As a result we had to move him into one of our guest huts, awaiting snake removal in staff quarters. We put up papyrus mats as an extra ceiling, to avoid snakes falling onto the beds. The snakes were as a matter of fact harmless house snakes - but in any case…

We'd now been living in our first guest hut for exactly one year. So much had happened during that year. When we arrived in the village at the end of 1996, the site was a dry and dusty maize field with rocks and stubble. No trees and no grass. It was difficult to imagine that now.

During the past year, the growth of plants had exploded and many different species of birds had found their way to us. Butterflies of all kinds were fluttering around among all the flowers we'd planted. We had three huts. One was surrounded with plants in different shades of red, one with only blue flowers of different kinds and one with only yellow ones. A restaurant building was finished, surrounded by enormous groups of hibiscus, red bottlebrush trees and Nandi Flame trees and a veranda framed with vines of golden showers. A building with WC's and hot water showers and an enormous septic tank, hidden amongst banana plants. Unbelievable! The kitchen garden was full of all sorts of vegetables. Hundreds of passion fruit plants were climbing on the fences. Around one hundred papaya trees and many avocado trees were already several metres high. The eucalyptus plants had grown big and the plant with Queen of the Night planted at the side of our pit-hole toilet, in order to minimize any odour, was impressive where it stood, secreting a fabulous fragrance.

It had become a paradise. In only one year!

I couldn't believe we'd lived in the thirty year old banda. Even less, could I believe I'd been able to stand it for six full months.

## 47. Travel journalists

We relaxed in the lounge in front of a blazing fire while a terrible storm was raging outdoors. As usual, I was afraid that our eucalyptus, so tall it seemed to be almost reaching the sky, would be hit by lightning and fall down onto our main building.

Playing patience in the light of the kerosene lamps, I thought of how we got the firewood we needed. We had a number of eucalyptuses on the compound and had also planted many small ones. Eucalyptus is a nice tree. If we cut off a branch, a couple of new branches soon grew out. It would, however, still be a long time before we could start using wood from our own trees for the fire.

Six months ago, a boy from the other side of the valley wanted to borrow money from us in order to buy a donkey. Using the donkey, he'd go to the forest to pick up old wood, fallen from the trees, and transport it home on the back of the donkey. He wanted to repay us by giving us firewood. We agreed that twenty loads would be enough as repayment. In this way, we were now constantly getting firewood and every load was ticked off on a paper in the kitchen.

"Bertil, somebody's knocking at the door," I suddenly remarked. "I think I heard a car, a moment ago."

It was half past eight in the evening and it was pitch-dark outside. Normally, we didn't get any visitors at this time of night. Bertil opened. A soaking wet and unhappy European was standing on the entrance veranda.

"Come in," Bertil said in English.

The man entered, leaving a trail of water on the floor. He introduced himself as Jack, a travel journalist from England. He'd been to the rainforest and had planned to stay overnight in their guesthouse. He'd looked for someone to notify, without success. Since he hadn't found anyone and since there was no water in the bathroom, he left. He continued looking in the bars along the road, until someone told him about Riverdale Gardens. That was why he'd now come to us.

We invited Jack to join us in front of the burning fire and served him a glass of whisky so that he got warm inside. After a while, he was in a better mood. During our conversation, he showed us articles he'd written for Sunday Telegraph and Financial Times. I cooked him an improvised meal and suggested he should stay overnight, as our guest, which he happily accepted.

Our conversation wore on and we told him we liked gold panning. He thought that sounded thrilling and asked if he could test it the following day.

Next morning, we brought Jack to Sotanini where he crushed and grinded stone, soon becoming friends with all the villagers. On our way home, we made a stop in the rainforest where we introduced him to one of the rainforest guides so that he could have a one hour guided tour in the forest - a must for any travel journalist.

After lunch at Riverdale Gardens, Jack wanted to pan for more gold. Bertil took him to close-by Nianini where he got a quick lesson. Testing with the pan, he got some gold grains which we placed in a small plastic bottle with a cork. Total happiness. Jack left content and cheerful.

A couple of days after Jack's visit, once again a travel journalist knocked at the door; this one from Germany. He'd biked all over Africa and written a biker's guide. Now, he was making a guidebook of Kenya. He talked and talked and wrote and wrote.

When he wanted to put up his tent to spend the night on the compound, we offered him a room and dinner on the house. The German was lyrical about the view from the veranda and would have loved to spend a couple of days with us, but he was unfortunately on a tight schedule.

It was so strange. We really lived in the middle of nowhere, but yet four travel journalists had found us so far, although Riverdale Gardens wasn't in any guidebook. That would, however, soon change as all four journalists had promised to include it in their future books.

I almost believed that the village medicine man had put a curse on Riverdale Gardens and us. It was evening-time at the end of the month. Petrus had just informed us that the man from whom we bought electricity for our freezer in Petrus′ shop was planning to cut off our electricity. He obviously thought he could get millions of shillings as extortion money. We paid him three hundred shillings a month, although our monthly consumption was for less than sixty shillings. He knew how important the freezer was to us and was hoping to get more money through blackmail. We must quickly find another place for the freezer, before he carried out his plan and destroyed our food. Petrus promised to help us with this, because without a freezer we couldn't receive any guests.

I wondered if the medicine man might have included our shamba boys in a possible curse. One boy had earlier cut his leg when cutting grass. It needed surgery, injections, stitches, many re-visits and sick leave. Fred had now done more or less the same and Bertil had to take him to hospital. Happily enough, there were no floods of blood this time. The second most common cause of death in connection with accidents in the countryside was, according to the Danish doctor, blood poisoning. Subsequently we made sure that those who got injured got an inoculation against tetanus.

Speaking of horrible things. One day when the boys were digging up an old tree stump on the compound, a forest cobra slithered away at high speed. Continuing to dig, they found eleven snake eggs, which they quickly picked up. We could certainly not have a lot of cobras loose on the compound, risking our guests and dogs.

"Gunilla, the post office in Wulushi just called. They'll soon be putting up the telephone wire," Bertil said on his way out from reception to the veranda.

"Oh, that's why your English was so good," I said. "When you're angry, your English becomes fantastic. You should hear yourself speaking. But didn't the wires come down several weeks before Easter? Now we're in June."

"Yes, the telephone wire has been lying on the ground for about eleven weeks. I won't believe that it'll be put up on the poles again, until I see it."

It wasn't only the telephone company men that made us desperate. The old waterman, Kabeji, made me see red. Not only was he almost always drunk and stinking of dirt, he was also the most corrupt of all corrupt Kenyans. He almost beat our chief in that respect. In spite of us obediently paying for water at the end of every month, we got none. The rains were coming to an end and the situation was getting acute. Kabeji took advantage of that. He knew we were in desperate need of water, especially when having guests. He therefore came several times a month to tell us he needed money for diesel. We'd noticed that even if we paid him this extra money, we didn't get any water. If, contrary to expectation, we got water it would only be run for a short while. Then he turned off the tap, claiming the money was finished.

Last time water was "finished" in the reservoir, we climbed all the way up and looked down the opening. The tank was almost full. A few hours later, he put a padlock on the hatch.

All these water problems were infuriating. Only we had paid for the digging of the whole ditch and the laying of the pipes and only we were paying for diesel. Kabeji didn't care. He sold water along the pipe to the villagers. After that, he redirected the water to his water kiosk in Wulushi, where he sold water too.

It was unbelievable that I'd given this ungrateful old man Christmas presents: a thick blanket, a shirt, one kilo of meat and some other small things. It would make you sick.

"Kee, ee, ee, ee, ee…"

I looked up from my book. I recognized that sound. It was Elvis. I scanned the sky with my eyes and there, immediately above me, I saw him circling round. He'd probably soon come down to land on the roof of hut number one. Subconsciously, I'd already lowered my glance towards that hut. There, on the roof, sat another

Long-crested Eagle. Had Elvis already found himself a fiancée, a Priscilla?

During the following days, Bertil and I looked for the eagle couple, so obviously in love. We were lucky at last. They'd built their nest high up in our biggest eucalyptus. Now, they were flying together or one was sitting waiting for the other, either on the roof of the hut or on one of the fence poles.

It was really wonderful to see all those birds of prey. We lived at high altitude so eagles, falcons and hawks were very often seen - and that at close range.

At the beginning of summer, we had nine Dutch guests for a couple of days. It was nice to notice they were having a wonderful time with us as well as in the rain-forest. They really loved our food and our veranda. According to them, it was something special that they were allowed to make a note themselves of whatever they took out of the bar.

"How can you trust your guests to this extent? I've never seen this before in Kenya," one of them asked me.

"We actually don't trust all our guests, but our intention is to make you feel at home here," I answered.

The Dutch people promised to recommend Riverdale Gardens to the Dutch colony in Nairobi. That promise rapidly gave a positive result and increasingly more Dutch visited us.

## 48. Three small birds

A few days later, Kees, a Dutch friend, turned into the compound. This time, he came by car instead of the motorbike he usually rode. We knew him from Kakamega, where he was head of a Finnish forest project which unfortunately now was coming to its end. Bertil and he had become friends since both were interested in minerals.

He brought a rickety birdcage with three sweet small Love Birds as a gift. He was busy emptying his house before his return to Finland, and he'd earlier given us a lot of plants. The small birds were lovely. You could almost call them "the colour palette of the Lord". Dark-brown head, yellow and orange collar, dark-green wings, light-green body, black wing-quills, green feet, red beak, white eyes with big black pupils. They were unbelievably colourful. We didn't like birds to be kept in cages but couldn't refuse to welcome these small darlings. We knew that Love Birds were regarded as pest in Kisumu, since they ate the crops, but they were so fantastically beautiful.

Before our friend disappeared, he explained, "You must move the birds to this other bigger cage I'm giving you. This is only a transport cage. Please, also remember that they must have the company of each other, otherwise they'll die."

They were so charming, sitting close to one another on a branch.

"Three small birds sitting on a branch...," Bertil sang to me. (A travesty of a famous Swedish song)

We asked the staff to move the birds. Disaster! They made such a mess of things that one bird escaped, flying out through the open door. Having recovered from this shock, we foolishly asked them to move the other two birds. Veronica was impatient and banged hard on the cage to make the birds fly into the other cage. This scared the birds so much that one of them dropped dead. We almost had a nervous breakdown. Only Doff was left (we'd named the other two Ole and Dole, after a Swedish nursery rhyme). How could we avoid Doff dying, now that he was left alone?

One of the forest guides, who came to visit us, told us Love Birds were sold at a market this side of Kisumu. We got into the car together with Fred and drove towards Kisumu. On our way, we stopped at several marketplaces to ask if they sold this kind of bird. Finally we found a man who claimed he knew where to find them. We gave him a lift so that he could show us. After approximately ten kilometres, we came to another marketplace and started to look around. No birds.

When the man showed signs of wanting to leave the car, Bertil got so angry that he turned the car homebound again. He wasn't letting the man out of the car, until we were back at the market where he'd joined us. He'd only tried to cheat us into a free ride home to his village, but no way. He'd have to walk back along the main road.

No birds. That was the gist of several hours driving and searching. We could only hope that the bird that had escaped would return to look for his mate. Otherwise, we'd have to free the last poor darling so that he could find his friend living free in the open.

Hopefully David, who would soon come on his second visit, would have time to see Doff, before we let him out of the cage.

It was four o'clock in the morning. Outside, it was pitch dark and really cold. After a quick cup of coffee, we got into the Land Rover and tried to drive towards the gate. In spite of the four-wheel-drive, the car glided so that mud was flying in every direction. Bertil blew the whistle and the night askaris turned up to push the car.

After a while, we were on our way to Kakamega. Because of the bad state of the roads, we chose the inner road to town. Hopefully, it would be easier to drive on. We were going to meet the Akamba-bus coming from Nairobi. David, our youngest son, was on it.

After getting stuck in the mud a number of times, we arrived at the Akamba bus station in Kakamega, eager to embrace our youngest one. But where was the Akamba bus? The bus station looked deserted. What had happened? Had the bus had a traffic accident on its way from Nairobi? My nerves were on edge. Where was my son?

"Calm down, Gunilla," Bertil said. "They might've parked around the corner."

We turned around the corner at Kakamega Primary School. And found the bus - completely empty. A metre away, a uniformed Akamba-driver was standing smoking. We pounced on him.

"Have you seen a young man, a mzungu, on the bus a moment ago?" Bertil asked.

"Yes, of course," the driver replied. "He came on my bus. He asked if it was possible to get a taxi. He said his parents, who were supposed to meet him, weren't here. He's probably caught a taxi to your place."

"No!" I exclaimed. "He has absolutely not gone to Wuasiva in a taxi. He's not that stupid. He'd risk his life going into the countryside in a taxi. He knows that. He must be somewhere in town."

"Golf," Bertil burst out. "He'll of course be at Golf Hotel. Let's go there."

Said and done. We got into the car and drove up to Golf Hotel. The night receptionist was on duty as it was only around six o'clock in the morning.

When we came into the reception area, the receptionist, whom we already knew after many visits to the hotel, remarked, "The boy you're looking for is sitting in the lounge. He seems awfully sleepy."

"Heellooo there," a deep voice said and I was swept right into David's arms. Bertil also got a bear hug. Within a moment, we were sitting on the sofa speaking all at the same time.

David was hungry, so we ordered breakfast for all three of us. We weren't in any rush with the return trip, as we preferred to wait until daylight. Maybe the roads would then also have time to dry up after the night's violent rain.

At home again, I tried to make David go and lie down for a rest. He'd travelled on the night bus and ought to be tired. My suggestion wasn't accepted. David walked into the reception, fetched the rocking chair, carried it out onto the veranda and sat down. Without a word, he kept staring at the valley.

"How is it possible?" he finally asked. "How is it possible? When I was here in March last year, this was only a dusty field? It's so beautiful, so extremely beautiful!"

We laughed happily. Who doesn't like to hear praise for his creation? It wasn't thanks to us it was so fertile but we'd indeed planned, bought and planted lots of trees and bushes. And we, too, found it very beautiful.

David should in fact take all the credit for the houses. They were, after all, his architectural creations.

That nothing had been built according to Swedish standards was no fault of his. We'd bought the timber on root (while it was still a tree). Then it had been felled and hand sawn in the traditional local way. We hadn't given any thought to the fact that timber shrinks when it dries, so it was fortunate we didn't have a Swedish climate, since in such a case we'd have frozen to death. The spaces between the floor boards, now a centimetre wide, meant that at night the temperature inside the house was as low as outside.

After a short rest, David opened his luggage and handed over a blueberry bush, a small piece of a blackcurrant bush and roots from rhubarb. These were to be planted, as an experiment, in the kitchen garden but they'd probably not survive. He also took out some delicacies my mother and father had sent along with him. Herring and other things typical for summer would be eaten this Midsummer when Johan, one of David's best friends, would also come for a visit.

When David had spent a while cuddling and playing with the dogs on the veranda floor, Bertil took him on an inspection tour of the compound and introduced him to our staff. They were eager to meet him since in fact only Johannes had met him earlier.

It was extremely convenient that David had arrived in June. We were planning to extend the restaurant building, adding a small private apartment at one end of it. Until now, we'd been moving around without having any really private place to ourselves.

David quickly threw himself into the work, drawing up plans for the extension. He'd spend a month with us and as much as possible needed to be done during that time. David told Daniel, our fundi, to get concrete and off-cuts for the plinth moulds at once. They would be cast as soon as the material had arrived.

We had a lot to plan and discuss. We wanted, for example, to reduce use of the generator. It was, as a matter of fact, mostly used for the oven, which we needed a lot when we had guests. For the rest, we usually used solar power. The public electric cable stopped only four hundred metres from our compound. The Electric Company wanted an equivalent to around 20,000 US dollars for the connection to our place, so that was out of the question. Instead, we hoped that later on we'd get electricity through the national programme for rural development.

## 49. The death of a child

Bertil banged his fist on the table, so hard that our coffee cups jumped. Then he roared, "Get lost and never show up here again. You're a bloody murderer!"

Johannes cowered, shielding his head with his arms. Did he really believe Bertil would hit him? Actually, I felt almost capable of hitting Johannes. He was absolutely inhuman. An egoist beyond comparison. Prison wouldn't be enough punishment. Unfortunately, my better self won and I remained on my chair. I was on the verge of tears. David and his friend Johan were walking around, kicking everything in their way and seeming just about in tears. The rest of the staff were silent and diffident and didn't know in which direction to look.

"Get out of here," I hissed at Johannes. "You can be sure we'll tell the chief we consider you guilty of your daughter's death."

When Johannes, who had been one of our shamba boys since our arrival in the village, had sneaked out through the gate, I asked the others, "Is it only me needing a whisky right now? I'm so angry and upset I'm shaking."

Bertil and the boys also needed something to calm them down so we sat down on the veranda with a glass in our hands. We were all silent, thinking of what had happened.

"Explain to me why you're so angry at that boy," Johan suddenly said. "Of course, it's horrible his daughter has died. But you really seemed pissed off, not only sad," he added.

Johan had recently come down to us to meet his old friend David. He wanted to celebrate Midsummer with us here in Africa. He was studying medicine and an hour ago he'd been listening to Sharon's heart with his stethoscope, just a short moment before the four-year old girl died.

Bertil and I related, both speaking almost at the same time, the story of Johannes. How the chief had asked us to lend Johannes money, so that he'd be able to get his dead wife's body out of the morgue. He was to repay that debt by working for us. When we later heard that his banda was leaking and that it rained onto Sharon's bed, we went to his home. The banda was almost falling down. They had neither beds nor mattresses. The beds consisted of wet removal boxes, lying directly on the wet ground.

Our fundi had calculated the cost for building a new banda for Johannes. Because of Sharon, we lent Johannes the money needed. He was to repay that debt too, by working for us. When the banda was ready, we gave Sharon one of our beds, a mattress, pillow, sheet and a blanket. We agreed with Johannes that each week he'd get flour, tea and sugar to take home so that Sharon would not starve. He also often got eggs and milk. That way, we ensured that his small motherless daughter would not starve or be cold. All our employees knew that we paid medical care for them as well as for their closest families. So we felt fairly sure everything would be working for the little girl.

A couple of days earlier, Johannes had come and asked for a loan of two thousand shillings. Sharon was ill and he wanted the medicine man to treat her. We refused to lend him money for a visit to such a man and instead suggested he should take the girl to hospital. A little later, we sent Veronica to Johannes' home to check on Sharon. She came back and informed us the girl was very ill, needing medical care. According to Veronica, Sharon seemed undernourished. I immediately asked her to take the child to hospital. Johannes, who didn't want her to go there, refused to come along.

When Sharon's treatment had started at the hospital, we found out little by little what had happened. Things we hadn't known about. Johannes had found a new wife approximately a year earlier, when his new banda was finished. She moved into it and within a short time, they had a baby. Sharon then had to move into her grandparents' banda, which was leaking like a sieve. The stepmother kept the bed for herself. That way, Sharon was once again sleeping on the wet ground without bedding or mattress. The stepmother ate the food we gave Johannes to bring home and Sharon didn't get any food, either from her father or her grandparents.

During the last few days, we'd been to the hospital several times, checking how the girl was getting on. Johannes' mother had been staying with her around the clock and we'd given her money for food. But Johannes himself hadn't visited his daughter. The doctors told us the only way for the girl to survive her undernourishment and pneumonia was by remaining at the hospital

That morning, Johannes had shown up at the hospital and taken his daughter away in spite of the doctors protesting. Nelson turned up at our compound and told us the girl was lying dying outside Johannes' banda. Together with David and Johan, we ran there. Nelson examined her and declared there was a very small possibility to save Sharon, with an expensive medicine. In that case, it had to be bought at once. The boys declared they were willing to pay for it, and Nelson ran off with his bicycle to buy it but before he was back, Sharon died.

“So,” I said, "we find him guilty of his daughter’s death. I feel sick just thinking of him."

"Yes, and as usual we’ve to give up any hope of getting back the money he owes us. We promise each other all the time never to lend money to anyone. But what can you do, when people are suffering so much?" concluded Bertil.

At that precise moment, there was a call at the gate. Johannes' father was coming down, starting to beg for help. As usual, the discussion ended with us lending him money, without any hope of being repaid, for a coffin and funeral clothes for little Sharon.

## 50. There is no gratitude in this world

Our villagers were so damned ungrateful. It didn't matter how much we helped them. We still always got a stab in the back.

Bertil came out onto the veranda, where David and I were having tea. Even from a distance, it was easy to see Bertil was angry.

"Njombo isn't quite right in the head," he hissed. "What a little bastard. Can you imagine? He refuses to pay any rent, so he's moving out this afternoon."

"It can't be true," I exclaimed. "He's lived rent-free for eight months. And he's making a fortune just from us and what we buy in his kiosk."

Bertil got out the calculator in reception, made a few calculations and then uttered, "Yes, on soft drinks alone he makes at least nine hundred shillings a month profit. Then add all the other things we buy daily: bread and milk, Blue Band and cigarettes. And he has a steady stream of clients at his kiosk."

"How high is the rent?" asked David curiously.

"Only five hundred shillings."

"Yes, and to think we built the kiosk for him. His drunkard father attacked him last year, chasing Njombo with his panga, having smashed his old kiosk in his parents' home, to pieces. He almost lost his life on that occasion. I remember he got a cut on one arm. He came crying to us, asking for help. So we agreed to build him a kiosk on our compound, up at the big gate. It's so big he can even live in it. And it's a fine kiosk, nicely built with a tin roof."

Bertil was still upset, as he stopped talking.

David looked quite shocked and I told him such things often happened to us here. Gratitude didn't exist. It went without saying that we, white people, should help everyone. On top of that, we had to gladly put up with the knife stabs that inevitably came. There was surely no gratitude in this world. Now we had an empty kiosk. We had neither time, stamina nor the money to run it ourselves.

The days passed quickly and it was fun to have David around. He mixed with the guests and entertained them with stories from his motorbike journey in South East Asia. It was actually very nice to see how polite and kind he was and how everybody seemed to admire him, both the guests and the staff members. He also helped us a lot with practical things like washing up, cooking dog food or picking vegetables. It was such a pity he had to return home just a week after Johan's departure. It was therefore important to make the most of him – to gain maximum pleasure and advantage - before he left.

David was happy, when we asked him to come along with us down to Kisumu in search of a car for everyday use. Our Land Rover consumed far too much petrol, so we had to have a cheaper car as a run-around. Our Belgian friend Olivier had a second hand red Suzuki Samurai convertible. It was fun, but it wasn't recommended driving an open car in Kenya, what with all the thefts and assaults. But that problem could be solved by getting a hard top made for the car, so in the end we bought it.

The car was driven up to us a couple of days later, when our Dutch friends came on a visit. Just as I'd imagined, David threw himself into the car and was in seconds behind the wheel, out through the gates on a test run. I'd thought it was my car, but I was sure it would turn out the same way as with the rocking chair I got on my 50th birthday. Everybody except me sat in it. I seldom had time to sit down.

The rainforest guides were important for the marketing campaign. They had to recommend places to stay for forest visitors, so it was important they knew what our place looked like. Most of them had already been there including, now, Smith. He was an ornithologist and in close contact with the professor at the Ornithological Department of National Museums of Kenya. He told us, to our great joy, that this professor now included Riverdale Gardens in the book and map which had been published for bird watchers. Not many places in Kenya had that honour.

We needed to prepare so much for future guests. The more activities we had, the longer they'd stay. Our Dutch friends from Kisumu would, for example, soon return to pan for gold with their children. So we had to go to Sotanini to prepare a full-day tour in the village. Panning together with the villagers seemed to attract a lot of people and was regarded as somewhat exotic.

Unfortunately, the gold prospectors had a new problem. The last problem, lack of oxygen, Bertil had already solved for them. Now the mine and shafts had started to fill with water. My father and Bertil corresponded eagerly about the new development. The water was probably following the gold veins all the way from the open air mine. How could this be solved? The solution must be cheap and simple, since we were talking of poor villagers.

As we were getting more and more guests, Max's trainee period with us was unfortunately at an end and it was time for him to return to the catering school. We hoped we'd have him back later on because he'd certainly done a fantastic job and was a natural at cooking. Since David had now also left, Bertil and I had to act as managers, cooks, waiters, plumbers, guides, night askaris and entertainers. Sometimes at the same time. It was important to grin and bear it, whatever happened. We had, for example, difficulties in keeping our laughter in control, the night we chased a small mouse between the kitchen and the dining room, while the guests were eating. It was like an episode out of "Fawlty Towers" with John Cleese. It goes without saying, the mouse won. Another night, just before we'd serve the guests, thousands of brown beetles landed in the middle of the already plated serving dishes. We searched desperately for tweezers and finding a pair each removed the monsters one by one. That evening, we learnt never to leave the kitchen door to the veranda open while cooking.

Talking about insects; we would soon have our own honey. An American missionary couple from Kakamega came for lunch one day. They brought a computer with a will of its own that Bertil repaired. They thanked us by giving us a lot of children books, bibles, jigsaw puzzles and family games as well as a beehive to be hung between a couple of trees. I thought the hive looked somewhat macabre - like a child's coffin - but it had to be put up. We had an extremely high number of bees on the compound and it would be stupid not to take advantage of the possibility of getting our own honey. Our shamba boys assured us they knew everything about bee keeping, so we'd no doubt manage this occupation, quite new to us.

## 51. A lady?

"Bertil, can you check in the container for that Indian cook book we were talking about yesterday?"

I called Bertil from the kitchen, probably interrupting him where he was sitting comfortably on the veranda, with his feet on the rail and Rufus on the floor at his side. But he was probably happy for a break in the boring work of writing payment slips for the staff.

We were going to test a dish out of the Indian cook book and I needed it urgently.

“Just a moment, I’m on my way up.”

Bertil came jogging onto the patio outside the restaurant and continued up through the now high grass to the white-painted container.

"The boys must cut the grass again,” he muttered. "What a pity the ground is so uneven we can’t use the lawnmower we bought in Kakamega."

Arriving at the container, he noticed that a new bee swarm had made its home under it. It was really big. You could judge that from the swarm of bees continuously humming on the left side. Bertil managed to open the heavy door and a swarm of small bees, the size of banana mosquitoes, swarmed around his head. They usually didn’t sting. They seemed to have built a nest in the rubber strips of the container door and honey was pouring along the edge of the door. It had a mild and sweet taste but the production seemed, alas, not sufficient to use.

Bertil suddenly realized that the bees he’d seen outside the container were much bigger than the ones he saw at the door. What was this? Did we have two different kinds at the container?

He found the cook book without any problem. He saw his battery-operated drilling machine, with a six-millimetre drill, lying on a table. Feeling mischievous, he picked up a screwdriver and put the point of it towards the floor and his ear at the other end. By moving the screwdriver around, he could quite quickly locate the centre of the new beehive.

He cautiously drilled a hole through the wooden container floor right down to the bees. They didn't notice. Then he grabbed the cook book and came down to me, where I was standing in the kitchen talking with the temporarily hired cook.

"Here's the cook book," he said. "I'll try to remove the hive from under the container. Those bees are huge."

"Have we got bees there again? Be careful, remember they could be African bees," I said worriedly. "These are dangerous."

Bertil grabbed the spray with the 'Doom' insecticide from the store. Back in the container, he held a short metallic tube over the hole in the floor. He could hear distant buzzing. Putting the spray bottle's mouthpiece in the tube, he pressed the spray button and released a large dose.

For a fraction of a second, he believed he'd missed the hole, but the buzzing quickly increased into a terrible roar. He'd misjudged the situation. At daytime, plenty of bees were at home. He bolted out through the container door, inside a black cloud of angry African bees. I was outside the kitchen, watching him.

Bertil yelled at me, "Run to the car. Be quick!"

He was already on his way there. We arrived approximately at the same time. Inside the car, we saw with horror how the bees started attacking everyone in the vicinity. Bertil got three stings on his right arm, but I managed to avoid any. The bees found their way into the car, through different crevices, and outside we saw people running in all directions, gesticulating wildly. Bertil started the engine and drove away.

"What will the neighbours say? I saw the bees spreading to our neighbour's banda," Bertil exclaimed. "I guess, we had better have dinner at Little Home instead, so the bees and the neighbours have time to calm down."

Since Max' return to hotel school, we'd been testing a new star in the kitchen - Ella. According to her documents, she was number one in her class at the school. She was, however, a really strange person, if I can put it that way.

Her first morning with us, Fred stood giggling outside the kitchen. I looked up towards the row of staff apartments and saw a scene that seemed taken from "Gone with the Wind". Ella was mincing down the lawn in a long light-blue dress with lacy sleeves, reaching all the way to her fingertips. Linda carried the train of the dress, in order to avoid dirtying it. I kept staring. How on earth would the girl be useful in the kitchen, wearing a dress like that? I asked her in a firm but friendly way to go back up and put on normal clothing, unless she'd brought chef clothes.

Muttering crossly, she disappeared, after having told me she wanted to be beautiful when meeting our guests. I answered her that clean and neat was enough and that her place was in the kitchen.

The start of our relation was, in other words, not very good. Bertil and I tried to improve matters. Maybe she was just nervous and for that reason had got off on the wrong track? Hence I spent a lot of time in the kitchen with her, asking her, among other things, about her family.

"We're one lady - that's me - and seven gentlemen in the family," she stated.

"Oh, so your mother is dead?" I asked.

"No, but she doesn't count," Ella answered and continued to tell me about her nice family. She'd recently attended the funeral of a relative. The deceased was a rather tall man and they'd taken the wrong measurements for the coffin. It was too small. The coffin cost 20,000 shillings and they didn't have time to make a bigger one.

"But," Ella said, "it was easy to make room for him. We cut off a piece of his head."

Sometimes, you wonder if you have a hearing defect. But her little story was perhaps merely a not too successful attempt at joking. One would at least hope so.

When we were without guests for some days, Ella completely went off the rails. Bertil and I usually ate in the dining room when being alone, served by a house girl or cook. Our meals weren't remarkable but we wanted them to be nice looking, neat and tasty. This was one of our ways to train the staff.

Ella didn't cook what we wanted for dinner and she just threw some food on our plates, although we'd told her we wanted to serve ourselves. We pointed out her imperfection, as usual in a kind and polite way. She then said that she should of course also sit at table with us and be served "as the lady she was". When she didn't get it her own way, she slammed the doors and stormed out. At that exact moment, her time with us came to an end.

When checking with the restaurant school, we heard Ella had already been reprimanded about her bad temper on several occasions.

Thank heavens, Max was coming back to work for a wage for a few months. Since he didn't have enough money for school fees, he wasn't able to take his exam in September, as planned. Since it was a matter of a lot of money, we couldn't lend him the sum needed but we'd succeeded in persuading his headmaster to let him take the exam in March instead. Until then, he might make the money he needed working for us.

Ole, the Love Bird that escaped some months ago, suddenly appeared one day on our compound. The bird landed on the cage and started talking to Doff. Then it disappeared again.

Since we'd been worried over the fact that Doff was alone in the cage, we promised a reward of 500 shillings to the person catching Ole. Injehu, Daniel's carpenter assistant, told us he often caught small birds, using a special bird adhesive that he put onto sticks. We let him try his method. As a consequence, we soon had a lot of these sticks lying on top of the cage, which was daily carried into the shade at some distance from our house.

One morning, Ole was seen in the neighbourhood again but he disappeared as soon as someone approached the cage. No luck for hunter Injehu. But Doff would probably solve the problem himself. He was frantically gnawing holes in the net. It would actually be the best solution, if he escaped by himself.

Injehu suddenly asked if he could catch a grey parrot from the rainforest for us. We had by now already, on a couple of occasions in Kakamega, been shown illegally caught parrots in rucksacks. It was completely awful to see these poor birds kept prisoner like that. We got upset with Injehu and explained our point of view. We also informed him, it was illegal to catch and sell parrots, but that information only seemed to go in through one ear and out the other. He was probably thinking how he'd become a millionaire by catching birds.

While standing talking, we heard an awful noise coming from down the village road. Some tractors and lorries were passing with material and timber for the clinic construction. After a lot of bureaucracy, something was at last happening. The work would start the following week, so we planned to be present by that time to document it.

## 52. A big family

"Fred, could you help me for a while, please?" Bertil wondered. He and I were standing at the telephone pole beside the container. "Can you climb that pole and fasten the cable up at the top?"

Astonished, I looked at Bertil. No human being could climb a smooth telephone pole, could they? I was still more astonished as I saw Fred in a jiffy sitting at the very top of the pole fastening the radio antenna according to Bertil's instructions.

"But Fred, how did you do that? Where have you learnt to climb like that?" I asked when Fred, laughing, was back on the ground.

"All the village boys must know that, at least those who've been circumcised."

"What more do you have to know? Do you have more manhood tests?"

Our questions rained down on Fred. He was uncomfortable. Finally, he explained he wasn't allowed to divulge that. It was a secret.

A couple of weeks later, we were reminded of that incident. Rather late on a dark evening in August, we heard songs and laughter from the public area. We walked up to the gate to see what was happening, and then we saw a lot of teenage boys dancing and singing on their way down to Wushiye. From the explanation our night askari gave us, we understood they were singing circumcision songs. It was, it seemed, important for the villagers to behave extra well during circumcision times. Otherwise the boys would compose songs about the misbehaving person which would then be performed in public.

Merry had become fat during the past month. Sometimes, I wondered if she would burst. Wouldn't she soon give birth? Taking out the calendar, I started counting. I saw that time had passed really quickly and that the moment was close. Sixty-one days had already gone by.

"Bertil, it's soon time for Merry. She probably has only one or two days left," I said and looked at him over my teacup.

Bertil at once bent down to pat Merry. She'd just finished her breakfast and came up to her master, starting to lick him.

"My little girl, are you going to be a mother? But you're so childish yourself."

"What if the vet won't come here? What do we do then?" I wondered.

It was time for our beloved dogs to become parents for the first time and for us to become "dog grandparents".

"Mother wrote that we shouldn't worry," I continued. "The bitch normally takes care of the whole thing herself. Her Bustra had three puppies in the garage in Sri Lanka. In spite of mother being present, she didn't have to do anything. But I'm nervous."

"Don't forget that in our dog book there are several pages dedicated to whelping," Bertil answered. "Everything will be alright. And furthermore I'm quite sure the vet will turn up."

"Can you ask Fred to make the puppy box today?" I asked, when I'd finished breakfast with a small "monkey banana" - a small kind of banana that we liked but which wasn't appreciated by the villagers.

On August 7th, Bertil and I gave birth to in total eight puppies. Merry was of course also involved. Poor little soul. It wasn't easy for her, but it wasn't easy for us either. The labour started already at seven o'clock in the morning. Then we called the vet. No answer. The hours passed and Merry got increasingly uneasy. We spent several hours at her side, nervously studying the dog book. Time after time we called the vet. Still no answer. The first puppy didn't arrive until three o'clock in the afternoon, proudly welcomed by Merry. We'd earlier sent Rufus up to the big house, so that he wouldn't bother Merry. The first puppy was jet black and seemed lively. When Merry gave birth to puppy number two, things were almost fatal. Merry was careless and bit off the umbilical cord too close to the body. Blood was streaming. Barefoot I ran uphill to the restaurant to get sewing thread, then back to the hut, where we finally succeeded in tying the puppy's umbilical cord. Having calmed down and after another fruitless attempt to contact the vet, we continued the birthing. Puppy number two was identical to number one. Then out came what seemed to us identical puppies number three, four, five, six, seven and eight. All of them jet black. A couple of them were a little smaller than the rest. When the whelping was finished, we tidied the puppy box and then Bertil went up to get us a whisky each. Quite exhausted, we sat on the floor admiring our extended family.

The night wasn't much easier. Bertil and Rufus moved up to the restaurant with mattresses and everything else. I was lying tense all night, once in a while checking that Merry wasn't squeezing the eight small puppies to death. Every peep felt as if someone was turning a knife inside me and made me grab the torch to inspect the puppy box.

Some days later, we had a vet visit. Young and nice and very fond of dogs. He examined Merry and the puppies carefully, stating we had two bitches and six males. They all seemed healthy but he pointed out that we should keep an eye on one of the bitches that was much smaller than the others.

One evening, I took a quiet stroll around the compound together with Bertil, in order to take a break from the kennel work. We decided to count banana bunches. Around thirty-five plants of sweet bananas and the same number of cooking bananas together had around half a ton of fruit. The initial 250 banana plants had now multiplied so much that we already had 1,500 – 2,000 plants. Imagine when even more plants would be bearing fruit at the same time.

On top of that, we had 200 plants of passion fruit, on which the fruit was already showing, and around 100 pawpaw trees, out of which many already bore fruit. The avocado trees we'd planted as stones, less than a year ago, were already two to three metres high. But it would probably take another few years before the orange and mango trees bore fruit. We counted on having wonderful feasts with newly pressed fruit juices in a not very distant future.

We really missed smoked food, so we built a smoke house and smoked tilapia fish from Lake Victoria. It was delicious. We also put joint and belly of pork in brine in the refrigerator, as we planned to experiment and see if we could smoke them, getting something like smoke-cured loin of pork and bacon.

Once in a while, a frenzied longing for Swedish food seized us. Since, after many tries, we'd at last been successful with the dill cultivation, we prepared dillströmming (Baltic herring in a tomato-dill sauce) from tilapia. One day we feasted on shrimp sandwiches, made of tinned Thai mini-shrimps, home-made mayonnaise, our own dill, salad and a bottle of white wine. But I'd have paid a fortune for a ring of falukorv (a typical Swedish sausage, originally from Falun in Dalecarlia) and a box of Kalles Kaviar (a very popular Swedish caviar in a tube).

When longing for restaurant food, we went to the Golf Hotel in Kakamega and ordered a Chicken Tropicana. That was perhaps the only dish on their whole menu that we found edible. One day, our appetite quickly disappeared. A number of Marabou storks which normally gathered at the rubbish heap behind the hotel, came walking among the tables. They were so disgusting. I told Bertil the thought of a Marabou stork on a chocolate bar made me sick. (In Sweden the chocolate company of Marabou used to have a Marabou stork as its symbol.) It was strange the hotel management permitted the staff to throw food remains to the birds walking on the lawn. That way the storks probably thought they were welcome guests.

## 53. Bomb blast in Nairobi

At midday on August 7th 1998, we were sitting at the pavement café of Franca Hotel in Kakamega having a tepid beer after a visit to the marketplace. Suddenly, we saw some journalists hurrying up to the phone booth at the pavement edge. They were urgently discussing something and almost fighting to get first in line for the telephones. The atmosphere seemed tense. Something must have happened. Bertil and I looked at each other and then Bertil stood up and walked up to one of the men, whom we knew from our press luncheon. He told Bertil that terrorists had blown up the American Embassy in Nairobi. At that point that was all that was known but, as the days passed, we heard more and more details.

The frightful bombing paralysed the whole of Kenya, in all respects. It also hit us hard, since foreigners in Kenya - diplomats, UN staff and people working in different NGOs (help organizations) - who hadn't gone to their respective countries on the usual vacations during July and August, were now unwilling to go on vacation within Kenya. They preferred to stay at home. Since we didn't know what impact the bombing would have on foreign tourism to Kenya, we kept a low profile and decided not to waste a lot of time and money on marketing. But our economic situation was becoming rather acute. We hadn't had any guests since the middle of July and money was just pouring out without any coming in.

All the same, we didn't rest on our laurels. No, we worked hard on different improvements to the guest huts, the main building and the compound.

Towards the end of August, guest hut number three was painted white on the outside. We'd by now given up hope of getting the cement floors glossy and polished, so we let one of our boys paint them with red paint on top of the red cement. Then they turned out more or less as we wanted them.

After purchasing some more furniture, we had three huts with a total of six big guest rooms. Around this third hut, we'd planted only yellow plants and flowers.

The kitchen garden needed a lot of work. As soon as we'd harvested one vegetable, the soil must be turned and manure added. Our first harvests had been much more abundant than the ones we were getting now, so we'd probably have to start with crop rotation.

One morning, we harvested haricots verts. We felt luxurious when picking this delicacy that would be put in the freezer to wait for the guests. It was a pity the sugar peas weren't doing well any longer. The first harvest had been superb but by now the soil probably had the wrong PH-value.

"Do you remember," I suddenly asked Bertil, "when we picked sugar peas? How difficult it was to see the plants? The supporting sticks had also developed roots and with leaves on them it wasn't easy to see what was what."

"A couple of days ago, I was up with an axe chopping off twigs from part of the fence. It has also rooted," Bertil answered.

A few weeks later, Bertil was off to Nairobi with the Suzuki in order to have the glass fibre top, which we'd ordered for the car, attached. Edgar, our friend from the car repair shop, accompanied him on the trip. I'd have to manage alone for a few days. Any boredom would probably be shaken off with the help of our eight small puppy terrorists.

The construction of our private apartment was advancing rapidly. The living area was approximately 48 square metres plus roofed verandas of 43 square metres. This area included a big room for us plus a small bedroom for private guests as well as toilet and shower. It would be wonderful, when finished.

The puppies spent the days up on the new veranda. The construction workers weren't so happy about that. The puppies ran around, playing, growling and barking - with some pathetic squeaks in-between. They weren't yet allowed to be anywhere open to the sky, since a bird of prey - for example black kite, eagle or hawk - could catch them. A favourite game was to bite the construction workers in their feet, which wasn't so funny if you weren't wearing shoes.

I'd fallen ill with malaria once again. The usual malaria medicine, Fansidar, didn't help. Hopefully I'd manage until Bertil returned and could buy some other medicine for me. In spite of the illness, I was supervising construction carpenters, co-workers and ten dogs. I felt actually rather proud of myself.

After a few days, Bertil returned home with my small red Suzuki. It had a white top and looked like a mobile hot dog kiosk. My lovely husband also brought one kilo of boiled crayfish tails. They only cost 250 shillings per kilo. You could buy live crayfish, which people said were delicious, for 70 shillings per kilo and you could actually have them delivered by bus from Lake Naivasha, paying a small additional cost. But why buy whole crayfish when the most delicious part of it was the tail?

We quickly made a marinade and put the crayfish tails in it for some hours. Then it was time to start feasting on them. The rest, approximately 700 grams, were put in the freezer.

In the evenings, I used to sit in a comfortable chair in the lobby reading until my poor eyes couldn't stand the weak light of the kerosene lamps any longer. Then I switched to playing patience. Since Bertil had his short wave radio in reception, he often sat talking on it. Sweden had about ten thousand active radio amateurs. In Kenya there were only twelve and hence people were interested in contacting Bertil over the radio. It was exciting to listen to Bertil's talks with other radio amateurs all over the world but when someone, at times, mentioned strawberries with whipped cream or mushroom walks in the forest, I felt stabs of homesickness.

It was comforting to have the radio as an extra security. If we had an emergency, we could always reach the outer world through it.

## 54. Runaway kerosene lamps

"Gunilla, we must count our remaining kerosene lamps, before the guests arrive next week."

"How many do you think there could be left?" I wondered.

"We've bought approximately eighty lamps. You remember, don't you, that we usually buy twenty lamps at a time. Let's count them."

Having finished counting, we concluded we only had nine working kerosene lamps left. So we'd have to buy at least twenty more.

Oh, these lamps. I got tired thinking about them. It was an eternal problem. Running out of kerosene, replacing the wicks, staff forgetting to refill them, broken lamp glasses. We found lamps everywhere but now discovered they were all broken, impossible to repair.

"Instead of a hotel, we should've started a factory making kerosene lamps."

"Yes, and a nail factory too," I answered wearily. "Why can't they stop stealing everything from us? The whole village nowadays must have nice kerosene lamps. Maybe we should check if any of our employees has started a lamp shop. They might be selling our lamps."

We'd have to go to the furnishing shop in town, where we usually got quite a decent price for the lamps. They'd probably laugh when they saw us.

"This time we'll mark the lamps," Bertil suggested.

"A good idea," I answered. "How?"

"I was thinking of engraving 'RG' for Riverdale Gardens on the bottom."

"That's good, I hope," I answered.

The truth was that the lamps continued disappearing. Unfortunately, we couldn't go to our employees' homes and turn the lamps upside down. The kerosene would spill out. But we'd probably paid for the kerosene too.

Elections had been held in Sweden. We received a letter from the Swedish Embassy only two days before the elections. They informed us we could come to Nairobi to get a voting card. You could obviously cast your vote somewhere there. It was such a pity the Embassy didn't understand that all Swedes in Kenya didn't live in the capital. So, for the first time in our adult lives, we'd thus neither voted nor knew the outcome of the elections.

It had happened before - in connection with the Kenyan elections, when it was said they could cause riots in the country - that we'd been called to an information meeting in Nairobi. Going to the capital was in fact a rather long and troublesome journey for many white people living in the countryside, especially if it was a matter of riots because at such times you didn't want to be on the roads unless extremely urgent. It wasn't so far to Nairobi, only five hundred kilometres, but they were tiresome kilometres. It took us about seven hours to go there if everything ran smoothly.

Several months had passed since our last visit to the hairdresser and it was time for another visit. On our way to Kisumu, I thought about my first - and only - visit to a hairdresser in Kakamega. I'd seen a sign outside a hair salon close to the Golf Hotel saying they also cut European hair. Full of confidence, I entered. Just to be completely sure I checked, before sitting down in the chair, that they really knew how to cut

European hair. Oh, of course they knew. A girl started cutting my hair. She was really quick. Suddenly I discovered what she was up to. With one hand nonchalantly glued to her side, she used the other hand to at random cut off big tufts of my hair - without using a comb or any similar tools. Violently protesting, I flew out of the chair. Naturally, I refused to pay and ran out. My hairstyle was very strange - in certain places my hair was a couple of centimetres long, in others about twenty. My head looked like a straggly floor mop. The only way to make me look normal again was to steer the car towards Kisumu and an Indian hairdresser. Thank heavens; they could fix the catastrophe, so from then on that was the salon we used.

While in Kisumu, we had a good lunch at our favourite place, a Chinese restaurant on Oginga Odinga Street. After lunch, we went shopping at the Nakumatt store. It was important to take the opportunity when you were in a city that big. We could for example find tuna fish and lots of other delicacies here, something we couldn't do in Kakamega.

As usual, we shopped for a fortune without actually getting much. We also bought half a litre of milk and a big loaf of bread for the street boy watching our car. It was always the same boy. A glue sniffer around ten years old. It was so sad to see all these small children, who sniffed glue. They were mostly either orphans or ill with AIDS. We'd earlier given the boy some money but had been told he'd buy glue with it. We thought he might drink the milk and eat the bread this time, but the store guard declared the boy would run to a place around the corner and exchange milk and bread for glue. What could you do? How should we act in order to help?

On our way home from Kisumu, we stopped, as always, at a small marketplace high above Lake Victoria. Before stopping, we wound up all the car windows. Within a few seconds, women carrying baskets and buckets surrounded the car. Everyone wanted to sell us fruit and they all asked for the same price.

Bertil carefully lowered the car window a little, pointed at one of the women and said, "Avocado."

Then he cautiously opened a little more and the woman emptied a big basket full of avocado through the window. Avocados were rolling everywhere in the car. About seventy shillings for around thirty avocados. Although we'd already bought a basketful, the rest of the women begged us to also buy from them. Our dogs and we loved avocado, so we had a rather big consumption of them but thirty fruits would last for a long time. Before leaving the marketplace, we stopped the car to adjust the rear-view mirrors the women had knocked out of place.

Bertil was marketing himself as the computer expert that in fact he was and got a quick response. After a couple of days, he already had several assignments. That was a relief, even though he was paid only a fraction of what people had paid him in Sweden. If he could get some odd jobs here and there, we'd soon become less vulnerable. We were actually really optimistic, since everybody having hardware problems in this area until now had been forced to find expert help in Nairobi. And, moreover, no one else in Western Province had such a good knowledge of electronics.

Our happiness over Bertil´s success increased when we got our first guests in two months. And a few days later, fourteen American youths spent twenty-four hours with us. They were, as a matter of fact, only paying half price but it was still money. We furthermore received a lot of lunch guests, which added to our income. Dry smoked tilapia from Lake Victoria with dill-boiled potatoes and Rhode Island or Tartar sauce had become popular. Judging by the demand we got for this dish, we were obviously the only place in Kenya serving it.

As an extra topping to the positive things happening, we noticed that our custom clientele - foreigners residing in Kenya - had now returned from their vacations and seemed interested in visiting. Our problems would surely be solved.

Our staff behaved extremely well, when we had guests. We actually felt rather proud of them, but to our surprise we found that as soon as the guests had left, they immediately started to act strangely. By the end of the month, we yelled at everybody and the mess they were making. Things broke or disappeared, written instructions regarding the puppies weren't followed. If the puppies didn't burst from too much food or the wrong kind, it wasn't thanks to our employees. They didn't seem to understand that jet black clouds meant rain was approaching and that they should hurry to fetch the laundry hanging outside.

We didn't understand a thing. Why were they acting like this? Didn't they have enough stamina to behave well for longer periods? Or perhaps they wanted to demonstrate their power over us - that we were dependent on them? To tell the truth, we sometimes wondered if, as time went by, we understood less and less of the people around us instead of the opposite.  Or was this maybe their normal behaviour?

But since we also had causes for joy, we shook off our staff problems. We and our ten dogs would soon move up to our new apartment in the extension. It didn't matter that the inner doors were still missing as well as interior paint, toilet and shower. I was quite content to have a wall with wardrobes in our bedroom. The puppies would live in the biggest room to start with, because from there we could easily let them directly onto the veranda via the double doors.

Daniel, the fundi, proudly showed us his work. The apartment was really nice. He'd made the interior door linings, facing the veranda, very well and we were impressed by his work.

We closed the door and went to the veranda, where Daniel was waiting for his final payment. He was shining like the sun and had prepared his account really well, specifying it with good basic data. He knew that both he and his assistant, Injehu, would get a bonus for the good work.

When we'd made the final payment and Daniel had left, we returned to the puppies. I was the first to enter the room and didn't understand what I saw. What was that thing laying on the floor? Then I roared, "Bertil, come and look."

Bertil came and within a moment both of us started laughing. With united forces, the monsters had succeeded, in fifteen minutes, to tear down the door linings and chew them into fragments. They must have been standing on each other in order to reach all the way up. The doors looked awful. A reddish dust covered the floor. Where did that come from? The lunatics had started to dig out the bricks in the wall, where we had planned to have bookshelves in a near future. It almost seemed as if they'd made small stairs in the wall, crevices in the bricks, so that they could climb higher up.

"Thank God Daniel's left," Bertil said. "He'd probably have started to cry if he'd seen this."

"I don't think we'll repair it until we've sold the puppies," I answered.

## 55. Language confusion

"James, please put some firewood on the veranda."

The weather was nasty and I intended to light a fire in the fireplace later in the afternoon. The firewood at the house was finished, so I asked for help as James was passing by. He was the boy who had cut his hand when he was almost bitten by a snake in the forest and he was also one of the gang we usually hired, when it was time to cut the grass.

"Yes, ma´m," he answered with his beautiful English accent. He disappeared towards the firewood store to fetch the wood I'd asked for.

I sat down for a while on the veranda to relax a little. It was hard work walking uphill from the huts. I wasn't young any more.

"Gunilla, did you really ask James to light a fire on the veranda?" Max looked out from the dining room with a questioning expression in his face.

"No, absolutely not. I only asked him to put firewood on the veranda? Why do you ask me that?"

"Well, James has just arranged for a fire on the veranda. He came to me and asked for matches."

Oh my God, imagine if Max hadn't reacted but had let James light a fire directly on the wooden floor on the veranda. I'd forgotten to double check with James what I had said. He must have thought I said "put on a fire on the veranda" instead of "put some firewood on the veranda". James, like so many others, pretended to understand English. Instead of admitting they didn't understand, they did whatever they thought you'd said. Why had he not questioned my order to put on a fire on the veranda?

I remembered another incident due to language confusion.

One day, Bertil wanted to make pesto, so he needed some basil. He asked Fred to fetch some and then forgot the whole matter. After a long while, we saw Fred, Max and Petrus coming with armfuls of newly harvested basil. Unbelievable amounts. They'd harvested all our basil. For a little pesto.

The misunderstandings weren't always due to bad knowledge of English. Sometimes they arose because we didn't know enough about the villagers' life. I remembered an episode with Mark, one of our night askaris. He asked for a couple of days off.

"My mother's died," he told me, "and I've to go to the funeral."

"Poor you, of course you can be off duty," I answered. "Didn't your brother also die recently?"

Yes, the brother had died and now the mother too.

Some weeks later Mark came to me, asking, "Can I have a few days off, I've to attend a funeral?"

"Oh, I'm so sorry. Again? Who died this time in your family?"

"It's my mother, who died."

Now I was almost angry. Did he really believe I'd accept that?

"Mark, your mother died rather recently. She can't die several times, can she?"

"My mother died again. It's true, she died again."

When he'd spent a long time giving explanations in his almost non-existent English, I understood that it was his father's second wife, who had passed away this time. It was quite probable he'd come more times telling me his mother had died, since I didn't know how many mothers he had in his family.

This was called 'extended family'.

Language confusion happened also, when speaking about time. As Europeans we were rather used to the Spanish mañana-mentality but the Kenyan one was even worse. We'd daily, for what seemed like an eternity, been told that the clinic construction would start the next day. Now it had at last happened.

It was inaugurated with traditional local rituals that, among other things, included a short sermon and a longer prayer. After that, the oldest man in the Clinic Committee "broke the soil", which meant he took the first dig with the spade. That man was so old it seemed uncertain if he had enough strength to lift it.

We'd have to wait and see how far the construction could advance with the money we'd managed to collect in Sweden. The villagers must also keep their promises about their own contributions. A lot of people had promised to contribute with food, work, bricks and similar things but they were, at the chief's request, reneging on their promises. That was, of course, exactly what could be expected. We'd now told the Clinic Committee that we wouldn't collect one more shilling in Sweden for the project, until the villagers themselves contributed in kind, but they didn't seem to believe this threat.

Since we didn't want to be accused of corruption, we'd been careful to exclude ourselves from signing for the project or withdrawing money from the bank. If the project failed, it wouldn't be our fault.

Being at the hospital for a new health control after an attack of malaria, we also paid a visit to our friend Elisabeth, married to the Danish head of the hospital. She gave me a small plant that she and her husband recommended I take for future malaria attacks. Malaria medicine usually didn't cure me. She told me she'd received a couple of plant cuttings from a Philippine pharmacist, who had brought the plant to Kenya and replanted it in the Kenyan climate. At the hospital, they'd been successful testing it for milder malaria attacks. If you boiled seven leaves and drank such tea for three days, the malaria was cured. It would be exciting to see if that was true with me. We planted it in the garden, and put big sticks around it so that nobody would mistakenly tread on the small plant.

Suddenly a man offered us a small office in town to rent at a low cost. In it, we'd have electricity and a telephone connected to a better switchboard than the one we already had, and could start up our computer network. We could offer email-service to the public, something which wasn't found in Kakamega, have a booking office for Riverdale Gardens, maybe some private computer tuition for high bank and hotel employees, sell some fruit from our garden, offer desktop publishing and so on. Our right-hand girl, Veronica, who these days was dealing with puppy poo, washing up and cleaning (in spite of her computer training), should be able to man the Kakamega office, with Bertil and me backing her up.

Since we had no guests for several weeks and needed additional income, we accepted the offer after a lot of thought. With our modern computer equipment and our knowledge, this office should make a profit.

Unfortunately, we had to wait with the moving in since the company we'd be renting from couldn't let us move in until they'd moved onto the next floor. They couldn't do that until the electricity had been connected. The Electricity Company refused to connect until they'd received "something small", that was to say a small bribe, from our landlords. That was the way things worked.

We'd lately made many trips to Kakamega and had been in close contact with Kenya Wildlife Service, helping them to write a presentation of tourism in Western Province. In it, we made suggestions on how to increase the number of people touring. The Provincial Commissioner appreciated the presentation and invited us, with a ceremonial card, to a full-day seminar led by him. He wanted to meet the owners of all the most important hotels in the area. On the invitation card was written, "Please be on time. The meeting will start at eight o'clock." As obedient and well-educated Swedes, we were of course on the spot already at half past seven. We almost believed we'd come to the wrong place. Nobody else was there; we were all alone. We waited and waited. Gradually the rest of the participators slowly arrived. At eleven o'clock, the P.C. turned up and the meeting could start. A lot of talk and few issues of substance. At three in the afternoon, the meeting was finished. Not even a cup of tea or a bottle of water to drink during the whole day. The result of the meeting was that a Western Tourism Association would be founded and that all the hotels would be members of it.

The local manager of K.W.S. (Kenya Wildlife Service), Eunice, was impressed by our establishment. She especially appreciated that construction had been from local materials. The guest baby cot, made of plaited and lacquered banana leaves, took her completely by surprise on her first visit to Riverdale Gardens.

"Boom, boom, boom..." A black lava stream flew around the veranda corner. Bertil threw himself onto the floor. In a jiffy, he was covered with crawling, licking and barking puppies. Once in a while, he moaned when the puppy teeth bit too hard. They chewed on everything that came in their way and were unbelievably active.

The puppies were now weaned and that was a relief, since Merry had had increasing problems with suckling and was getting stressed by them. She often vomited. Furthermore her nipples were causing her pain, since the small monsters had bitten her really hard. She was happy to go back to a normal dog life: escaping, cat and hen chases and everything else she loved.

The little rascals were still fond of climbing. The chicken net we'd put up as protection, so that they wouldn't fall between the poles in the higher part of the veranda, had instead provided some help for them when they climbed. They quickly learned to put their feet in the wire mesh and that way they climbed up the fence. We had to put plywood on top of the net. The plywood had to be so high that the puppies couldn't stand on their hind legs, gripping the upper part with their front legs in order to heave themselves up. So little by little, as they grew, we had to move the plywood upwards and finally, get bigger boards.

Three of the puppies had new homes. We selected the order in which they'd leave us, by cutting a little of the neck fur on the one who was most alert and aggressive. When it was time to deliver a male dog, we always took the one we'd cut. Then another male became more dominant and we repeated the procedure.

The first puppy leaving us got a new home with an Indian ironmonger. He wet himself several times in my lap on our way there. Since I couldn't appear among people with clothes covered with dog pee, we went first to the second hand market to buy a blouse and a pair of trousers. When we arrived at the hardware store, the puppy started off his new life by peeing all over the counter.

Now we had only five puppies left. We'd keep one of them but still hadn't decided whether it should be a bitch or a male. It would undoubtedly be nice when the rest had left, since unfortunately we lived in the same apartment - without inner doors. The puppies were usually awake at five in the morning with an enormously active morning temperament.

## 56. Terrible news

I almost fainted. My head was spinning. From a distance I could hear my father's voice over the telephone. He couldn't be telling the truth, but I still understood he wouldn't lie about something like that.

"Gunilla, you must come home at once. Mother's got a brain tumour. She won't live much longer."

I felt I couldn't grasp the situation.

"But I recently got a letter from Mother. I told Bertil her handwriting has changed." Then I added, "Although Per Göran has also told me Mother hasn't been feeling well this past summer and that you've been worried."

"Yes, unfortunately," said Father. "The doctor told us this yesterday. And according to the doctors, the tumour is inoperable. Mother only has very few weeks left, maximum."

Now, I'd managed to control myself a little, even though tears were running down my cheeks.

"I'll come to Sweden as soon as possible."

Father informed me that Per Göran, my eldest brother, would get me a flight ticket and that I was to keep in contact with him. We said goodbye and then I immediately gulped down the whisky Bertil had poured me.

My elder brother was able to book me to Sweden at the beginning of the following week. Time went awfully slowly. I just wanted to be with Mother.

During the weekend, I was forced to pull myself together and try to focus on our guests. It was difficult. At the same time, I tried to pack some clothes.

As if it wasn't enough constantly thinking about my dear mother, I also got malaria again. It was verified a couple of days later at the hospital.

During the flight to Sweden, I noticed that, in spite of the medicine, I still had a fever and felt faint, but that was the least of my problems. Far more distressing was the fact that my younger brother, Per Erik, was somewhere in the Amazons, not knowing Mother was ill. I sincerely hoped the travel agency would be able to locate him, so that also he would be home in time.

## 57. Back in Kenya

The bus drove into the Kakamega terminal and with a hissing sound the doors opened. Bertil was waiting impatiently. I gave a sigh of relief both at seeing him and at being back in Kakamega.

The journey had been difficult and tiresome, above all the last section from Nairobi with the Akamba bus. You needed a reserved seat on it. Hence I'd been looking forward to reading and sleeping on the bus, but no way. The employees practised Kenyan Corruption. As soon as the bus had left Nairobi, they started using the principle "stop at every waving person, demand twenty shillings and squeeze them on standing". The consequence was that those of us, who thought we'd paid for a comfortable trip with a good book, were instead getting elbows, knees, people, handbags and hens in our faces and everywhere else.

The bus was stopped a couple of times by the police. It was absolutely forbidden to have standing passengers on these buses and we had about fifty persons standing in the gangway for several hours. When the police officers had received their bribes, they let us continue. Just outside Kakamega, the bus stopped again. All the illegal passengers without a ticket then had to leave. At the arrival at the bus terminal, everything looked nice and legal. The extra money collected was, of course, put in the pockets of the driver and the conductor.

"Where are Mathias and Gunseli?" I asked Bertil, while we were loading the luggage into the car.

Mathias was one of Per Erik's sons and also a cook and Gunseli was his girl friend. Immediately after my mother's funeral, they'd gone to Riverdale Gardens in order to help us for a couple of months.

"They're at home, holding the fort."

On our way home from Kakamega, we got a quick glimpse of "our" small street child, Andre. He seemed ill and had a badly infected eye. He walked crying on the street. I was so tired I couldn't bring myself to ask Bertil to stop the car.

After a wonderful three-course dinner, I found it difficult to sleep. I was lying in bed thinking of the little street boy. I had a bad conscience. He was absolutely not our responsibility but when we saw him, we usually gave him a coin or a piece of bread, some bananas or some milk. He never begged - merely looked at us.

I got up in the early morning, listened to bird song and watched the sun rise. Bertil brought breakfast. The young ones were still asleep.

"Gunilla, I've something unpleasant to tell you," said Bertil suddenly.

"No, no more wretched things. I can't take anymore. My nerves are frayed."

"I'm sorry, but I have to. I didn't want to spoil your first evening at home by informing you yesterday. It's important that you know."

"OK. Tell me."

"Max has stolen twenty thousand shillings. Furthermore he's probably stolen my video camera." When I tried to interrupt him, he added, "The money was stolen one evening, when he and I were the only ones present, so there's nobody else we can suspect."

I stared at him. How could that be possible? Our wonderful cook that we had trusted one hundred percent.

"Does he know that you know?"

"No, he doesn't. The youngsters don't know either. We have to pretend nothing has happened, until we know what to do. I think we should check with Elena what she suggests, maybe also with the police."

"Bertil, didn't you write to me that Max has moved? That he no longer stays in staff quarters?"

"Yes, that's true. He, once again, found a couple of harmless house snakes there and now refuses to stay up there. He's rented a room in Wulushi market."

I agreed with Bertil we shouldn't show Max what we'd found out, but I was boiling inside with anger when speaking to him a little later. But it was important to grin and bear it, so that he didn't suspect anything.

Suddenly, Nelson turned up asking us to drive him to town. He had to get a seven-year old boy, weighing only fourteen kilos, to hospital. The boy had tuberculosis and possibly AIDS. He seemed to be dying. We were of course willing to help so Nelson, the boy and the boy's grandmother got into the car, where they had to share the small space in the back.

When we'd left the boy and his grandmother at Kakamega General Hospital, we went downtown with Nelson to try and find little Andre. We heard he had no parents and that he was lying ill somewhere in an alley. The street children didn't dare to divulge where he was. Someone claimed the police had arrested him because of theft and that he was in prison. Ill and unhappy.

Nelson continued looking for Andre. We drove to our friend, Elena, to consult her. What should we do with Max and what should we do with Andre? We got some advice from her and her Kenyan husband. Then we continued to Police Headquarters where we talked to a C.I.D. inspector about Max. We asked whether we should first speak to his parents and thereafter contact the C.I.D. again. The police officer agreed that was a humane plan. When we asked whether Andre was in prison, we got a firm denial. The inspector told us they never ever arrested children that young and we believed him.

We drove to the home of Max's parents and talked to his brother and mother. The father was out working. We told them the whole sad story and decided we'd meet the following afternoon at Riverdale Gardens, with also the father present. If we didn't get our money, we'd notify the police.

When we were about to drive home, we ran into Nelson. He informed us he'd left a message for Andre telling the boy he should keep a lookout for us, so that we could help him to the hospital. Now it was up to him if he wanted our help. We couldn't do more for him.

During the return trip to Riverdale Gardens, Bertil suddenly asked me, "How's your malaria? Is it over? You wrote you were going to Tropical Medicine at Huddinge Hospital."

I laughed, somewhat sarcastically. "Yes, listen. I actually marched out from there after having met the most conceited doctor you could imagine. When the nurse took my blood sample, she said the blood looked exactly like malarial blood, that's to say extra thin. She thought it was very typical of malaria. When I eventually saw the doctor, he claimed I neither had malaria nor ever had. He believed my fatigue was due to anxiety during Mother's last days. It's quite possible he's right about that. But I made him look at my dossier from the Missionary Hospital and he just laughed at it. You must have a high fever, if you've malaria, and counting 'rings' is a stupid way to test malaria. He even said 'Doctors down there in Africa don't know as much as we do, here at Tropical Medicine at Huddinge.' An arrogant idiot, in other words. I hissed at him I thought he should practice in the bitter reality in Africa, so that he might learn something."

We were back at home around five-thirty in the afternoon, quite exhausted after an intensive day. Mathias had, minutes earlier, discovered some exciting things: a live metallic- blue snake, a Brunton compass and a refractometer. Hidden at the fence by some employee for retrieval at the end of the workday. Life was really super.

We were, as a matter of fact, now forced to divulge the truth about Max to Mathias and Gunseli. Hearing about the theft of the video camera and the money they were, just like us, extremely surprised. They, too, had thought that Max was a nice boy.

When we told them Max was hysterically afraid of snakes, Mathias spontaneously exclaimed, "How strange. He was down with me, searching for the snake. Maybe he wanted to check if I'd found those hidden things that belong to you, Bertil."

When discussing the different thefts, we discovered that the only explanation must be that not only Max but also Linda and probably at least one of our shamba boys were involved. I felt as if the whole house had fallen down on me. I couldn't stand any more. We'd all been united as one happy laughing family for quite a long time. Once again, people had cheated us. Would this never end?

I called Elena telling her about the new development. Full of sympathy, she suggested we fire the lot, threatening them with taking fingerprints on the things found on the compound and possibly going together to Police Headquarters in town. She, who'd lived in Kenya for twenty years, thought that was the only sensible thing to do. At the same time, she said that we, Bertil and I, Mathias and Gunseli, by taking care of everything ourselves could show everybody that we knew how to bring things to a successful end.

We sat discussing the matter for a while.

Suddenly Bertil exclaimed, "No, no way! We call the police and ask them to come here tomorrow morning. I'm so sick and tired of us always being so kind."

Said and done. Bertil got hold of the inspector we'd met earlier and informed him about the afternoon's happenings. The inspector agreed that enough was enough and that a house search needed to be done, at least in Max' and Linda's homes.

Two criminal investigators, Mike and Lynn, arrived early in the morning and we went together down to Wulushi market, where Max was living. On our way there, they asked us where Max originated from. When we said he came from Kisumu, Mike at once exclaimed that Max was the guilty one. All Luos were, according to them, thieves. We actually were quite distraught at this remark in spite of knowing that only he could be the guilty one, and demanded that the police at least should do a house search before arresting him.

Max was awakened by the knocking at the door and was noticeably nervous when he understood the police intended to do a house search in his new home.

All four of us entered and among the first things I saw was one of our suitcases. It was opened and inside it we found a Swedish one hundred kronor note plus a couple of receipts from a furniture shop. The receipts stated the purchase of a group of sofa and armchairs and a couple of coffee tables. They were sure enough standing in the room and were of high quality, far beyond what a poor young man could afford. The receipt was dated the day after the money theft and the sum was 18,000 shillings.

"Yes, Max, no more evidence is needed to prove you're the guilty one. It depends on your employers if you go to jail or not," commented Lynn.

We asked Max to come to us in the afternoon and at the same time we notified him that also his parents would be present. We'd then discuss what had to be done.

Back home, the police officers explained to Linda they wanted to check her house to see if she had any of our property. We gave them descriptions of a number of things that had disappeared without a trace. After a while, they returned telling us they hadn't found any of those objects in Linda's home, hence we couldn't accuse her of theft without getting in trouble ourselves. We couldn't even fire her and that was a strange feeling, as we knew for sure only she could have been inside our apartment to steal the video camera.

When the officers had left, we assembled all our employees and informed them about what had happened. We also declared that we were almost certain that one or more of them were involved. If one more thing happened, all of them would be sacked and kicked out. If someone helped us to get the culprit, that person would of course keep his employment with us. This measure certainly didn't improve harmony among the staff.

During the afternoon talk with Max and his parents, a document was written, which stated we'd notify the police about the theft, unless we'd fully recovered the stolen money at the latest on December 29$^{th}$.

While Mathias and Gunseli were playing monopoly, Bertil and I sat down together trying to relax for the first time since my return. When walking around on the compound an hour earlier, I'd found a round flower bed - quite new - down to the right of the veranda. Bertil now explained that he - in memory of my mother - had planted a lot of white lilies there and that among the lilies he planned to put some beautiful green stones, which we'd found in a quarry. What a wonderful idea - a small memorial grove for my mother.

"Bertil, thank you so much for all the emails you've sent me. I've actually just had a quick glance at them. I've not been able to engage myself in the life down here. Can't you tell me what's happened here? You can use your emails to me as a reminder."

Bertil took out the emails and his diary notes. Using them as a starting point, he informed me about what had happened during my absence.

"I've been busy a big part of the time, arranging things at our Kakamega office," he said. "Daniel's been ill with malaria, so I brought Veronica and Fred to town and had them wash and paint the walls and the ceiling. It looks really nice now. When Daniel was well again, he and Fred made a nice counter and an Internet surfing table. I've installed the alarm and all the computer equipment and Veronica's walked around in town handing out leaflets, so rumour about the Europeans' Internet café has spread quite well."

He recounted that, when he'd started the server, which hadn't been in use since Sweden, and switched on the electric current, he heard a big "bang". The current was set on 115 Volts instead of 230. Maybe it had switched position owing to the vibrations the container had been subjected to or maybe one of the removers, unable to resist, had touched it. So we had one server less. But as by now we were quite accustomed to losing things, it didn't really matter, did it?

A lot of people obviously wanted computer help. They needed harambee-cards, invitation cards, sign-posts, letters, email and calendars with scanned photos. All types of assignments, but this was a poor country and the profit was unfortunately low, especially when you took into consideration all the work you had to do on every printed item. Bertil had a much better income from the rather many service turnouts he made to the Rainforest Retreat, the supermarket and the Missionary Hospital. At the Missionary Hospital they were even talking about attaching Bertil to them through a running service agreement.

According to Bertil, the clinic walls were now a little more than one metre high – after many rounds with bribery attempts and similar things. To try to do something in Kenya without paying 'something small' mean that everything took much longer, if it was finished at all.

He also told me more about the accident in Sotanini that he'd mentioned in one of his emails. The Sotanini mine was now temporary closed after the tragic incident in a neighbouring mine. A mine owner's son one morning went down the forty foot deep shaft to secretly check on the work. He climbed down and his brother, who remained on top waiting for the signal to come down, waited in vain for a long time. He didn't understand the silence could be an indication of something being terribly wrong, so he decided to climb down to see why he hadn't heard from his brother. The reason was that his brother had suffocated and now also the second brother suffocated. Lack of oxygen works very quickly. The brothers weren't used to the mine and had forgotten to bring a candle to control the amount of oxygen in the hole. Bertil happened to pass the place of the accident together with our guests, when the villagers had just brought up one of the perished brothers.

Our Mazizi, one of the two bitches, had moved away from home during my absence. It was love at first sight with an American Peace Corps girl, so now Mazizi lived in Kipkarren River. Before my trip to Sweden, Bertil and I had decided we'd keep Musse, one of the male puppies, instead of one of the bitches and that seemed like a good choice, because he was absolutely adorable.

## 58. An unforgettable Christmas

This year, as we had Mathias and Gunseli visiting us, we decided to celebrate a real Christmas in the middle of all the sadness.

George, a combined carpenter, taxi driver and butcher, found us fresh ham and spare ribs. We also had a couple of tinned herring, a bottle of mulled wine and some punch and schnaps essence. Said and done. We salted the ham lightly, boiled red cabbage from our own garden and waited for Christmas Eve to arrive. The day dawned and we sat down to a fantastic breakfast buffet table. At that precise moment the telephone rang.

"Good morning, Gunilla. This is Mr. Singh speaking."

"Good morning, Mr. Singh. How can I help you?"

Mr. Singh was the wealthiest man in the whole province. He and his family had had dinner at Riverdale Gardens on several occasions and they'd really appreciated the food. Now, he wanted to celebrate Christmas, on Christmas Day, at Riverdale Gardens. It was going to be a party for fifteen relatives. Most of all he wanted turkey, but I explained that since a turkey wouldn't fit into the oven, it had to be some kind of chicken. As some of his relatives were vegetarians, special food must be prepared for them. A drink before the meal and the best wines with the food. The dessert was important and the whole table should be decorated with party hats, serpentines, toy trumpets and confetti. As usual, it didn't matter how expensive it was. The important thing was that it was splendid. We discussed some more details and then we said goodbye. I returned to the breakfast table.

As soon as Bertil saw me, he started laughing, "Aha, so we won't be celebrating Christmas on our own this year?"

"I hope you understand I had to give Mr. Singh a positive answer. It means a lot of money to us, so I couldn't refuse."

"I don't understand. Explain," Mathias interrupted.

"OK, this is the situation," I continued. "We'll have fifteen guests for Christmas lunch tomorrow. It must be the best meal in the whole province. Furthermore our guests want a lot of party things, like toy trumpets, party hats and things like that. You know - more or less like a New Year's party. And worst of all, we can't find those things in Kakamega. Subsequently, we have to go down to Kisumu – now."

"But it's Christmas Eve today," Mathias and Gunseli stammered out almost in chorus.

"It doesn't matter. If you have a hotel known for serving the best food in the province, then you have to," Bertil said. "But first of all we have to decide on the menu. Mathias, get Grandma's cook-book."

We sat down together at the table. We'd completely forgotten our Christmas breakfast. Quickly, we checked the list of the things we had in the freezer down in Wushiye. Mathias suggested a menu based on the discussion Mr. Singh and I had had.

"Now we are ready," I finally declared. "For entrée: prawn tails from Naivasha, marinated in garlic and served with avocado and a fresh salad in coupe-glasses. For main course, coq-au-vin and for dessert, rhubarb pie with vanilla sauce. We can dry-smoke some tilapia-fish, and serve it with a nice cold sauce for the people who don't eat meat. What do you think?"

We quickly made a shopping list, stowed away the unfinished Christmas breakfast, got dressed and rushed off in the Suzuki down to the Southern Hemisphere - Kisumu. We hoped we'd have time, later in the evening, to have some Christmas food.

Coming back from Kisumu at five thirty in the afternoon, we immediately started preparing lunch for the following day. With only a ham sandwich each in our stomachs, we tumbled into bed, dead tired. That was the end of our Christmas Eve.

Christmas Day began with a standing breakfast after which we started cooking, laying the table and blowing up balloons. At one o'clock, fifteen members of the Singh family arrived. They got together on a sofa group down under the big eucalyptus, where they were served mulled wine. They'd never had that before and they liked it so much the whole bottle was finished. We'd obviously not have any ourselves this Christmas.

Lunch was served on the veranda, where we'd laid a long table and hung serpentines. They put on the party hats, sounded the toy trumpets and threw confetti. They evidently enjoyed their food hugely, while laughing and talking. Suddenly we discovered that Mr. Singh's old mother, so beautiful in her embroidered sari, was only eating cucumber. She told us she'd promised not to eat even potatoes with the cucumber many years ago in the temple. We asked one of our shamba boys to quickly run down to the kitchen garden and pick all the cucumbers he could find. The old lady should at least get a bowl full of cucumber. With their coffee, they were served ice-cold Swedish punch, made of essences bought in Sweden, which they also seemed to like very much. According to Mr. Singh, who was a gourmet, this lunch was the best and most exotic he'd ever eaten and he said he wanted Mathias to train his chef.

While our lunch guests were having coffee, twenty-five other Indians came dashing in. They wanted to be shown around and have something to eat. Since all of us were now feeling extremely exhausted, we kindly declined their visit.

We didn't get much to eat this day either. After a couple of whiskies, we fell early into bed, having decided to celebrate Christmas Eve next day.

On the morning of Boxing Day, four Dutch people with children stood suddenly at the gate. They wanted lunch, dinner and an overnight stay. Mathias had the day off, so I improvised pizza for lunch and meatloaf with mushroom sauce and some other nice things for dinner. When the guests had finally gone to bed, we also went to sleep with neither dinner nor celebration.

Life as a hotel owner was tough. On December 27th, when the Dutch had checked out, four Belgians, who had made a reservation, arrived. They checked in, handed over the voucher from the travel agency and told us they'd go and spend a few hours in the rain-forest. They'd bring their luggage to the guest hut, once they were back from the forest. We headed into town to shop for some more food, since all our stores by now were empty. Mathias prepared lunch for the Belgians. A couple of hours later, we heard the guests had left a message at the gate, saying one person in the group had become ill and that they therefore were forced to return to Nairobi. I quickly discovered, however, that the voucher they'd left me earlier in the day had been stolen back by one of the guests. As we suspected they'd lied to us, we threw ourselves into the car and went to the Rainforest Retreat, where we discovered the guests had checked in. Arriving back from the forest, the Belgians seemed to shrink when seeing us. They finally admitted the theft, returning the voucher without which the travel agency would never have reimbursed us.

A sandwich for breakfast on December 28$^{th}$, a rush into town to shop now that the shops were open again, omelette for lunch. In the afternoon four Britons came for an overnight stay. We prepared a nice dinner for them and we ate leftovers from the day before.

On December 29$^{th}$ the guests had an early breakfast. A sandwich for us a little later. We prepared a picnic lunch for the guests to take to the forest and then they checked out. A couple of hours later, a group of Finnish people, who had suddenly decided to have lunch at Riverdale, turned up. We improvised again, since we were lucky to have a freezer as well as vegetables and fruit growing on the compound.

All of us were completely exhausted, so we cuddled up in the armchairs as soon as the lunch guests had passed the gate on their way out. Even though we now had made quite a lot of money, we wondered if it had really been worth the effort.

"What became of Christmas?" Mathias exclaimed confused.

"Yes," Bertil interjected; also he looking quite dazed, "I bet all of us have lost a lot of weight."

## 59. Assaulted

"Can you show me the airport?" Gunseli wondered when we were ready with our errands in Kakamega.

We'd had lunch at the Golf Hotel and were on our way home where Mathias was alone, holding the fort. He'd probably appreciate being relieved.

"Calling it airport is exaggerating. It's, more or less, only a strip for taking off and landing," I laughed. "Of course we can take that road home."

Bertil turned onto the road passing Kakamega General Hospital.

We were talking animatedly, while Bertil was carefully zigzagging; trying to stay on the parts of the road that still had some tarmac left. The road was really bad. Cattle, people, bicycles, potholes…

To our left, on a small peninsula in the river, we saw one of the newest hotels in the area. A lot of wonderful bamboo of different kinds was growing in its garden. We'd bought a big part of the bamboo for our construction here.

"The former manager of this hotel bought one of our puppies," I said.

When we were driving up the hill just past the hotel, Gunseli suddenly shouted, "Gunilla, look out!"

I craned my neck forward and noticed a man just a metre from me, diagonally to the right. He was in the process of throwing a big stone and seemed to be aiming at my head. The stone flew through the air directly at me. I ducked. Bertil stepped hard on the brakes and the stone landed in front of me on the windshield, which exploded. If Bertil hadn't braked, the stone would have hit me through the open side window. Glass splinters rained in on me and I could feel sharp bits everywhere, including in my face. How fortunate I was wearing my glasses.

Sick with shock, I tumbled out of the car. Bertil was equally fast on his side. Gunseli wriggled out of the back seat and came up to me. She was deathly pale and hugged me. People gathered around us, laughing and pointing at us. The man, who had thrown the stone, disappeared downhill. I guessed he'd seen Bertil′s facial expression.

Shaking, I leant on the car and felt I needed a cigarette. When I lit it, with tears streaming down my cheeks, a man started nagging me that he wanted one. I screamed hysterically at him.

Gunseli took a few staggering steps away from the road and started vomiting. A couple of Africans followed her and laughed at her, while she was throwing up.

She returned to me; suddenly she screamed and threw herself on a man who, behind my back, was leaning into the car to steal my handbag. She tore it from him, hissing he should be ashamed of himself.

Bertil asked Gunseli to go to the hotel and phone the police. She must ask them to come as quickly as possible. Bertil assembled some Africans and started chasing the guilty man.

After a while, Gunseli returned and told us, "The police officer was very rude to me. He asked why I called them. He thought we should catch the villain ourselves and then bring him to the police station. I explained to the officer that I thought it was their job and that we weren't trained to catch culprits. I said we'd most certainly be lynched if we, as whites, captured an African. But the police officer continued to refuse, so they won't come."

Gunseli was quite confused. She'd hardly believed her ears during the telephone conversation.

Meanwhile, some men had caught the stone thrower and brought him back to our car where a hectic discussion started. People commenced to yell at us. We understood they wanted to be paid. When we couldn't, since we were out of cash money, they released him and he disappeared.

The situation soon worsened. The atmosphere was beginning to be threatening. A lot of women started gathering big stones that they probably intended to throw at us. We felt extremely threatened. They all looked as if they hated us. The hotel manager, who had heard the noise, came out to talk to the mob and managed to redirect their attention so that we could steal into the car and start it.

As we left towards town, Bertil pressing hard on the accelerator, some women began to throw stones at us. Gunseli and I, who were now both sitting in the back seat, pressed ourselves down onto the car floor in order to avoid being hit. Thank God, the stones missed us.

We went directly to Police Headquarters and reported the attempted murder. The police officers weren't in the least interested. Not until Bertil started talking about contacting the Ministry of Tourism. Then they said they'd try to catch the guilty man. Having talked for a long time to the police officers, Bertil asked them to accompany him out to the car in which Gunseli and I were still sitting.

One of the officers leaned in through the side window and, looking at me, he asked, "So what's happened to you?"

Then Bertil exploded. He'd, in fact, just spent a long time explaining to them what had happened to me.

After the visit to the police, we drove directly to the Missionary Hospital. I needed help to remove all the glass splinters in my face, on my neck and on the rest of the body. They'd penetrated my clothes and I had splinters also in my backside. The hospital staff members on duty were quite uninterested in helping. We left and decided to try to remove the splinters at home, using pincers and torches.

It took an eternity to find all the small glass spears stuck in me. I felt like a packet of needles. It was a true piece of detective work. Afterwards, I took a shower and washed my hair twice. Not until then did I feel completely clean. The floor now glittered with tiny glass fragments. We wouldn't be able to use that shower again until the floor had been thoroughly swept.

One of these days the hospital manager would come to lunch and he would certainly not be happy when I told him how his employees had neglected their work.

Bertil sat down at the computer and wrote a letter to the Minister of Tourism. He should know that we didn't find it safe for tourists to go to the rainforest. He would also be informed about the mob that had attacked Per Erik and Bertil in Kakamega the previous year and that we found the Kakamega police very nonchalant and uninterested.

"Bertil," I said later in the evening, while having a cup of tea, "I'll never again go to Kakamega by the inner road. We don't even know the people there. Why do they hate us so much?"

"Yes," he answered, "that's something you may well ask. We do whatever we can to help them. We are poor as church mice. And what we don't give them voluntarily, they steal from us. I really wonder why we came to this place."

"Yes, right now I only want to leave. I can't face another hostile act."

Thinking about what had happened during the day, my tears started falling again. Why this too? Hadn't we had enough misery already?

A couple of weeks later, we were called to Police Headquarters. We suspected that the Ministry of Tourism had contacted the police, demanding an investigation of the case. The police informed us that the man throwing the stone had been captured on the evening of the assault. He was evidently known for throwing stones at passers-by. It was probably not meant as an attack on us as white people, in contrast to the mob's attack, which we believed was just that and that was really frightening.

At the police headquarters, the police officers subjected us to idiotic interrogations. We did whatever we could to be uncooperative and refused to sign the interrogation protocols, until statements had been added about the unwillingness of the police to help us. The car was photographed but we'd have to pay the cost for the windshield ourselves.

## 60. Why are we here?

We'd run out of steam. We were so low in spirits that we actually didn't feel like doing anything at all. Our water and telephone problems remained unsolved. We were ill with malaria and had different stomach problems. Hospital visits were frequent.

During January, the guests had been conspicuous in their absence and that was just as well. We'd had more than enough of them during Christmas and New Year, so now we needed to catch up with ourselves. But it was such a pity that everything felt so negative.

Oh, it would be so wonderful to have Father with us again. I missed him so much. I remained in bed under my quilt, delaying the decision to get up. Nowadays, I really had no wish at all to leave bed. If I did, there would certainly only be misery. It felt as if each day only brought new sorrows. I had nightmares every night. In them, I saw threatening faces expressing hatred and stones flying towards me. I was suddenly afraid of people. I didn't want them to come close to me, because they could turn into dangerous monsters. That was how I felt. The most rotten thing about it all was that Bertil and I were, in no way whatsoever, racists. We'd come to Kenya to help, then why were people so racist towards us? The flash of hatred we sometimes saw in their faces: why? I thought about what one of our half African friends had recently told us, when we'd told her about the assault on us.

"In spite of being half African and half European I, too, am afraid of the mob. I know how quickly mass hysteria takes hold and I always keep a distance when something happens. I know I could be in trouble, be attacked. Imagine you're driving your car in a street when a cyclist falls. Even if you're a hundred metres from the incident, press the accelerator and quickly drive away. They're capable of suddenly deciding you're involved and have caused the accident. Don't ask; don't show compassion - just get out of there."

Those were really tough words but they were maybe worth remembering.

At last, I finally got out of bed. We had to go down to Kisumu, Bertil and I, to hand over our immigration documents to Olivier, who would take them to Nairobi. Our entry permits would expire within more or less a week, so this was really an urgent matter.

The youngsters stayed at home to rest. They were regaining strength after an attack of typhoid fever and they were still under medical supervision, taking medicine. They grumbled about the horrid salty drink they had to take in order not to become dehydrated.

Their typhoid had been unnecessary. Even though it hadn't been a severe attack, it could have been avoided. The scheming waterman had sold our water, for which we'd paid him, to an African bigwig, building in the neighbourhood. He'd refused us water for more than a week, during the recent heat wave. Our dishes, as a consequence, had probably been washed in dirty water. Damned corruption.

Before leaving for Kisumu, I gave orders in the kitchen that all our crockery had to be washed again, this time with boiled water. I told Mathias we intended to buy the water filter we'd seen in Kisumu. From now on, it would be used for our drinking water. The water would of course be boiled first, as we'd always done. Furthermore, we'd have an obligatory Sunday meeting, led by Nelson, about hygiene. We'd act strictly towards anyone violating the rules.

Once Father had arrived, we'd sit down with him to try to find a solution to our future water supply and how we could more easily heat water for the kitchen. It was obvious our employees had cheated us, not heating water properly in the pan on the stove.

On February 4th, we celebrated Bertil's third birthday in Kenya. The years had passed unbelievably fast. Mathias and Gunseli had prepared a delicious meal, set the table at the barbecue place and decorated it with garlands. They'd also made a very funny festive hat for the hero of the occasion. They handed that over to Bertil together with a live hen, something that caused a lot of merriment. Fred had made a hand-carved key ring for Bertil and I gave him a bottle of sherry and some sweets.

It was a real feast. Barbecued minute steak with savoury butter and baked cooking bananas together with a salad and tasty claret.

What had we done the previous year on Bertil's birthday? I tried hard to remember. Then, I suddenly recalled.

"Did you know Per Erik was here exactly one year ago? It was he and I, who celebrated with Bertil last year; we had lunch on the veranda then."

"It'll be fun, when he comes down again. I think he'll turn up at the end of March," said Per Erik's youngest son, Mathias.

We'd have a couple of relative visits during the next few months. Father would be arriving soon and after that, in March, Christian, our eldest son and his girlfriend Kicki. As far as I understood, they wouldn't stay for long, but it would be wonderful to receive them here. They'd actually not visited us before.

"Suppose we receive paying guests at the same time, where will everybody sleep then?" asked Gunseli.

"No problem, we'll sleep in a row on the dining room floor and in front of the fireplace but Father-in-law will have a nice bed in our apartment. He won't have to sleep on the floor." Bertil explained.

The exquisite meal was completed with coffee and liqueurs, served on the veranda. It was unusually hot and stuffy. Even in the shade of the veranda, the air was quivering so much it was almost impossible to be outside.

Unfortunately, we had been stupid painting the tin roof red. Red attracts heat. All the roof paint was also starting to peal off and therefore we had to put a grid on the gutters, during the rainy season, in order to avoid having the water tanks filled with flakes of paint. According to what we'd heard, we ought to have waited for a year before painting and we should, in fact, have painted the roof white, but it was now too late to do anything about that.

We could, however, do one thing soon in order to lower the temperature on the veranda: make a ceiling with an air slit between the roof and the ceiling. Hopefully, the air would circulate more that way and, with a ceiling of papyrus mats, it would, in fact, look cosier. Our golden shower plants had grown enormously, so if we led the long flowering shoots to the papyrus mats and fixed them there, it would look exotic. Why hadn't we thought of that earlier?

We quickly gave up our attempt to sit on the hot veranda and moved down to a group of armchairs on the lawn, in the shade of the house, to spend a pleasant afternoon. When it was cooler after dinner and sunset, we returned to the veranda to listen to music. It was cosy and the sight of all these kerosene lamps along the twenty-two metre long veranda must have been beautiful from the other side of the valley.

Listening to Barbra Streisand, we devoted ourselves to Bertil´s and my evening hobby. We took turns interpreting the tree silhouettes on the opposite hill, describing the details at length. We'd done that on many an evening. When we moved to our African village, a rather big area on the opposite valley slope was still covered with the original rainforest. That area was now extremely small. People didn't care it was illegal to cut down rainforest trees. Hence, the silhouettes changed often. We spent a couple of pleasant hours laughing and joking, trying to visualize dragons, princesses, castles, ballet dancers and similar things, standing out against the evening sky.

## 61. The chameleon

I was dusting the bookshelves in the lounge, when I suddenly heard a terrible yell from the lower part of the compound. The dust cloth fell to the floor and I dashed out onto the veranda to see what had happened.

Linda and Veronica were screaming, their hands in front of their mouths. They looked quite shocked. My first thought was that a snake had bitten them. At this point, also our shamba boys had reached the girls. The boys weren't shouting but looked upset.

"Has anyone been bitten by a snake? What's happened?" I asked.

"No," Fred answered, "but the girls were passing through the gate down to the huts, when they saw a thing like that ..." he paused and pointed, "sitting on it."

I burst out laughing. What he pointed at was a cute little chameleon. We often sat, with binoculars, on the veranda studying them, when they were walking around in the bushes or on the telephone line. They were so beautiful with all their colours.

"But, honestly, they're not dangerous. Just look at how beautiful it is."

"No," they all said, almost in chorus, "we Kenyans don't like chameleons. They're horrible and mean bad luck, and they probably bite."

Then I happened to think about something I'd just read about chameleons in Kenya. It was from the book "The Flame Trees of Thika", by Elspeth Huxley. In it, she tells the story of how, together with her parents, she arrived in Kenya in 1913 as pioneers. I loved that book and had read it several times. I remembered quite well the passage where the story of a Kenyan chameleon is told, so I wanted to let our terror-stricken staff hear it.

After telling them a little about the book, I started, "One day, she wants to give her friend - I think his name is Njombo - a chameleon as a gift. He steps away from her with a fearful grimace, full of detest.

'Those are bad animals', he utters, without explaining why. She doesn't understand his dislike, since chameleons only do good things and since they neither bite nor burn.

One of her friends finds an explanation in a book about Kenyan legends and, as soon as she hears it, she passes it on to Njombo. It seems, the chameleon has been ordered by God to deliver an important message to the first man, who lives somewhere close to Mount Kenya. God declares to the chameleon he's forbidden to linger at the roadside, because it‘s most important the chameleon delivers the message, before the moon disappears.

To start with, the chameleon trots on, but he soon forgets the reason for the walk. Different adventures happen to him, but one day he remembers his errand, resumes his walking and finally arrives at his destination. But, at that time, the time limit has been exceeded.

God is upset with the chameleon and roars 'Look at what you've done. The purpose of the message you were to deliver was that the moon would stop disappearing every month and that man would stop dying. Now it's too late. From now on, the moon will disappear monthly and all men and women will die, sooner or later - and all this happens because you've not followed my instructions.'

So, ever since that time, the poor chameleon that could have saved humanity has been detested."

Veronica and Linda and the others laughed a little at the story, but declared they were still as afraid of the poor little chameleon as before. I, in turn, found it amazing to see that what was written in the book coincided with reality. Kenyans were indeed afraid of chameleons.

We'd spread the message we needed a new cook and houseboy. In consequence, a steady stream of applicants had come. Some seemed qualified, others not. This time, we'd be very careful. Not another Max. We intended to check their references thoroughly and the person in question would also have to be tested for a while.

If you were to believe all letters of recommendation, in Western Kenya you could find an abundance of chefs, having worked at coastal hotels, embassies and wherever. We, however, no longer believed all the documents people showed us. We'd, on several occasions, been asked to write letters of recommendation, at the office in Kakamega. Asking us for a computer printout, the clients gave us an unused original letterhead from, for example, a hotel. Talk about faked references. We'd naturally never been willing to do that.

Anyway, one day we got another visitor, aspiring to the position of cook. A young, handsome and pleasant but rather shy boy. We immediately liked Bernard. He worked in the kitchen of the Rainforest Retreat, but was looking for a more qualified job than the one he had there. The kitchen staff at the Rainforest Retreat had nothing but praise for him. Bernard was quiet, hard working, loyal and willing to learn. They told us they actually wanted to keep him. Hearing all these positive remarks, we decided to hire him on probation.

Having Bernard proved to be a big relief in the kitchen. To begin with, we worked together preparing the meals, but it wasn't long before we gave him bigger and more difficult assignments to solve on his own. He enjoyed it and was happy working. He said his father was a cook and that he himself had always wanted to become one.

Standing in the kitchen talking to Bernard, I heard a horn sounding at the gate. I asked Fred to quickly run up to open. I thought I knew who was arriving. I put on my shoes and ran uphill at full speed. Bertil had already parked the Suzuki and jumped out to help him out of the car. Father had at long last arrived.

Yesterday evening Bertil had gone to Kisumu to meet him. On arrival, they checked into Imperial Hotel, so that Father could have a night's rest before the drive upcountry. He looked healthy but a little worn out, but then he was 81 years old. It was quite an achievement to fly alone all the way from Sweden at that age. He was going to spend about six weeks with us and that would be absolutely wonderful.

I guided him, after all the hugging - his grandson Mathias with his girlfriend had also appeared to welcome him - to the veranda, where he was served a bottle of cold mineral water.

I felt melancholic seeing Father on the veranda. Last time he sat there, Mother had been with him.

## 62. The Ambassador who disappeared

After Mother's death, Father decided to build a family house on the upper part of our compound; a house where he and my brothers and their families could stay part of the year. David and he had together made drawings of a fantastic brick house. It even had a veranda with a place to sleep up on the roof, so that you could enjoy the wonderful view. I felt a little doubtful about the whole idea - Father being so old. Should he really embark on such a big project? Would he, at his age, stand being in the heat during longer periods? But as long as he was content, he could do whatever he wanted as far as I was concerned. The loss of Mother had been tough for him, so it would be good for him to become engaged in something.

I saw Father on his way to the upper part of the compound, where he had a meeting with Daniel on the construction site. His hands were full of drawings and he was full of enthusiasm. The work with the foundation-laying would now begin. Daniel and Father had many long talks. When Father heard it was difficult to find a lorry that could bring sand for the cement, he told Daniel about the donkey caravans he'd used, during his work with school construction in Ethiopia. Daniel quickly found some donkeys and we soon saw a donkey caravan, loaded with sand, coming from the village in the direction of Yala River, where the sand was fetched. It looked really picturesque.

A little later in the day, Father asked me to accompany him to the building site. He wanted to tell me about his plans and show me how he visualized the future house. After a lot of pointing and talking, he said, "Yes, we'll build over there. A comfortable cosy house - not big but airy. Imagine the view of the valley. What do you think, Gunilla?"

"It sounds wonderful, Father. And the view is so fantastic. But …"

Fred interrupted me, saying a man was on his way down from the gate and that the man didn't want to divulge his name or errand. Fred was irritated. The man came up to us where we were standing in the high grass. He was tall, slim and nicely dressed and looked authoritarian. Shooing Fred away, he asked who Father and I were. Then he introduced himself as Chief of Criminal Investigations Department in Kakamega.

"You've a reservation for tomorrow here at the hotel," he stated and continued, "I've come for that reason."

"No, we've no reservation at all for the nearest future," I answered.

"Yes, you have. I know what I'm talking about," he persisted.

Father suddenly intervened, "Gunilla, the telephone line is out of order. Those wanting to make a reservation might not have reached us by phone."

"But what do you want? What business of yours are our guests?" I asked surprised.

"I've to check the security, before the arrival of the guests."

"That responsibility belongs to my daughter and my son-in-law and they take very good care of it," exclaimed Father, now as irritated as I was.

Bertil turned up and was quickly updated by both of us. We understood absolutely nothing. We hadn't received any booking, and why was the head of the C.I.D. at our compound?

"Who is the person supposed to have made a reservation here?" asked Bertil.

"I can't answer that; it's a secret," the man answered. "But you should know the security issue is extremely important, therefore you must let my policemen in so that they can check the whole hotel. Remember that their instructions must be obeyed. You must at all times follow their orders."

"This is ridiculous," I objected. "We don't know anything about the alleged reservation. We don't know for how many persons or for how many days the alleged guests are supposed to stay. We can't work this way. We don't even have a functioning telephone."

"A functioning telephone is a necessity."

The man took out his communication radio, bawling some orders in Swahili. After that, he said to Bertil, "When you're in town shopping, you have to go to the Telephone Company and check that they've solved the problem."

"Should we be open as usual to tourists coming to the gate asking for a hut, or should the whole place be reserved for these unknown and unbooked guests?" Bertil wondered, in an ironic voice.

"I can't answer that question. You might get an answer later," the man hissed. "Now I'm in a hurry. My men will return later today to check the fences and other security issues. Margie, one of our female police officers, will also come. She'll be your contact person - and remember - all this is secret. You're not allowed to tell anyone about this visit."

The man said goodbye and disappeared up towards the gate and his car. We stared confounded at each other and walked together to the main building, where we sat down on the veranda with a glass of beer.

Thoughts were swarming in our heads. It took a while before anyone started talking.

The staff were curious and tried to stay close to us, in the hope we'd inform them about what was going on. We gave them some chores down in the garden and explained the visit by saying that the police wanted to know what Riverdale Gardens looked like and that they wanted to check our security routines, so that we could feel safe.

We asked Mathias and Gunseli to join us, since we now needed to have a family meeting. How would we deal with this strange situation?

All this hush-hush indicated that an important person would be staying with us. Who could be so important that we weren't even allowed to know who it was? Could it be the president himself? No, hardly. But - our discussion continued – we'd recently had a Nordic Ambassador having dinner and lots of embassy people staying at the hotel. Could we possibly be talking about a diplomat?

Our discussions were interrupted by the aforesaid Margie, turning up in complete police rig-out. She wanted to discuss details with us and inspect the guest huts. She asked us to order our employees out of earshot and then we proceeded down to the huts.

"Is this where they'll be staying?" she asked, when we entered one of the huts.

"Maybe, but first we have to know how many persons we are talking about and if they should have single or double rooms. Are you actually sure these secret people are coming to us? And do they really know that the toilets and showers are in a separate building?"

"Yes, the guests are coming to you," Margie answered. "Four persons will stay one night at Riverdale Gardens."

"But will they have single or double rooms?" Bertil wondered. "And should any of them have a whole hut?"

"And what kind of food do they want?" Father asked. "And what do they drink?"

"I've no idea," Margie answered. "You'll have to prepare something delicious. You'd better buy some different good wines and the best varieties of spirits. Make sure, one hut is reserved for the most important person in the group. I'm sure everything will be OK."

"But please, Margie," I intervened. "We need to know what people we are talking about - this is ridiculous. We are trusted to have these persons as guests, but we are not allowed to know who they are."

"OK, tomorrow I'll tell you. It's unbelievably important you won't divulge it to anybody, not even your staff. Now you must go into town to check with the Telephone Company that they've fixed your telephone. I'll be back tomorrow. See you then."

Margie left and Bertil and I made preparations to go to Kakamega. Before leaving we had to write a shopping list. What would we serve?

We decided to offer almost the same menu as the Indian family Singh had had on Christmas Day: first a coupe with garlic-marinated crayfish tails that we, thank heavens, still had in the freezer in the village, decorated with a small salad containing amongst other things small pawpaw balls; for main course coq-au-vin; followed by homemade passion fruit sorbet and for dessert rhubarb pie with vanilla sauce. Our best wines with the food, and a drink served with small filled croustades, before dinner. Coffee and brandy afterwards.

Having decided the menu, Bertil and I jumped into the car and drove towards town. Turning onto the Kakamega tarmac road, we met a Telephone Company car loaded with telephone workers driving towards our village. Maybe it was a reaction to the telephone order issued by C.I.D. We'd tried for three weeks to convince the Telephone Company to repair the line, but as usual in vain.

In Kakamega, we stopped first at the Telephone Company. The man at the client reception asked which telephone number we wanted repaired.

"21651. A police officer has probably already phoned, giving you details about the number," Bertil answered.

"21651," the man shouted loudly to the woman behind the counter. "What is the situation? Somebody answer, it's urgent. It has to be working today."

The woman looked stressed and started going through her papers. "They're out working on the line. It might be ready, I suppose," she said nonchalantly.

"Might? This is top priority. It must be in order today, otherwise we'll be in trouble."

Bertil and I looked at each other confused. What on earth had the police officer in civilian clothes told the Telephone Company?

In the evening, we made detailed plans for the following day, in the light of the kerosene lamps. Who would refurnish the huts? In one hut, we'd make a living room instead of one of the bedrooms. Who would pick and arrange flowers for all the vases? At what time should we start preparing food? We must not forget to give our employees orders to stop all other possible guests already up at the gate. We made checklist after checklist. Everything had to be perfect. Finally, we felt ready to face tomorrow.

Before bedtime, we relaxed over a drink. Then the speculation started again. Who could it be? In the end, we all agreed that it was the American Ambassador.

The following morning passed quickly. All of us worked like mad with the preparations and the food turned out really delicious. Now only the guests were missing but we felt full of confidence.

Margie arrived in the early afternoon. She and her men walked around, checking the whole compound, the huts and the main building. They ordered us to keep our dogs locked in, so that they wouldn't disturb the guests. Our employees were getting quite sullen not knowing what was going on. Therefore, we told them that some famous Swedes would have an important meeting at Riverdale and that they'd be staying overnight. They must not be disturbed in any way; that was the reason for this hush-hush.

The time for the guests' arrival approached. Margie was standing in the door opening of the blue hut, now called the Ambassador Hut, with the communication radio in her hand. She'd revealed to us that, sure enough, it was the American Ambassador that was coming. Standing dressed up at her side, we waited for orders. She started talking energetically over the radio. Bit by bit, she gave us information as to the position of the Ambassador's car convoy.

Finally Margie jubilantly exclaimed, "They've turned off into your road and will be here within a couple of minutes. Hurry up to the gate, so that you can welcome the Ambassador when she arrives."

We hastened, full of expectation but at the same time enormously tired after all the preparations. Our neighbours obviously suspected something was going on, since people were gathering on the public land. Time dragged. We waited and waited - nothing happened. Why didn't our guests come? It was strange. What had happened?

Half an hour later, we returned down to Margie. She was as surprised as we. The radio contact had been cut off and she didn't get any answers to her calls over the radio. Alarm was spreading. Had the Ambassador been assaulted? Could that really happen on our small road? We'd, actually, already had reports informing us the convoy had turned into our road. No other roads were going out from it.

An hour later, Margie decided to go out in search of the Ambassador, together with her subordinates. Bertil also wanted to help an Ambassador in need, but was persuaded to stay at home. Margie promised to contact us, so that we'd be prepared when the Ambassador turned up.

All of us had run out of steam and the food would soon be destroyed. We dared not have any drinks as we ought to be sober when our guests arrived. We walked around like lost souls.

The hours passed and we heard nothing. Finally, after four hours, we got a very short telephone call from Margie.

"The Ambassador is at the Rainforest Retreat. That's where they had reservations. Obviously, there must have been a misunderstanding. The Rainforest Retreat also has bungalows, also lies in the rainforest and the name also begins with an R." And then she put down the receiver.

What a rollercoaster ride.

The evening was strange. One whole hour passed before we even talked to one another. We'd run out of steam. We hardly touched the food. Everybody was walking around alone, muttering to themselves. First the worry about what could have happened to the Ambassador and then the stupid explanation.

Bertil finally pulled himself together and assembled us all on the veranda. We sat down, lit kerosene lamps and candles and poured ourselves each a glass of expensive whisky. Slowly, we started communicating.

Was the whole thing a diversion? Had we been used as a decoy? Had the Security Police used us and Riverdale as bait?

We didn't know what to think. We were upset, disappointed and furious. The whole farce had cost us a lot of money.

Father calmed us down and suggested we first check with the police if they would reimburse us. If they rejected, we should immediately contact the American Embassy.

Hungry and sulky, we went to bed. But, first, we sent our employees home with the scanty explanation that the expected guests had been prevented from coming by some other engagement.

The following morning, Bertil called the Security Police and talked to the head's third assistant, counting from the top. The head himself didn't want to talk to us. Bertil asked if the invoice should be sent to the police but got an angry reply that the police were in no way involved. Bertil was advised to contact the American Embassy.

A diplomatic but questioning letter was sent to the American Embassy in Nairobi. After a couple of weeks, we got an icy reply from them. They denied all knowledge of the incident. Their suggestion was we contact the police in order to be reimbursed.

Whether it was the embassy or the police that had conned us was still an open question, which would probably never be answered.

## 63. Airline without service

Petrus came towards me, waving a letter in one hand.

"This is for you and Bertil," he declared. "I just got it from a police officer, who lives in Wulushi. He said it's important. But he wants money for it - at least 500 shillings."

"May I see it?" I said and took the letter. I opened it and read that we - Bertil, Gunseli and I - had been summoned to Kakamega Law Court, where we'd evidently testify against Peter, the man that threw the stone at me. If we didn't appear in Court, we'd have to pay a fine.

"No way! We are not going to pay the police one single shilling," Bertil exclaimed, when he'd finished reading the letter. "It's his duty to deliver this summons to us. Or don't you agree, Petrus?"

"Yes, of course it's his duty. I agree on that, but please remember this police officer is a bad man and that it could be dangerous to offend him," Petrus finished.

When things like this happened - when I saw how corrupt people were - my body started pulsating. It was throbbing and pounding and I felt as if my blood pressure was sky high. I'd better calm down. Otherwise something might happen - maybe I'd have a stroke. Could you get that from anger and frustration? I pulled myself together and sat down on the veranda, where Christian and Kicki were having breakfast. As Christian looked a little white about the gills, I asked him how he'd been sleeping.

"Not so well," he answered. "That awful malaria prophylaxis I'm taking, I think it's called Lariam, gives me nightmares."

"Yes, he's raising hell at night," Kicki exclaimed, "and the worst of all is that we don't even know if the medicine prevents malaria. We heard Mathias has had malaria, in spite of taking Lariam."

"Yes, he has," I answered. "The mosquitoes here seem to be resistant against most prophylaxi. You can forget normal chloroquinine tablets. For some people Lariam works but for many they have no effect whatsoever. I hope, anyway, both of you are wise enough to use the mosquito nets over the beds."

Christian asked if the malaria in our area was of the most dangerous kind. He was reassured, when I informed him that type wasn't found in our region. The malaria was of course dangerous, but it couldn't be compared with the severe highland malaria found around Kisii. Nasty epidemics spread among the people there and many died.

Christian and Kicki had now been spent a couple of days with us and would soon be leaving to continue to Madeira on vacation. It was the first time our eldest son had visited us and I was so happy to see him. The two of them weren't, in the same way as our youngest son David, used to exotic places, although they'd been on vacation in Kenya before. To see us in these surroundings was certainly a rather big change for them. The step was, without any doubt, big between a terraced house in Täby and life in an African village - especially taking into account our age.

In the evening, Christian and I ran away from the others to have a private openhearted talk between mother and son. I didn't believe in withholding, especially from grown-up children like Christian, how you were feeling deep inside. I told him, after he'd promised me he wouldn't pass this information on to Grandfather, how bad I was feeling after the assault and all the deceits we'd been subjected to. I divulged I wasn't feeling well mentally and that the malaria attacks were particularly trying for my body. He made me promise him, we'd leave our project the day we couldn't stand any more without feeling it was a failure.

A couple of days later, it was time to drive Christian and Kicki down to Kisumu, where they'd catch a flight connection to Madeira. Since we arrived with plenty of time, we decided to go to Imperial Hotel and wait there. They'd take the airport bus from the hotel to the airport so that we wouldn't have to drive all the way back to Riverdale in darkness. The airport bus always stopped at the Imperial where the driver used to fetch the passengers in the lobby.

Time passed and no airport bus arrived. Time after time, we asked where it was but nobody knew. Suddenly, somebody said it had passed quite some time ago and that the departure time of the flight had been brought forward one hour. Christian and Kicki threw themselves into a taxi and left for the airport. We also went there by car, in order to make sure they really caught the flight. Arriving, we couldn't see the youngsters anywhere. The aircraft was still on the ground. Finally Christian and Kicki turned up, very much delayed. The taxi driver had taken the wrong road. The entrance road to the airport had recently been changed, something we knew but obviously not the taxi driver. Together, we rushed to the check-in counter and tried to persuade the staff on duty to let them on board. No way. In spite of the aircraft still being on the runway, it was too late. No attempt at persuasion would help.

The aircraft took off and the four of us were left standing on the ground. Swearing. We renamed the airline "Shame of Africa". Christian and Kicki hadn't been given any information about the timetable change, in spite of having reconfirmed their flight. A V.I.P. was obviously onboard the flight and he wanted to disembark at Eldoret. That was why the flight had been rerouted that day and the time of departure brought forward.

After a lot of quarrelling and fuss with the staff, we made them realize they really had to help us get a hotel room in Kisumu. Unfortunately, everything was fully booked, because of a big Indian wedding in town. Finally, after several hours, they found a room for the overnight stay. We parted and Christian promised to contact us next day from Nairobi to tell us if they managed to get a flight to Madeira, where friends were waiting for them.

The telephone exchanges between us the following day were intense. To our astonishment and dismay, we heard that also the airport staff in Nairobi were unwilling to help. Only after having spent twenty-four hours at Jomo Kenyatta International Airport could Christian and Kicki manage to get a flight. Their planned vacation on Madeira would, as a result, be just a couple of days long.

"Bertil, what's wrong with Veronica? She's usually laughing and now she's as sour as a lemon and she's been like this for several weeks now."

We decided to talk to her to check why she wasn't happy. When we sat down together, her behaviour was brusque and arrogant. She informed us she wanted a written reference and a couple of days off. She was secretive and actually quite hostile but we couldn't convince her to tell us what was wrong.

Within a day, she got her reference and declared she wouldn't work for us any more. She said it in an unpleasant way. We didn't understand anything. Had we done her any wrong? We'd really been content with her, up until lately when she'd been sulky, and we'd believed she was happy with us. It was strange.

We soon heard Veronica had gone to Nairobi and had got a job there. Bertil discovered, within a couple of days, she'd apparently taken my laptop along too. What she didn't know was that it was completely destroyed by leaking batteries and that it would never work again. Yet another person, we liked and trusted, had betrayed us. Would it ever end?

Father's construction work had advanced as far as he'd planned for this visit. He'd continue building on his next stay.

Since Father couldn't stand being idle for more than a few minutes at a time, he decided to dedicate his last two weeks in Kenya to another project. He'd repair the village road, the one kilometre between Wushiye and our compound, including the ravine-like sector so gruesome during the rainy season, when you could slip off the road and slide down into the tea plantation.

Being a constructional engineer with road and canal experience, he knew the course of action. He had, furthermore, practical experience in the tropics - from his years living in Sri Lanka and Ethiopia. With Daniel's help, Father soon had a group of young strong men. When he'd ordered sand and big stones, the work started.

It was fantastic to see my 81-year old father, in shorts and hat, standing for hours in the road with a stick in his hand. He pointed with it and the whole group of workers followed his orders. He explained that the local method of putting soil in the holes didn't make much of a repair. The rains washed the soil away. You should instead clear all the soil from the road, dig the holes big enough to be filled with stones, then add twigs and branches and top with concrete and sand. This kind of filling would stay put even during the heaviest rains.

This was a quite new technology in this area and people gathered just to look at the old mzungu and his strange way of repairing the road. The ravine disappeared in a couple of days, having been converted into a very normal piece of road, fit for driving. It would be interesting to see if the road would remain intact during the rainy season.

## 64. The hotel is closed

"No, enough is enough. We are closing for guests," Bertil angrily exclaimed, having once more tried the tap to check if any water was coming. "These people don't want any help."

We'd had a terrible and expensive problem getting enough water into the tanks. The people we normally hired as extra workers to carry water from the spring had been busy working in the maize fields. And, of course, precisely when the supply was difficult, we had guests, who unfortunately loved to shower at odd times of the day.

As usual, Kabeji - the old waterman down in the village - was causing trouble. Bertil had spoken to the man from the Water Ministry and he'd promised to sort things out. In spite of that, we'd still not received any water. Maybe he, too, was in our chief's pocket? Chief Weaky didn't want us to be successful, even though guests meant more money for the villagers. Bertil had been in Wushiye, on several occasions, to be present at the Water Committee meetings but they'd all been cancelled, since Bertil had been the only one to show up.

In this situation, we could hardly receive our guests with a clear conscience. We'd expose them to health hazards, unless we could keep the place clean enough. Water was a must, especially when the elements were completely unreliable. In April we should have heavy rains, but the sun was baking all day long.

It was ironic that Travel News, published by the biggest travel agency in Kenya, in its April issue, had a positive article about us. Having read it, all sorts of people had started calling to reserve rooms, so now the telephone was ringing non-stop. But since we no longer accepted reservations, we had to answer, "Closed for guests since April 6th due to local corruption." That was tough.

Father returned to Sweden at the beginning of April. He left a huge emptiness behind. In spite of his advanced age, he'd contributed in so many aspects to the improvement of our situation. The village road was now fit for traffic, although we planned to continue improving certain sectors of it. He'd given us an outdoor, roofed kitchen - an extension outside the kitchen - with a cast-iron range with two hobs and an oven. It was mainly used for heating dishwater, cooking dog food, preparing staff lunches and other similar things. The oven also functioned, which was quite a relief, since the oven in the kitchen didn't work any longer.

Father was really generous. When he heard that our freezer, down in Wushiye, had been full of food and left without power for a week - something the landlord didn't care to inform us about - he bought us a large gas freezer which we could place on one of the verandas. What a wonderful gift. We only had one small problem. The temperature in it never went below minus five degrees Celsius. Unfortunately that wasn't enough, so we had to call the Nakumatt store in Kisumu and ask them to fetch the freezer. They agreed and reimbursed all the money, except for a small deduction to cover transport. That was really kind of them.

The first court hearing regarding the assault was unpleasant. Seeing the mad man, who had thrown a stone at me, made me relive it all. The court was full of curious people and I felt quite sick having them so close. One of our journalist friends was sitting with us in the courtroom. He pointed out that, during the witness hearings, we shouldn't say the police had refused to come to our help. If we did that, the police could take their revenge on us and we could be in serious danger. Bertil was the only one of us, who needed to give evidence, and he told them what had happened and identified the culprit, Peter.

When the hearing came to an end, the judge told us to return to Court at the end of April. In the meantime, Peter would undergo an examination, conducted by a forensic psychiatrist.

On our way home from court, we saw our friend Glenn, from the Sotanini mine, walking on the main road. We stopped and asked him where he was going and if we could give him a lift.

"I've been summoned to a police interrogation," he said. "About a month ago, I found a dead baby in the Yala River and informed the police about it. Now they summon me time after time. Each time I arrive, and I can't afford going by matatu, they declare the interrogation has been postponed and that I'll have to come back. If I don't show up, I'll get a fine."

"Oh, my God," I exclaimed. "Do you know to whom the baby belonged?"

"No, I've no idea. As far as I know, it doesn't come from my village. I just happened to find it."

We drove Glenn to Police Headquarters. On our way home, we talked about the strange behaviour we often saw with the Police. Witnesses and victims alike were regarded as guilty. We could understand those who refused to give a statement or inform; to do that only led to trouble.

## 65. Thunder and lightning

Once again, Bertil and I were all alone. It felt empty and boring. Per Erik, who had been down here for only a short time on this trip, had left together with Mathias and Gunseli. No more family visits were in sight. The hotel had been closed for guests. Everything was very depressing. I just wanted to pull a blanket over my head and wake up in some other place.

The weather gods sneered at us. We'd closed the hotel because of lack of water, caused by local corruption. Now that it was closed, the rainy season had truly started, with daily thunder and lightning and water tanks spilling over.

The thunderstorms weren't exactly harmless. One evening, Bertil was standing with the telephone cord in one hand in order to connect it to the modem. We heard an enormous bang and lightning jumped from his left index finger. The lightning had hit the ventilation tube of the water heater, which was standing about fifty metres from the main building, and from there jumped on to Bertil. I don't know which one of us was most scared: Bertil with flashing and cracking fingers or me, hearing the bang not knowing what had caused it. Thank heavens Bertil was quite unharmed, but certainly shocked.

Deaths in combination with lightning weren't uncommon in our area. The tempests were horrible with cloudbursts so violent you couldn't see anything, even at a metre distance. Gusts of wind, constantly changing direction, tore down the trees and, just recently, our TV-antenna. Heavy thunder sounded like a giant releasing huge piles of wood onto the roof. Flashes of lightning brightened the whole sky. The devastation after a storm was often great and the roads looked like flooded mud fields - quite impassable.

One evening, we had a hailstorm. The hailstones were as big as golf balls. When the storm had died down, the hail was piled up in drifts on the veranda. We let the dogs out and, at first, they were surprised and suspicious, but after a while they ate all the ice they could manage. It was very popular.

I looked up at the sky. Dark clouds were piling up. Would we have thunder today? No, it seemed to be a false alarm.

I put on my flip-flops and, as a safety precaution, I grabbed an umbrella and walked down to the toilet.

Having philosophized down there for a while, I smelled the pronounced odour of ozone and got a sharp metallic taste in my mouth.

Strange. I hadn't heard any thunder yet, had I? I hardly had time to finish the thought, before I noticed my hair was standing upright. It tingled, like when you hold a charged comb near your face. A crackling sound turned into an enormous crash. At the same time, a blue-white light, so bright all details were wiped out, encircled the ground outside the toilet. What was this? It didn't sound like thunder. The whole thing happened in a fraction of a second and then both the ground and the toilet building started shaking. Those were actually flashes of lightning. Everything was so unreal. I didn't understand I was sitting in the middle of a stroke of lightning. Then an uneasy silence followed. I took a deep breath. Was that the only flash? No, it wasn't. The flashes of lightning continued, though not as close as the first one, which had probably struck the water heater's high ventilation pipe.

I saw flashes of lightning in every direction and the thunder clashes were horrifically loud. Yes, now I remembered. It was this building that was struck by lightning, on one of the occasions when Bertil got such a nasty shock in his hand. Oh my God, I wondered if Bertil knew I was down here.

By now it had also started to rain. What should I do? I absolutely refused to step outside with my umbrella unfolded. The lightning could strike.

I cowered on the floor close to the door, expecting the worst. Was the lightning attracted by water or was it the opposite? I didn't know what time it was, but I felt I'd been there for an eternity.

The thought of the high ventilation pipe also made me nervous. Imagine if the lightning struck it again, in spite of people saying lightning doesn't strike the same place twice. I sensed I was getting more and more hysterical. Tears started running down my cheeks. I'd been here for so long. Why wasn't anybody looking for me?

After what seemed like an eternity, the rain diminished and more time elapsed between lightning and thunder. Dare I run up to the main building? Nobody seemed to have heard my cries for help.

Suddenly I gathered courage. I left the umbrella in the toilet and ran uphill over the slippery, muddy lawn. A flash of lightning made me stumble and fall. I was soaking wet, muddy and dissolved in tears, when I finally opened the door to the reception. Inside, Bertil was sitting, reading.

Seeing me, he said, "Oh, I was just wondering where you were."

I felt like killing him. Looking at the clock, I realised I'd spent more than an hour down in the toilet. He hadn't noticed until now.

## 66. Enough of it!

We had to sell Riverdale and get out of here. My father's dream of a meeting point for the relatives was probably just that - an unrealistic dream. I walked up to look at the construction he'd started during his last visit. My heart ached. Deep inside he had, no doubt, understood what a hellish situation we were in - in this wonderful paradise we'd created out of a maize field.

The question now was how we would find a buyer. We asked everybody we met if they had any suggestions, so the rumour we wanted to sell was spreading. One day, we visited our Indian friends to get some information on how we should proceed with the sale. Before sitting down to talk, they took us on an inspection tour of their big palace-like house. What luxury. We really felt like the poor country cousins. Unfortunately we only got some general advice to take home. Our Indian friend, however, promised to keep his ears open in case he heard of someone wanting to buy.

When we walked towards our car, two loudly barking big Alsatians came up to us. Our friend warned us they were dangerous watchdogs. Without thinking I stretched out my hand to let them smell my scent. Next moment, I had two wonderful beasts near me, just wanting me to scratch their necks. Love at first sight. Our friends looked irritated and I was pretty sure both the dogs and their handler would be scolded, after our departure. It was probably not their intention people got to know how nice and kind their dogs were.

We decided to try to keep ourselves afloat while waiting for a buyer to turn up. Deborah, who was now helping Bertil in the town office, seemed to manage quite well on her own and actually made some money.

To keep our spirits up, Bertil and I tried to spend as much time together as possible. The dogs were wonderful company, even if Merry was in heat again and we had to keep Rufus and Musse away from her. She slept in the small bedroom and the males slept together with us in the big room. That worked pretty well now, which hadn't been the case earlier, when one of us had had to sleep with Merry down in another hut during her periods in heat.

One evening when I walked into the small bedroom to say goodnight to Merry, she was gone. Had she managed to escape? Where could she be? And with her being in heat. Different possible and impossible scenarios flew through my head. I ran into the living room and shouted for Bertil, "Bertil, Merry is gone."

Bertil rushed over the veranda into the apartment and the small room. In my haste I'd closed the door behind me. He probably thought the same as I had. Then I heard laughter. And thereafter, "Little girl, you've really made a nice bed."

My heart started beating again and I hurried into the room. Look. Our darling was lying there, only showing the tip of her nose. She'd jumped up onto one of our shelves and pressed herself close to the wall. Since the shelves were deep, she'd found a big space in which she'd prepared a bed of T-shirts and other stuff. Oh, how comfortable she was. As she had to sleep alone, we didn't have the heart to push her down.

Quite suddenly and like a bolt from the blue, we got kicked out of our office in Kakamega.

The computer training company we were renting from had acted unfairly and meanly. They'd used Bertil's name to get ranked as a proper computer college, including computer repair training. Now they didn't need Bertil any longer.

We'd introduced and marketed both email and Internet in Kakamega. Our landlords had now made a better agreement with another Internet entrepreneur, who could offer email service for five percent of our rate. They could afford to do that, since the biggest part of their income came from their training courses. This meant we'd never make a profit, should we choose to open the office in another place. So the only thing we could do was to close our office and sell all our things.

Now a really strenuous period started. We struggled so hard we almost killed ourselves. To town early every morning and back home at sunset without anything to eat during the whole day. High costs for petrol and a never-ending stress, as all the computers must be fixed before they could be sold. We had at our disposal a couple of square metres in premises belonging to our friend John, so we'd moved all our computer things there and Deborah and John were helping us to sell them.

It wasn't a nice feeling being paid five hundred shillings for something unique here and for which we ourselves had paid fifty thousand. We sold the only scanner in Kakamega, the only binding machine and the only colour printer. The need seemed enormous. The customers told us, "You should sell the stuff for next to nothing, because you can always buy new things." We tried not to do that, but the consequence was that the daily income hardly covered the petrol costs for going to Kakamega.

In some cases, we also had to install the computers we sold. One of our clients, who had bought a computer from us, had difficulties in making the printer work. When we visited them, Bertil discovered the transformer to the printer had burnt. Checking the mains power, he became quite nervous on discovering how high it was. It should be 230 volts but it oscillated between 245 and 275 volts. The Electricity Company didn't care, unless you bribed them.

The corruption contributed to our feeling that we could no longer remain in Kenya. Since we were living out in the bush as private persons, without any organization behind us, people exploited us from left to right. Regardless of how much good we did, helping the village and the villagers, we always got stabbed in the back instead of being thanked. We didn't want to become hard and insensitive people, so we chose to move away before all our ideals had been destroyed.

The last theft we'd discovered was rather unusual, at least for us. The previous year, we'd bought several hundred hedge plants and planted them along the fence on one side of the compound. We'd also bought around fifty eucalyptus plants for the lower part, near the stream, from the same man.

One day, some children came with lots of hedge and eucalyptus plants, which they wanted to sell to us. According to Fred, the plants we'd dug down a year earlier hadn't done well, since the planting had been done during the dry season. Hence Bertil and I decided to have another go. We bought the plants from the kids and planted them. When Petrus arrived later that day, I told him this.

With a sigh he said, "What a pity I wasn't here. I would've stopped you from buying."

We, of course, wondered why. He explained that the children's father was the person who originally sold us the plants. Later on, he'd sent his children to dig up the plants and sell them to us once more. So, we'd actually bought the same plants twice. I gave up.

It was evening and we were sitting talking on the veranda. At our feet, two of our three darlings were lying, newly washed and smelling of chemicals from the special shampoo used against fleas. The third one, Musse, as usual, had climbed onto his master's lap.

We'd spent the whole day at home, since Kakamega had been without electricity during the weekend. Now the Sunday had almost come to its end. After a whole day with rain and thunder, the sun finally appeared for a few minutes immediately before sunset.

The weather hadn't bothered us, since we'd been quite busy sorting papers and emptying boxes. Less than ten boxes now remained in the container and almost all the heaps with documents and computer software, which had earlier been spread all over every table in the restaurant and in our apartment, had disappeared.

We'd also tidied up the apartment; painted it, nailed up pictures and put in flowers. We must have a home, especially now that times were hard. Quality time was so essential during our remaining time in Kenya, regardless of it being short or long. We had no time schedule yet. The day would probably come when we, if we hadn't sold Riverdale, would have to stop trying to sell it and instead pack a couple of suitcases and some boxes and just leave. We were okay, but all this was a great drain, both on our physical and mental reserves. Our joints, necks and backs ached and we felt rather worn out. We hadn't had a single day of real vacation in more than two years.

Yes, Riverdale Gardens had to be sold, but a nasty premonition told us it would be difficult and that it would take considerable time to find the right buyer. The estimated value of Riverdale Gardens was many millions of shillings, but to find someone who was able to pay in cash would probably be impossible. We'd, anyway, now made a beautiful hardbound pamphlet with newly scanned photos and the first copies had already been put in the mail to prospective buyers.

It was tough. We'd done everything in our power in order to remain here and we'd stood much more than most people would, but now we'd reached the limit.

It felt like an extra slap in the face when, on top of all other worries, we got a problem with the renewal of our entry permits. We'd received them a little more than two years earlier, in a quite correct and official way. When they now were to be renewed, the officials in Nairobi denied their existence and accused us of being in the country illegally. They threatened to expel us with only twenty-four hours notice.

That must not happen. Everything we owned was at Riverdale Gardens. We must immediately find a person, who could help with this mess. Our nice Belgian friend Olivier volunteered and the permits were now ready, having cost us astronomical sums. It was a nice feeling as we otherwise would have been illegally in Kenya from the following day.

We certainly didn't wish to relive the same misery, in two years time. When not even the official receipts from the Immigration Office were considered proof that you were legally in the country, alas you couldn't do much. Now, we had the necessary documents but, on the other hand, such documents had existed last time too.

We couldn't avoid discussing the hopeless corruption, as we sat on the veranda.

"Gunilla, do you realise we've only had water on seven different occasions during April? According to my calculations, we've had water for a total of twelve hours - often with very low pressure."

"Yes, it's absolutely insane," I answered. "The Water Committee was founded at the beginning of February and it hasn't had one single meeting yet."

"And that horrible man, our Chief, certainly doesn't understand that the village is the loser if we leave. Doesn't he understand we are supporting many of the villagers?"

"He's the most corrupt of them all. He only cares about himself and how he could benefit by others, without having to do anything for them. I'll never forget, when he told us 'As a chief, I first have to see to the needs of me and my family.'"

Bertil looked furious, when I repeated the words the chief had uttered at the beginning of our time in the village, when he insisted we employ his own relatives before hiring anyone else. We'd of course opposed that.

## 67. The nightmare

Summer in Sweden. How wonderful that sounded. I was longing so much to once again experience evenings full of light; full of the scent of bird cherry and lilac. In Kenya, darkness fell more or less at the same time (half past six) every day all year round and it got pitch black in a couple of minutes.

If the roads weren't impassable during the rainy season, I'd actually prefer that season to the dry one. The air was much fresher then, everything grew so fast and we usually also got sunshine every day for a couple of hours.

That was of course easy for me to say. I didn't, like our poorest villagers, have to live in a leaking banda. Even though it was cold in our house, because of the cracks in the floor, it was at least dry. We could cuddle up in blankets and sit in front of the fire with a warm cup of tea.

Brr. It was really cold that day, only nineteen degrees Celsius. I decided to put on a sweater and long trousers and to light a fire in the fireplace. Then, I'd play patience for a while before going to bed where I'd cover myself up with the quilt.

At night, I dreamed about Sweden. In the dream, I wasn't allowed to return to Sweden but was being kept in Kenya, year after year, by mushrooms entangling us in their mycelia threads. I hoped this dream wouldn't come true.

Funerals were so common in the village. Funeral processions and drums, disco music and crying. They attracted people from far and near and everything else came to a standstill. People disappeared from work for weeks on end to attend a funeral. Once they were back at work, some other relative or friend died and they disappeared again.

Funerals meant party time. People ate and drank, dug the grave and danced. I remembered when our previous house-girl, Milly, sang with joy, because she was going to a funeral. The fact that it was a small child that had died wasn't enough reason for her to mourn. "She was going to dance anyway."

I also recalled when a man on the other side of the fence, about fifteen metres from our bedroom, had died a couple of months earlier. Just before dying, he was lifted out of the banda to die in the open air. If he'd died inside the banda, one of his brothers would have been forced to burn it down. Since the man died outdoors, it was according to local customs, enough if the banda was left uninhabited for one year. After that, somebody else could move into it.

That funeral went on for fourteen days. They hired two music set-ups and lots of car batteries. We had disco music and loud noise twenty-four hours a day for two weeks and hardly got a wink of sleep during that time.

One night, we saw a burning banda on the other side of the valley. It was our friend, who delivered firewood to us, that had set fire to his brother's banda. The brother had died inside it and therefore the house must be destroyed.

Also at Riverdale, people were ill. Our shamba boy Willy was ill with malaria. According to what we'd heard, he had one hundred rings, which is a way of measuring malaria. When Bertil and I were ill with malaria, feeling really lousy, we only had about eight. Now Willy was on a very tough quinine treatment that had nasty side effects with hearing and balance problems.

When we returned home after a visit to Willy's house, where we'd brought food and healthy vitamin drinks for him, we handed out mosquito nets to all the staff members and gave them strict orders to use them. We also informed them we planned to take them to the Missionary Hospital to undergo a thorough health check.

The atmosphere in our closest neighbourhood had become unpleasant. Somebody was stirring up people against us. Rumours said it was the chief himself, but we didn't know if that was true. We certainly noticed a difference, compared to earlier, when out with the car. On two occasions, children hit me through the open side window. Once, children threw stones when we passed and a small boy tried to damage the car with his panga. It wasn't easy to avoid crying the whole time. Sleeping pills and tranquillizers were the only things that helped.

In this situation, we felt relieved when men from the Telephone Company came to repair the telephone line. This time, we'd been without a working phone for twelve days. The reason for the trouble was that the line has been struck by lightning. When that happened, we heard a big bang in the reception and saw a flash jump between the telephone plug and the transformer for solar power. The latter died immediately and had to be taken to Kisumu for an estimate of the repair cost. Since it had cost as much as 50,000 shillings to buy, we felt somewhat crestfallen.

The telephone workers' excuses for not coming earlier were, as usual, most imaginative. The common ones were: no fuel for the car, no driver, no car at all and, of course, away at a funeral.

## 68. Bernard dies

Bernard, our cook and houseboy, and also a nice person, at our suggestion had started to spend the evenings with us, in the main building. Since he was fond of drawing, we'd taken out all our drawing material for him to use and in the evenings he now sat drawing at one of the tables in the dining room. He appeared to like our company as much as we liked his. It must be far less lonely for him than sitting alone up in staff quarters. He'd told us about his girlfriend in Wulushi and about their little son and sometimes he disappeared to see them.

We were worried about Bernard's health. He'd started coughing a lot and admitted he was feeling very weak. When we wanted to take him for a health check at the hospital, however, he categorically refused, so we suggested he should at least have some time off, in order to rest.

Finally, we succeeded in getting his permission to take him to Nelson's clinic in Wulushi. According to Nelson's diagnosis, Bernard had serious malaria. He was immediately given quinine injections and orders to rest. Nelson told us Bernard would get a total of eight injections during the next two days and asked Bertil to drive him to the clinic on those occasions. Back at Riverdale Gardens, we put Bernard to bed at once. He was now so tired he hadn't the strength to protest. We asked Linda to look after him, making sure he ate properly.

After a couple days, Linda reported that Bernard no longer ate anything and that he was being sick. I went up to him and was startled at how quickly he'd deteriorated. He was sitting on the threshold to his room, vom-

vomiting bile. I sat down beside him, put an arm around him and helped him as much as I could.

Bernard declared he wanted to go home to his parents, now that he wouldn't have any more quinine injections and would switch to taking quinine tablets for three days. During that time, he wanted to rest at home. Bertil and I thought he was looking extremely ill and, as he still refused to go to the hospital, insisted on his coming with us to see Nelson one last time. We wanted Nelson to give an OK to Bernard's being with his parents. His home was far off, at the edge of the rainforest and lay in rough terrain, so if something acute should happen it would take a long time to get him under medical supervision.

Helping Bernard into the car, we noticed that the whites of his eyes were all yellow and that he had difficulty in breathing. Now very frightened, we asked Nelson to try to persuade Bernard to come with us to the hospital.

"No," Nelson said, "he doesn't want to. I've already tried to convince him. He asserts he'll kill himself, if we take him there against his will. I don't know why. "

"Can we really let him go home? We can certainly drive him to the end of the road, but then he'll have to walk quite a distance. Will he have enough strength? He seems terribly ill."

"He's extremely ill, but he'll probably manage. You should know that quinine treatment is unbelievably tough for your body, but he should soon be better. He'll only take the tablets for three more days. After that, he'll soon recover. Let him go home."

Since Bernard was of age, we couldn't do much else but drive him to the end of the road. There, we wished him a quick recovery, before he started walking in the direction of the forest.

An early morning a couple of days later, Petrus appeared on his bicycle. He'd just heard from one of the boda boda boys from the forest that Bernard had died the previous evening. I couldn't believe it. Only two days had passed, since we last saw him. And now he was gone. A nice, sweet boy with the ambition to one day become a cook as good as his father. He hadn't, of course, been in our service so long, but we'd come to like him quite a lot. Incomprehensible.

We immediately decided to go to Bernard's home, together with Petrus and Linda, to express our condolences and say farewell to him. When we had parked the car at the end of the road, Petrus told us we'd only have to walk a short distance.

The walk took more than an hour, up steep hills and through maize fields in boiling hot sun. I wasn't feeling well and I was certainly not getting any more alert from the strenuous walk. Relatives and family friends welcomed us, upon our arrival. Bernard's bed was standing outside, under a shelter of banana leaves. In it, Bernard was lying peacefully, clad in the chef's uniform Mathias had given him and surrounded by photos and flowers. We greeted everyone present and walked up to the bed to put a couple of newly taken photos of Bernard in chef's uniform, on his chest.

As per tradition, Linda started wailing, offering her condolences. Thereafter, we all sang a tranquil psalm, which was finished with a prayer in Luhya - the local language.

Then we sat down with Bernard's father under a tree. With Petrus' help, we explained everything that had happened and that we really had tried to get Bernard to hospital, but that he'd firmly refused. The father told us that Bernard, the previous evening, had come out of the banda and said, "Now it's time to go, goodbye" to his parents and then died.

Before our departure, we handed over money to cover the funeral costs to Bernard's father.

All our employees got time off during Midsummer to be present at the burial. Since I was not feeling well and couldn't walk long distances through rough terrain, Bertil and I stayed alone at home. Linda and Fred, as our representatives at the funeral, would hand over a beautiful wreath and a farewell letter we'd written, on our and our family's behalf.

The following afternoon, our employees returned, having spent twenty-four hours in the home of Bernard's parents digging a grave, saying prayers and burying the boy. When they came back - neatly dressed - all of us said a prayer together in Bernard's room. Then the door was opened. It would remain open for three days and nights in order to chase the spirits away. Next morning, all the staff members came there to cook a rooster that we ate together and, a few days later, Bernard's relatives came to say prayers in his room. At that time, they were also allowed, according to local customs, to take with them the furniture Bernard had used.

## 69. Relaxation

To get away from all the misery and sadness, we made a full-day excursion to Iten. After driving for many hours on lousy roads, we were rewarded for our pains. The view of all views. The whole of Rift Valley stretched out, approximately two thousand metres below our feet, straight in front of us. The imposing blue mountains of Elgeyo Escarpment were diffusely silhouetted against the sky - in contrast with the bottom of the Rift with its sand dunes. We felt so small, where we sat on the lookout site. The view, in front of and below us, seemed taken from another planet. It was unbelievably beautiful.

When we returned home, rather late in the afternoon, Linda said with a wide smile that she'd made us dinner. She showed us a sweet-smelling chicken stew, rice and a paprika salad. Oh, how kind of her; we hadn't asked her to prepare food for us. As a matter of fact, we'd never even considered her working for us in the kitchen, where we hadn't had any help since Bernard's death.

Before dinner, we wanted the drink we'd been dreaming about on our return home. Bertil wanted to make us a Vodka Martini. We had some Kenya Cane remaining in a bottle. Two caps Kenya Cane and one cap Martini Dry and some olives. We raised our glasses and toasted. What was this? The drinks had a strange taste of perfume, maybe Bertil had poured too much Martini in them? That was easy to rectify with some extra Kenya Cane - the strange taste became even more pronounced.

I had a flash of memory.

"Bertil, didn't you recently mix liqueur in a Kenya Cane bottle?" I wondered suddenly.

Bertil tried to save the situation by adding the little gin we had left. The result was still stranger. It tasted almost like Cointreau - with olives - but dinner was wonderful.

"Bertil, I'm not feeling well. My heart is galloping all the time and I feel so weak."

Bertil looked worried and I, too, was scared. Having talked it through for a while, we decided to go to Kisumu to the Aga Khan Hospital. We'd been given the name of a good Indian doctor, who I found both clever and sympathetic.

I was submitted to a lot of tests but the test results we got the same day didn't show anything positive. As a precaution, however, the doctor told me to increase the dosage of the heart medicines I was taking and also gave me medicine to calm down the heartbeat frequency.

When I asked him what the cause could be, he answered that stress factors, in connection with the traumatic experiences of late, could be to blame. He told me about another Nordic patient, who recently had had to leave Kenya, because she was feeling ill after experiences like ours. The best medicine for my health would be to leave Kenya, he said with a serious face.

It wasn't a cheap hospital visit but the hospital was modern, the doctor competent and there was no queuing. The doctor even gave me his home telephone number in case I got worse and needed to get in contact with him.

It was time to end one of our donations to Wuasiva village. After working for almost three weeks, at a cost of approximately 40,000 shillings, we'd renovated the whole road from Wushiye to us in Wuasiva. All the work had been done following the method Father used during his visit. It had proven a good method, since the repairs he made had remained intact during the whole rainy season.

Everybody was happy. A lot of people along the road, who had sold us stones and concrete, were now probably rather well-off. I was sure they believed the stupid mzungu didn't understand that the villagers had stolen the stones, dug out at the roadside by us, and sold them back to us, either as stones or concrete. We quite understood what had happened, but we were so sick of fighting back. The whole repair work was finished with a big barbecue party for our employees and all the extra workers, hired for the roadwork.

Our neighbours waved at us when we were out inspecting the work. We could only hope they'd order their children to stop throwing stones at us, when they saw us driving down the road. Our chief was the only one, pretending not to notice anything.

The road repair would hopefully mean that possible prospective buyers wouldn't hesitate to buy our home because of the bad road. Once we'd left, maybe people would even remember us as those Europeans that repaired the road?

Talking about donations. We wondered how Nelson could suddenly have a clinic of his own. We hoped the money came from the extra work he'd been doing at some distance beyond Wulushi, and not from our clinic construction, which lay abandoned. When the Chief had persuaded the villagers to withdraw their contributions in kind, the clinic construction work had stopped. We'd decided that we, under no circumstances, would ask kind Swedes for more help as long as the villagers themselves didn't contribute.

My new medicine seemed to help. The heartbeats had been reduced but as the doctor had ordered me to rest in peaceful surroundings, we bought a lot of second-hand pocket books to read and also rented video films. We were, however, only able to watch a maximum of two per week, as it was cloudy outside and the batteries didn't charge sufficiently. We played with the dogs, made small excursions and tried to avoid getting irritated.

Bertil took care of me; he preserved cucumber, made tasty shrimp sandwiches, poured me wine and spoilt me a lot and I soon felt better.

To make our existence easier, we'd hired an advocate who would take care of the contacts with prospective buyers of Riverdale Gardens. During July, we showed our property to two different aspirants. Both wanted to start orphanages and both had foreign connections. Both of them seemed interested but "would only try to convince their colleagues," so we weren't too optimistic. You couldn't disregard the fact that we lived far out in the bush and that we had neither electricity nor a functioning water connection.

## 70. Dutch treat

"Welcome, welcome!"

Happily, I hugged my Spanish friend Elena and her husband Sebastian, while Bertil started carrying luggage and casseroles into the kitchen. Oh, what a joy! They, who lived in Kakamega, had dared come out to us in the bush. Elena and Sebastian were going to stay overnight and we'd agreed to share the provision of food. Like us, they didn't dare be out on the roads in the dark.

We unpacked the delicacies in the kitchen, clucking like hens. Then we joined our husbands, who were already sitting talking over a glass of beer on the veranda. The weather was beautiful, the dogs were nice and well behaved and all four of us were happy, being together in peace and tranquillity. Normally, we only made quick visits to our friends' wonderful garden.

Our employees had left for the day, so we didn't have to fear being overheard when talking in English.

After a while, we took a walk to look at the garden. Elena was very knowledgeable about plants, so we were sure to get good advice, both on vegetables and trees and flowering bushes.

A lot had happened on the compound since their first visit. Elena was obviously impressed. I asked for advice regarding the palm trees, as I couldn't get them to grow and they seemed half withered and limp. According to her, the reason was that our soil was the wrong kind. My dream about beautiful swaying palm trees quickly went up in smoke.

Then Elena said, "But what kind of tree is that? Isn't it jackfruit? You have to move that one soon. Hopefully, it will survive being moved - but it must be moved."

I looked questioningly at her. I thought we'd found a nice place for the tree - outside the entrance to the restaurant. The tree would be enormous - if we succeeded with it - and would be decorative. Suddenly it struck me and I started laughing. Of course it had to be moved. We were digging our own grave. If the tree grew too big, we'd never be able to use that entrance, without risking our lives.

"I see, what you mean," I giggled. "We've seen the tree outside the Kenya Seed Company. That one is a giant and carries millions of fruit. Every fruit weighs at least fifteen kilos. Bertil and I've talked about what would happen to the car, if a jackfruit fell on top of it, but that could be our heads if this tree bears fruit. Thanks for reminding us."

After a nice walk, during which we promised to exchange plants we each lacked, we went into the kitchen to prepare dinner. The meal was a combination of Spanish and Swedish food: Gazpacho as a starter, roasted whole fillet of beef with a sauce of funnel chanterelles as main course and pineapple cake as dessert. On top of that, good wines, of course.

It was wonderful to sit talking with friends at night. As things were, we could never stay overnight anywhere else. If we did, our home would be emptied of its contents upon our return.

We informed our friends about all our misery and that we actually wanted to give up, sell and leave. Elena thought the atmosphere amongst the population had become increasingly tough during the years she'd lived in Kenya. Corruption, as well as violence, was increasing. In spite of Sebastian being a Kenyan, he agreed. Besides, he also told us Wulushi was regarded as the place with the most violence, crime and corruption in the whole of Kenya. Really nice to hear. I wished somebody had told us that before we bought our land.

But we didn't talk only about negative issues. The hours passed and we had fun. Somewhat tipsy, we went to bed at two o'clock.

One of the askaris was having his night off and the other guard was home, because of a sick child. Subsequently, Bertil had to act as askari when the rest of us had gone to bed. Together with Merry and armed with a panga, he walked around the compound with his torch all night in the moonshine.

What a wonderful, relaxing and nice day we'd had in the company of our dear friends.

## 71. A new hobby

For a long time, it had been difficult to find mushrooms for cooking. We couldn't find any, either fresh, tinned or dried, not even in Kisumu. The mushroom factory in Eldoret had stopped their production, several months earlier. Before they closed down, we'd gone there to buy their last tins of mushrooms. Now those were finished, so we intended to combine business with pleasure and start mushroom growing. In the long run, it was boring to just sit waiting for the sale of Riverdale Gardens. It was better to do something meaningful, in the meantime.

After some real detective work, we managed to find a working telephone number to an oyster mushroom producer in Limuru. By telephone, we got permission to buy one kilo of mushroom mycelia, so we asked Petrus to quickly get on the bus and go and fetch it.

We had really no idea how you made mushrooms grow, but the trial-and-error method might work. Subsequently, we tested mixing mycelia with different substrates. We tried with composted grass, sawdust and other things. Nothing worked.

Bertil recalled that he could find information on the Internet and he actually found a discussion group for mushroom producers. The members were experienced growers, discussing subtleties, but when Bertil started asking about basics, these experts took pity on us and he got some good answers on how to proceed.

The substrate had to be pasteurised, before being mixed with the mycelia, and we needed much less mycelia than we'd used. Slowly, slowly, we advanced with our tests and, suddenly one day, we saw an oyster mushroom. Very small but nevertheless. Willy discovered it on the ground near our feet, when we were having breakfast with our staff in the breakfast area. We'd probably dropped some mycelia in that place.

Now we tried more in earnest. Who knows? We might succeed. It was important to find substrate ingredients, rich in fibre. We tried chopped banana fibres and chopped maize cobs; then we remembered that we were living in the sugar cane district. Waste from the sugar factories might do it, as it ought to be nutritious. Driving towards Mumias, the biggest factory, we soon found dumped sugar cane waste along the road which we loaded into the car. Now we could test mixtures of this and banana fibre.

We pasteurized substrate, mixed in mycelia and filled plastic bags with the mixture. Then the bags had to rest in the banda until the mycelia had spread through the whole substrate. That took up to a couple of weeks. While resting, the bags lay in darkness with the right temperature and humidity. We made a simple control for temperature and humidity, in our old banda. By covering the floor with bricks that the shamba boys watered a couple of times per day, we reduced the temperature by almost six degrees Celsius. At the same time, humidity increased. It would be thrilling to see how they turned out.

Bertil was enthusiastic and I tried to feel convinced this could be a success. But why should all the problems we'd had in all other projects not show up again here? I hadn't told Bertil about the mushroom nightmare I'd had. Maybe the curse the old man had put on us would involve the mushrooms too?

It was so typical. It felt like mockery. Now that we'd closed the hotel, the telephone exploded with demands for reservations. The coming weekend we could have been overbooked by more than twenty-five persons: insect researchers from Hawaii, a hospital group and several travel agency groups. The hotel in the rainforest was fully booked; those in town couldn't be recommended. Ours should really have been open. But without water, we couldn't do anything.

In addition, we now had more prospective buyers for our home. Besides the two orphanages, a travel agency and some rich Kenyans, with a background in the hotel sector, had contacted us. Everyone said how keen they were to buy, but then the money problem always came up. I didn't believe we'd ever be able to sell Riverdale Gardens.

We wanted to make sure that if we'd have to leave in haste, we wouldn't leave any personal belongings behind. Hence we cleared away everything we couldn't take with us. We could take a maximum of a couple of hundred kilos on the flight. All the Swedish software disappeared in flames, since nobody here understood Swedish. We also burnt thousands of photos, some of which had already been destroyed either by humidity or by termites. Unfortunately, a lot of the negatives had also been ruined.

## 72. Nature's pharmacy

"Pst, Gunilla."

I reluctantly woke up under the gorgeous down quilt and carefully put my nose out under the edge of the mosquito net. I wondered what Bertil wanted at this unchristian hour.

"Pst, are you awake? Come carefully. Don't wake the dogs. Put on your track suit. It's cold outside," Bertil uttered in a whisper. "And hurry up."

At the same time, we could hear a padding noise made by Rufus, Merry and Musse. They understood something was going on and wanted to join in.

"Nooo," I heard Bertil saying. "Back to your baskets all three of you - you can have a lie-in today."

On unsteady feet and muttering to myself, I staggered out and started dressing. After a small fight at the door, I managed to lock our three four-legged darlings in the bedroom and padded across to the veranda. Oh, it was so cold. It couldn't be more than ten degrees Celsius.

Bertil had set the breakfast table on the veranda and I was welcomed with hot coffee and some night cold papaya. It was dark outside and I wondered what on earth Bertil wanted.

It was rather silent and very cold. Suddenly something happened. The tree line on the other side of the valley was changing colour, turning into pink-orange.

Bertil smiled at me and whispered, "Now maybe you understand, why I get up so early in the mornings."

It was really fantastic. From one minute to the next, the sun rose, colouring our beautiful valley in the most unbelievable tints of red and yellow and, as if that wasn't enough, suddenly we heard the most delightful music. All our birds, of the most variable kinds, were joining in - almost as if each one of them had a given passage in the most wonderful of all concerts.

I forgot my fatigue and all our sorrows. It was as if I was given a sign to roll up my sleeves and try to see everything from the positive side again

After a while, during which we silently "drank in" the beautiful morning together with the morning coffee, Bertil went into the kitchen to make us breakfast. I remained seated and soon I started recognizing the different species of jubilant birds.

Even the Speckled Mouse Birds in the bougainvillea were beautiful in my new mood. This morning, a Hunters Sunbird visited our Bronze Sunbird in the papaya. On the veranda rail to my left, I suddenly saw a couple of small Red-cheeked Cordon Bleu, a species we'd discovered only some days earlier. They were enchanting and they could, according to hearsay, become tame so we were happy to have them. "The Telephone Bird" sounded like a ringing telephone and had made us run, many times in vain, to the telephone. It was usually hopping around in the eucalyptus. Our Black Bishops were, as usual, jumping about in our neighbour's maize field.

A sudden noise made all the beautiful chirping disappear.

"Shit," Bertil exclaimed, "the loudmouths are visiting us today too."

He had no more than finished the sentence before the birds, loudly croaking, invaded the compound. They were Black and White Casqued Hornbills, making an excursion from the rainforest, located at a small distance beyond our valley. Quarrelling and fighting, they landed everywhere among the trees. Their noise was actually only beaten by the Ibis, sometimes passing above our land, with a high screeching sound. When talking, I had difficulty in making my voice heard in all the noise from the Hornbills, or "bikers", as we called them, since they looked as if they were wearing a biker's peaked cap.

"Bertil," I asked, "do you remember the morning when the Ficus tree on the lawn was quite violet instead of green?"

"Yes, Violet-backed Starlings were eating the berries. I've never seen so many birds at the same time in the same place. You're right, the tree was all violet." He added, "Do you recall the name of the Ficus? Isn't it regarded as a holy tree here?"

"Yes, its name is Ficus Thonningii. A man was buried at its foot, a long time ago. And I know we are not allowed to cut that tree down, even if we wanted to. According to local traditions, a special person must do that. I wonder if it wasn't a brother of the deceased or somebody like that."

Yes, bird life was really fantastic. In Sweden, I hadn't been able to distinguish a magpie from a crow and now I was sitting all day long with binoculars and the bird book within reach.

"This pawpaw is really exquisite. It looks different from the normal one. It seems more elliptic and - look - the fruit meat has another colour," I said, pondering the matter.

"Yes," Bertil answered, "we've several different kinds of pawpaw, actually. I got some seeds from Elena, last year. I put them in the soil down in the kitchen garden. They must have been of a different kind than our usual pawpaws."

"Did you know," I asked, "that pawpaw isn't only good for the stomach. It has lots of other medicinal values. Wait, I'll fetch what I've written down about it."

I fetched my notes from my office table and then I read aloud, "Almost all parts of the plant are used in medicinal connections. The plant contains an enzyme, which kills worms and amoebas. If you're troubled with this, you should chew leaves and seeds daily. The fruits are rich in vitamin A, B and C. Vitamin A is good for eyesight, B for the nerves and C for the immune system. The roots are boiled in water, as treatment for diarrhoea and the leaves are smoked for asthma. The papaya tree is also used in dysentery, bronchitis and hepatitis. And we already know, both of us, that the leaves and the fruit meat are used for tenderising meat," I concluded my lecture.

"Your inventory of our plants is very exciting," added Bertil. "Let me take a bigger part in it, instead of only making number plates."

In the evenings, Bertil often projected numbers on greaseproof paper, tacked to the wall. With a pencil, he transferred the numbers onto special pieces of board that had first been painted white. Then it was my turn to paint the numbers black. The boards were fastened to sticks and placed at an example of each kind of plant on our property. I used the same numbers later in my inventory of the plants and their medical properties.

Linda had now arrived. As usual, she got a lot of kisses from our dogs before they threw themselves at their bowls. They also got breakfast and enjoyed their daily few drops of milk, with bread dipped in.

"Petrus and I will be discussing the vegetable cultivation today. Yesterday, he sent a message saying Benjamin from the forest is coming this afternoon. A boda boda brought him the message."

"Super," Bertil said. "Then you might get more information about the plants we planted last week. I gave them the numbers 52 to 58. Among them are a plant for snakebites and a new one for malaria. It wouldn't be so funny, if we got a cobra bite and used a malaria plant as medicine."

"Yes, talking about malaria, Petrus must check that the Philippine plant is doing well. It's important, since it was actually that one that cured me from my three month long malaria attack earlier this year. Think of all the different expensive medicines we bought, and then it was enough to drink a tea made of some leaves from it. Herbal medicine is so exciting," I said. "And we are really lucky it survived Merry's treatment."

"Yes, that was, what I'd call, a protest," laughed Bertil. "She didn't only knock over that heavy clay urn in the corner but gave the plant special treatment. She must have shaken it a lot, considering all the leaves on the floor. I didn't know she disliked us going to town that much."

The awful sight had greeted us returning from town. The plant had proven its worth at tackling my malaria, when all else failed: it was vital it now survived Merry's attack.

Bertil was off to the car workshop, also taking an order for meat. I talked for a while with Linda and the boys. Fred and Willy had been cutting grass, while waiting for orders from me. Everybody was well and in high spirits. I asked the boys to chop banana fibre and to put the sugarcane bagasse (the waste left when the sugar has been pressed out of the sugarcanes) in the sun to dry. We had to have plenty of crude material, always ready for the mushroom cultivation.

When they were having their morning tea, I told them we'd decided to have a joint work lunch, on the following day. Then we'd go through our plans for the nearest future. They were curious but I didn't want to say more than that the lunch menu would be nyama choma with kachumbari (grilled meat with a salad of fresh hacked tomatoes with onion and chilli). When I told them, it would fall to the boys to make the chapati, they shouted out of joy.

I took a walk around the compound inspecting the damage after the hailstorm we had a few evenings ago. Drifts of hail still remained the following morning, so we'd taken photos of Willy, standing with hail up to his ankles, while taking care of the hibiscus plants. During the storm, 160 windows were broken at Father Bede's seminar, just outside Kakamega. He was quite desolated by the havoc.

Now I noticed that also the hibiscus and bougainvillea - like the pawpaw trees - had been badly hurt by the hail and that their leaves were quite perforated.

It was good we'd started the mushroom growing. It was engaging all of us and also helped Bertil and me to keep our minds away from the hopeless sale issue. The Australians had no money. The Germans wanted to buy, but their sponsors thought it was enough with the orphanage they already had in Kenya. It seemed, we might have some other prospective buyers but we dared not hope any longer for a large amount. We intended to contact the lawyer again and tell him to sell, even if it was for a much lower amount.

No. I decided I had better think of the mushrooms, so I made an inspection walk down to the banda.

It was fantastic to see. Wonderful clusters of almost microscopic mushrooms had suddenly started popping up. Although we didn't intend to invest much money in the mushroom cultivation, it was still exciting.

On my way back, I passed the banana plants, where we usually threw discarded mushroom bags. I suddenly saw some oyster mushrooms, almost ready to harvest. OK, so the following day, we'd have sparkling wine together with our first home produced oyster mushrooms.

## 73. Lesson in the mushroom school

"Now, my friends, I'll give you some news," said Bertil, sitting at the table on the veranda.

Linda, Fred and Willy looked at him, full of expectation. Bertil looked happy, so they didn't need to worry. Furthermore, everyone's spirits were high after the nice lunch with a lot of nyama choma (grilled meat) and soft drinks we'd had together.

"Starting next week, we'll all dedicate ourselves to mushroom cultivation as much as we can. If your normal chores are suffering, we'll, once in a while, hire extra workers. We still have a lot of mycelia in the refrigerator but it‘s important we economize until we can make our own."

"What? Make our own mycelia?" Fred wondered. "Is that possible?"

"Of course you can," answered Bertil. "We've ordered books from the USA which show how to do it. Unfortunately, we won't get them for a few months. Marina, who is studying the monkeys in the rainforest, will bring them here in February."

"Don't forget the lessons," I whispered to Bertil.

"Oh yes, I almost forgot an important thing. Starting Monday, the three of you will start school again."

Bertil laughed at the questioning faces of our employees.

"And I'll be your teacher. I'm going to teach you about mushroom cultivation, two hours every forenoon. We'll be here on the veranda and you'll get pads and pencils from us. The two of you, Fred and Willy, will have to make a blackboard by Monday. I'll buy chalks in town."

Linda and the boys looked content. They'd get education on paid work time and they'd learn more about the mushroom growing they liked so much.

We talked for a while about technical issues regarding the mushroom growing and decided we'd build a cultivation room on the lower side of the banda. We'd, as a matter of fact, discovered that when we moved substrate bags out of the banda they quickly germinated mushroom clusters. As long as they remained inside, there were no mushrooms. Light was obviously important, once the mycelia had run through the bags. We could provide enough shade by making a roof of banana leaves on a net. Bertil did a drawing and explained what it would look like. To begin with and as a test, we'd let the cultivation bags hang. Then the mushrooms could come out all around them. Bertil would also build a sprinkler system with a manual pump for the watering of the cultivation room.

Our employees gave us many suggestions for solutions. Everybody seemed engaged in the issues, even Linda who normally was rather taciturn.

It was time to give the signal to rise from table and return to other tasks.

"There is something else," I said getting up. "We've forgotten to tell you, we are sending you on a study visit now. Bertil will drive you in a couple of minutes to the rainforest, where you'll get a guided tour for a couple of hours. Then three boda bodas will take you home. We think it's a pity that, living so close to the rainforest, you've never really been in it. We'll of course give you money for the return trip. So now you're free for the rest of the day. Have a nice afternoon."

They were almost dancing out of sheer joy, walking with Bertil up to the car. Imagine; they'd be able to see the forest they'd heard so many exciting things about, on working hours. That was where so many medicines came from. And everyone had heard the old stories about the different cures that used to be – and still were - collected in the rainforest.

In spite of the success with the mushroom growing and the positive spirits at Riverdale Gardens, not one single day passed without us hissing like angry snakes, when talking about corruption. It was really not making life any easier. It was one thing reading about corruption, quite another living with it. People said Kenyan corruption was ranked number three in the world and, at the same time, they joked Kenya had paid bribes to get that high ranking.

Our domestic telephone calls normally cost 300-600 shillings per month. On our last telephone bill, they came to 8,200 shillings. According to what we'd heard, it was common in Kenya that telephone company employees used client telephone numbers to make private calls. Their own telephones were blocked, only allowing local calls. Alas, you had seldom any hope of proving this, but we knew several persons to which it had happened. It was really atrocious, and if you didn't pay the telephone was disconnected. Now this had happened to us too.

Also we often had problems with the Internet. Post and Communications, earlier Head of Tele-communications, had been divided into several sections. The new company, TelCom Kenya, was incapable of handling the satellite station in Longonot, where amongst other things they'd forgotten to adjust the parabola to the small movements of the satellite. The violent storms, which caused trees to fall on top of the telephone wires, were another reason for the bad connections.

"Bertil, look," I exclaimed happily.

We were sitting outside Kakamega Post Office, where Bertil had fetched a parcel for which he'd received an official customs receipt. The parcel came from Gertrud, a nice Swedish dental hygienist who had visited us a couple of months earlier. Anchovy tins, tea, several tubes of Swedish caviar, three sausages, a packet of bread, a crossword puzzle magazine. What joy!

It was always fun to fetch parcels at the Post Office. Father often sent us pocket books. He weighed those, adding tea bags so that the weight was just below the postage limit. Sometimes he put in pieces of crisp bread. They were of course broken, but the dogs loved a piece, once in a while. Unfortunately, some parcels got lost. Envelopes containing seed bags were, as it seemed, predestined to disappear, since such parcels had never arrived. They were probably mistaken for envelopes containing money or drugs.

The Customs checked all parcels from Sweden carefully. When, at the beginning of our stay in Kenya, we received a big Swedish flag, it took the customs officer half an hour to check through all his books, before he finally arrived at the conclusion that we didn't have to pay any customs duty on flags.

Once again children were dying - one night three small ones on the other side of the valley. During a terrific storm, the children took shelter under a big tree. A flash of lightning struck it and all the children died.

At Riverdale Gardens, the same storm blew down two trees and three banana plants. Along the village road, five big trees and one of our telephone poles - including the telephone line - fell.

## 74. Where snakes are breathing

One day, a couple with a small son contacted us, wanting to make a reservation for November 9th. We answered that Riverdale unfortunately was no longer open; that we didn't know if we'd re-open it and that we might sell. We suggested that they instead should make a reservation at the Rainforest Retreat and informed them we could help them get in touch with that hotel. We also asked how they'd come to know about Riverdale Gardens and us.

The answer came quickly. They'd read about us in the Rough Guide - the well-known international guidebook - and fallen in love with Riverdale Gardens. They asked if we were serious about selling. The wife was born and raised in Kenya and they'd recently decided to move here.

The correspondence by email continued. The couple told us, they were looking for something exactly like our place. Money seemed no problem. They could take over our dogs, our employees and the vegetable and mushroom cultivations. They'd continue working in our spirit, as they liked everything connected with ecological life. They even thought the name of our property seemed perfect, since they were also big Tolkien fans.

We invited them to come and stay as our private guests for a couple of days in November. That way, they'd be able to see if they liked Riverdale Gardens as much in real life as in fantasy. It would be so exciting to see if we'd at last found our buyers.

While waiting for the new prospective buyers' arrival, we dedicated a big part of our time to the mushrooms.

Time passed faster that way. A small mushroom cultivation had been placed outside Petrus' flower shop in Wulushi. We'd put it there for people to see, with their own eyes, how the mushrooms grew. People gathered in groups, just staring at the beautiful mushrooms, growing so rapidly you could almost hear them. As rumour spread, more and more people came to look at the miracle. A lot of them were muttering about witchcraft, but at the same time everyone looked fascinated.

According to rumour, our chief had also been impressed. He was boasting it was his Europeans that were behind the miracle and had even told people he'd attend a course at our compound, learning to plant mushrooms.

People around here didn't believe you could grow mushrooms. They were convinced mushrooms only grow, "where snakes are breathing". By this, they meant that mushrooms only grew in places where there were a lot of snakes, places you stayed away from. Consequently, mushrooms were surrounded with mysticism; it was something they knew nothing about. To tell people you knew how to cultivate mushrooms was as likely as if somebody in Sweden claimed he could cultivate bricks.

The atmosphere at Riverdale Gardens was now good. Everyone was loyal and happy that we'd taught them how to grow mushrooms. Linda had harvested her first mushrooms and the rest of the staff would do so soon. In the past few days, we'd ourselves harvested 650 grams but we still had around 400 grams coming up. Each harvest was getting better, both regarding quality and quantity.

Our ingenious hand-operated sprinkler system for watering the mushrooms in our outdoor mushroom house was ready. As the mushrooms needed water also at night, the night askaris took care of that. It was really fun to grow oyster mushrooms, since they only needed about three weeks from planting to first harvest.

With enough water and light, the mushrooms "grew like mushrooms". Everything we produced was sold. One day, a chef came on his bike from the hotel in the rainforest and bought that day's whole production. Before disappearing, he told us they wanted to buy all our fresh mushrooms. It was a nice feeling being able to say that within a couple of days we'd have another kilo ready.

When the chef was leaving towards the forest, we'd persuaded him to buy eggplants, cucumber, squash and paprika; vegetables you couldn't normally find in Kakamega. He looked happy and was probably dreaming about a lot of delicious dishes to cook. "Keep up the good work," were his final words, before he rode out through the gate.

Awaiting the arrival of the English prospective buyers, we worked intensively on making Riverdale Gardens perfect. We wanted them to be impressed. Fred, Willy and Linda shouted for joy, when they got their new navy-blue uniforms and spent some minutes just strutting about in them. They probably felt their status had risen considerably.

It was still a secret that we intended to sell and leave. We'd only told the staff that our Englishmen were friends of some of our best friends and that we'd promised to take care of them, in the best possible way.

## 75. Hurrah!

The Englishmen arrived and seemed to be having a wonderful time with us, all three of them. Bertil and I were working hard preparing food, showing them around and entertaining them; all with support from our staff.

Before returning to England, our guests declared they were interested in buying. They, however, needed to think things through before making a definite decision. It was a big step for the family to move from England, even though the wife was born and raised in Kenya. Hence, they asked for a couple of weeks to consider. In the meantime, we'd have to bite our nails and dedicate ourselves to mushroom cultivation.

It was fortunate our employees were so interested and clever mushroom growers. For about a week, we hadn't had much time to dedicate to the mushrooms. The hotel was officially closed but we started making some exceptions to the decision not to receive guests.

First, three Swedish women having heard about us at Rotary meetings in Sweden. They were very nice and stayed for a few days. Linda was fantastic in the kitchen, making delicious and appreciated food, with only minor assistance from me.

Just when the Swedish women had departed, Father Samuel asked us to help him with overnight stays for four of his European friends. We must of course accept this, as he was such a wonderful man and had backed us up during tough times. On such occasions, we went down to the Church to talk to him and, at times, he visited us for a cup of tea or a glass of wine. The visitors were really nice and all of us enjoyed our time together. We'd never have guessed that our quiet friend, Father Samuel, could be so cheerful and merry, when off-duty and able to relax.

"Quite unbelievable!" Bertil burst out, as he joined me on the veranda after giving Father Samuel and his friends a lift to Kakamega. "Can you imagine, they're repairing the road outside the Catholic Church? Father Samuel told me the whole section between Wageya and Wulushi will be done now. What an improvement."

"Will they also change the camber outside the church?" I wondered curiously.

During the rainy season, I preferred not to go by car on that slope. It became incredibly slippery and since it was sloped steeply to one side, cars often slid right off. In spite of our four-wheel drive, we too had been close to ending up in the ditch.

"No, I don't think so, but we can always hope. They have nevertheless fetched big stones to put in the largest holes. That's always a step forward. They might have learnt from your father's methods."

Yes, it would be wonderful to write to Father, telling him the villagers for once had learnt something from him. To tell the truth, we'd often wondered whether all the information the locals got only went in one ear and out the other.

I was standing on tiptoe, holding the pruning shears, ready to start. I was in the middle of picking beautiful dahlias for a vase on the mantelpiece. The dahlias obviously loved our soil and got to almost two metres high. The flower heads were of an enormous size, appearing in all possible colour combinations.

Suddenly, I saw Fred coming hurrying over from staff quarters where he'd been busy preparing lunch.

"Gunilla, you and Bwana Bertil must come and have a look. We've found a strange animal."

I called Bertil, asked him to come and to bring the book "Larger Mammals of Africa".

Fred showed us the way to the animal, closely followed by Willy and Linda. It was in the staff lavatory where it was pressing itself hard up against a corner, looking terrified. It was actually quite cute.

All five of us crowded in the door opening, while Bertil flicked through the book, looking for a picture of the animal in front of us. All the while, it was waiting calmly in its corner.

"It's a Giant Rat," Bertil suddenly exclaimed. "Wait, while I read what they write about it." After a moment, he continued, "Aha, it‘s a thief. It says here, it likes to steal glimmering objects like coins that it hides in its nest. And it's apparently easy to tame and keep as a pet."

The rat was really big, almost half a metre long, excluding the tail which was long and naked like on a normal rat. The inner half of the tail was black and the outer half white, while the body was white underneath and brown on top.

Willy wanted to kill the rat but we didn't allow that. We asked them to leave it in peace so that it dared return to its nest, somewhere on the compound. The fact it could steal glittering objects wasn't enough reason to kill it.

I only had one thing going on in my head. Would they buy? Would they say yes? Would we soon be able to leave?

In order to make time pass faster, we made an excursion one day to Sabatia Eye Hospital, where a Finnish doctor and his wife were working. It was nice to make new acquaintances. We were impressed when they told us about their flights to Sudan. From time to time, they went there with a small aircraft from Kakamega Airstrip. In Sudan, they operated on blind people and in ninety percent of the cases the patients regained their vision. The operations were done in primitive camps out in the bush, using their own generator and medical equipment. All operations were furthermore free of charge. Talk about charity.

It was November 30th and we could expect an answer from England anytime. We were at sixes and sevens, thinking of the bottle of champagne lying in the refrigerator. We'd either celebrate drinking it or else drown our sorrows in it.

"Hurrah!"

Bertil had just checked the email. We ran into the kitchen to fetch the bottle of champagne and two glasses. The Englishmen had written we should open the bottle they'd brought us.

What a feeling! We wouldn't be back in Sweden for several months yet but everything now felt so much easier. We had a buyer. We could leave.

## 76. Turn of the millennium

The turn of the millennium. Here I was, all alone in the African pitch-black night, in the middle of nowhere. Who would have thought I'd celebrate the new millennium this way?

Except for my dogs and a night askari, I was completely alone at Riverdale Gardens. A couple of kerosene lamps and some candles lit up the living room. The dogs were lying around me, tucked in their evening blankets; only their noses could be seen: one dark brown and two black. Although the dogs were the worst watchdogs in the world, it still gave me a sense of security having them close.

I was too tired to prepare food. My consumption would probably be a couple of whiskies and maybe some wine. I also had plenty of fruit from our own garden: bananas, papaya, guava and some passion fruit.

A while earlier, I'd managed to start the TV. That astonished me, since I was probably the least technically-minded person in the world. I saw the turn of the millennium being celebrated on Guam and in Australia with big fireworks, but after only a few minutes the battery was dead. The only thing to do then was to take out a deck of cards and play patience, for a while. I couldn't read, as the push button lamp wasn't working. The kerosene light was too weak for my eyes. I was full of self-pity and actually rather low-spirited, but then suddenly I felt ashamed. For poor Bertil, things were much worse. On Christmas Day, he had to quickly fly back to Sweden. My father-in-law was dying. Bertil was informed a couple of days before Christmas but couldn't find any flight connections until Christmas Day. I hoped he'd arrived in time. I hadn't yet had any news as to how my father-in-law was doing.

Yes, again a Christmas had passed, like almost all our Christmases in Kenya without any specific celebrations or food. The only Christmas we'd had time to celebrate was the first one.

Having made some notes about the happenings of the day, I closed my diary. I walked out onto the veranda, hung up a couple of kerosene lamps and cuddled up in a chair. In the pitch-dark night, the whole valley was boiling with life.

Angry voices discussed in Luhya language from the banana grove a couple of hundred metres away on the other side of the fence. An illegal liquor den was hidden in it, like in so many other groves. Hopefully, the men wouldn't murder each other; they seemed so drunk. But it was quite possible that might happen. In our small valley, lots of drunkards had killed each other during the past year.

The worst of all was that they became so cruel towards children, when drunk. I wondered how many times Bertil had been forced to interfere in order to save children. I remembered one night, when our neighbour tried to strangle his small son, because the son wasn't strong enough to carry his drunken father back to the banda. On Bertil´s order, our night askaris intervened. The drunkard finally let go of his son who managed to escape. Next morning, we heard that thereafter a fight had broken out, during which the neighbours almost killed the drunken father.

There was no limit to violence, I reflected, putting a piece of pawpaw in my mouth. One of our first night askaris, Luke, who was also one of the village elders, was one night attacked by his own brother. When Luke was mediating in a quarrel between his brother and sister-in-law, his brother had hit him in the neck with a "rungo" (a wooden club). And now Luke was mentally disturbed for the rest of his life. I also thought of the boy who was murdered by his best friend going home from Midnight Mass. He was chopped to pieces and found in a ditch, on Christmas Day in 1998. That was why Father Samuel had stopped Midnight Mass; he no longer regarded it safe outdoors at night.

I was close to crying, so I decided to do something else. In the refrigerator, I found some chicken and boiled potatoes. I fried them and then went outside and called Joe, the night askari on duty. I heard nothing, until he was standing in front of me. Dear Joe, he was as stealthy as a cat. He was really delighted when he got a plate full of steaming hot food. Joe had earlier in the evening got his usual thermos of tea with lots of milk and sugar, so he was not expecting anything more. Chatting with him, I asked how his family was doing, if all the ten children were okay and if he was feeling well.

Joe was around seventy years old and had fought in Egypt during the war. He was so proud of the warm Swedish military coat, model 39; we'd given him and the other night askari. The old man had still got some go, in spite of his age, and became excited when we asked him to demonstrate how one night, using his wooden cudgel, he beat to death an enormous forest cobra, which was lying on the path down to our toilets. The following day, we gave him a big bonus.

When Joe had disappeared to his dining area, I returned inside to praise Merry, who was roaming the kitchen for mice. My eyes were smarting with bad light and fatigue, so I locked all the doors and brought the dogs into the bedroom. After some cuddling on the floor, I put them in their respective beds and went to bed. As a protective measure, I checked that the panga was under the bed and the torch below the pillow. Then I crawled down under the mosquito net.

"BOOM! BOOM! BOOM!" I jumped out of bed and the dogs started howling. What was happening? I dared not light the torch and, very afraid, sneaked over to the window. Why didn't Joe come? Had he fallen asleep on duty? The thoughts were whirling in my head and I felt completely helpless, but then I heard, amongst all the banging and noise, some merry voices and lots of children, so there couldn't be a major tragedy. I walked out onto the veranda with the dogs and saw all the villagers, running down the valley slopes. With sticks and stones, they were beating on all sorts of plastic cans, trying to make as much noise as possible. Then I understood, this was their way of celebrating the new millennium and that midnight had arrived.

## 77. Inventory lists

It was so empty here without Bertil. Restlessly, I jumped back and forth between different tasks. This was probably a reaction to the hectic time Linda and I had been having.

Last week, we had five Indians and two yelling children as guests for three days. The Indians were vegetarians; two of them were diabetics (no sugar) and two didn't eat eggs and, on top of that, the children needed special food all the time. Linda was a star. We worked well together and she prepared curries and pies and washed up. She stayed overnight for two nights and that was actually quite fun. The Indians were extremely pleasant and took part in the preparation of the meals with good humour.

As soon as the Indians had left, seven Africans came for lunch. We served them a mild Indian chicken curry and for dessert, beautifully carved pineapple with a circle of watermelon balls in the centre. It was a very tasty meal.

We were so lucky having such good and loyal employees. Linda's burden was enormous with cooking for all our guests, so Fred came to our help. He prepared dog food, washed and ironed sheets and washed-up after meals. He was really helping all he could. When, once in a while, he got half an hour free, he practised driving the Suzuki. Doing that, his face beamed like the sun.

I dedicated days without guests to work on the inventory lists. I moaned over them. What a job. I made them secretly. After all, our staff didn't know we were going to sell. The lists must be ready upon our buyers' return, to sign the contract, in the middle of January. I had no idea we owned so many things.

One early morning, I walked up to the gate. I wanted to see what our Rock Garden looked like after the last weeding. Mark was standing at the gate, putting on his greatcoat, since it was time for him to go home. He didn't notice I was on my way up to him. Suddenly I saw how he hid a kerosene lamp under the coat. I went completely mad. It was obviously not enough that he often slept or got drunk on duty; he was stealing too. You couldn't trust anyone.

Sneaking up behind him, I said as calmly as I could, "Mark, you're a thief."

He jumped about two metres in surprise.

"Mark, you can't work for us any longer. Don't you understand you're not allowed to take our things? We've actually helped you many times when you or your child have been ill. By the way, have you stolen any more lamps from us; we know there are many lamps missing?"

Crestfallen, Mark admitted he'd been stealing kerosene lamps, and some other things, for quite a long time. After a while, I couldn't stand hearing any more, so I asked him to go home and return in the afternoon. In spite of liking him, we couldn't allow him to continue working for us. That would mean we'd be giving the sign to everyone it was OK to steal. We had to fire him as a lesson to the others.

That same afternoon, Mark, with Joe and Fred as witnesses, signed a confession that he voluntarily quitted working for us, since he'd been drunk and asleep on duty, had stolen from us, had left the compound without permission and had lied to us. He didn't demand any compensation from us and knew that a copy of the letter would be handed over to the chief and the assistant chief. I, however, asked him to visit us when Bertil was back from Sweden. Then we could, if we felt like it, pay him something small in addition to the wages for the time he'd been doing a good job.

I asked Joe, who was the one we trusted most among the staff, to find us a new night askari. He at once suggested a man called Moses who, at least according to him, was honest. We agreed that Moses should come for an interview and that if I accepted him I'd take him on a trial basis until Bertil returned.

A few days later, around six o'clock in the evening when both Joe and Moses had started their night watch, we suddenly heard crying and yelling from the bandas on the other side of the public plot.

"My son has died," Joe cried out.

Without delay, I sent him home and, within minutes, Moses confirmed it was in fact Joe's young son who had died.

Next morning, Joe came to me and got an advance on his salary. To help him with the funeral expenses, I also gave him an extra contribution from us, his due holiday pay, sugar and two banana bunches. Later in the morning, Fred and I went to Joe's home to express our condolences. Fourteen persons lived in the smallest imaginable banda; everyone depending on Joe's salary from us.

I walked around shaking hands, saying "Merembe" to half the village and then I said a prayer, together with his parents, at the little boy's bed. Thereafter, I left Joe's home and the funeral preparations that had now started. Joe no longer felt like the lowest person of them all. It was, without doubt, very important for him that I had been there to show loyalty. He knew Bertil and I were backing him up. It had been an emotional day, but sometimes it was like that.

Fred and I were on our way to meet Bertil at the airport. It would really be wonderful to have him back home again, even though I was surprised at how well I'd managed the business all by myself. However, it was now getting too much. Since Merry was in heat, all the dogs had to be tied up. Rufus and Musse were howling. The noise was terrible.

Poor Bertil, he couldn't stay in Sweden for his father's funeral. The damned buyers ought to have understood that; they could have postponed their arrival.

I had made up my mind not to be afraid of Fred's way of driving, but it was difficult to abstain from yelling when he simply flew over the speed bumps on the road. I'd told him to take it easy and we'd left home in plenty of time for the drive, so that we wouldn't have to rush. I'd also told Fred that I intended to drive, once we arrived in Kisumu, since he wasn't yet used to city traffic. Although I didn't drive very often in Kenya, I'd had a driver's licence for several decades.

It was so wonderful to see Bertil again. He looked tired and worn out but that was not so strange.

I told Bertil that when our employees heard that Bwana's father had died, they had, on their own initiative, put flowers and candles at the small memory place we'd made for my mother and now also Bertil´s father. They'd also read prayers.

Once home again, three wild dogs, which we freed one at a time, jumped on their master as a welcome back. Judging by their violent licking, they'd missed Bertil a lot.

We spent the following morning on the veranda, planning everything that must be done. The buyers would arrive on Sunday, in two days time. They'd stay their first night at the Rainforest Retreat, where we'd pick them up. The following five nights would be spent with us. That was when the contract would be signed.

Yes, lots of things must be arranged before their arrival. We had to write introductory letters, draw up a suggestion for a contract and book meetings with lawyers, judges and chiefs. This was Africa, so most people didn't have a telephone. The only possible way was to look them up in person. Then they were, of course, away at a funeral or somewhere else and nobody knew when he or she would return. We'd have to wait or continue to the next person on our list. Everything was so time-consuming.

The temperature was 32 degrees Celsius, but we had so many important things to do that we took off in the hot car. Our first visit was to the rainforest to meet one of the guides working there. The guides were self-employed; they had no salary and had to survive on visitors' tips. The guides were dedicated and competent. The previous year, they'd started the project KEEP (Kakamega Environmental Education Programme). Every Saturday, school children from the whole province visited them to learn more about the rainforest and its importance. KEEP recently got a UN contribution of more than three million shillings for its project as recognition of their work and ideas.

Later in the day, we went to K.W.S. and spent some time talking to them. They were very sorry we had decided to leave Kenya and actually tried to talk us into staying. According to them, we'd contributed to their work with lots of good ideas and suggestions.

## 78. Falling flat

The buyers had now been with us for a couple of days. It was a hectic time with all the meetings we took them to. They wanted to be introduced everywhere, so we were running about, here and there, in the heat. Evening time we jointly prepared meals in the kitchen, having a really pleasant time.

The Englishmen had also caught a glimpse of reality in this country. A thief stole thirty metres of telephone wire in the middle of the day. As a result, we weren't able to send emails the usual way but instead had to send them using short wave, via a radio amateur in South Africa.

The English woman was dying to meet her old friends from her childhood in Kenya, so we offered them the use of our car to go and see them. While they were gone, we'd finish preparing all the documents we'd bring to court to register the sale.

When the buyers returned the following day, they were very upset with us. They'd talked to a lawyer, who claimed it was impossible that we'd received our title deeds in the correct way. They'd heard the President on the radio, saying foreigners weren't allowed to own agricultural land unless they invested money. That was actually not a problem in our case. We owned agricultural land but we'd, a long time ago, registered a specification of investments done as well as future ones and the authorities had approved it. It wasn't until then we'd received our title deeds.

Everything was so stupid. It made no difference for the buyers, whatever we did or said. We could in a perfectly correct way obtain certificates issued from every relevant instance, certifying that we owned our land, but they'd obviously decided we were lying; that we'd been bribing people and that our title deeds were false.

Finally the Englishmen declared, however, that they might consider buying if we could get written permission to sell from the Land Control Board. Unfortunately, it was impossible to get that at once. The Land Control Board only met a couple of times per month and had recently had a meeting, so their next meeting alas wouldn't be for a few weeks.

Consequently, the buyers returned home, without having either signed the contract or paid a deposit. Crestfallen and angry, we drove them to Kisumu Airport where Kenya Airways, "The pride of Africa", made a fool of itself once again. The return trip between Kisumu and Nairobi had been booked already in England. When the Englishmen showed their tickets at Kisumu Airport in the morning, the check-in staff informed them that there was no flight at 1.30 p.m. That flight had been removed several years earlier.

A few days later, we got the opportunity to speak to the Chairman of the Land Control Board. We told her what had happened. She assured us all our documents, including the title deeds, were perfectly in order and that she'd write the requested letter, but first she wanted the dividing up of our neighbour's land to be finished. We'd started working on that division, as soon as we arrived in Kenya.

When we bought our two adjacent plots in 1996, the seller told us that a small part of one of the plots wasn't included in the deal. The previous owner had sold that part many years earlier, but the buyer of the small area had never applied for a title deed. We'd talked to him on countless occasions, asking him to apply for the title deed, but he'd refused. We'd even brought the surveyor to measure his plot. Everything was prepared for the title deeds. Our District Officer and the chief had both explained to the neighbour that unless he got the deeds, we could claim we owned that land, since it was included in one of our title deeds. That was something we'd never do, but unfortunately our neighbour seemed to have guessed that, so he was in no hurry to get the document. Now we must persuade him to do it.

Like so many other months, January 2000 also came to an end without us having sold our land.

## 79. Colobus hides

We were still shocked and flabbergasted that the sale of Riverdale Gardens had come to nothing. The last straw was when I received the buyers' last email from England, which was full of nasty accusations. I answered that in Sweden there were people, who on Sundays went to real estate viewings, merely as a Sunday outing. I wondered if they'd been doing that. They'd, after all, been staying for free in our home and we'd even lent them our car.

The only thing we could do now was to return to everyday life and keep our ears and eyes wide open for new propositions.

It was Bertil´s birthday. It was unbelievable, how quickly the years had passed. It felt like yesterday that Mathias and Gunseli were with us celebrating Bertil, but a year had passed since.

I'd put a bouquet of flowers and a plate of cakes on the breakfast table on the veranda. The birthdays we celebrated out in the bush were really rather plain. Not even Christmas was very Christmas-like. Last Christmas, we'd ordered ham and spare ribs from George, who was going to deliver it all well before that Christmas. He'd never shown up. But that had perhaps been just as well, since Bertil had had to leave for Sweden, already on last Christmas Day.

In honour of the day, Linda had prepared a nice lunch with Chicken Tandoori. For dessert, a fruit salad. The chicken had been marinated for four hours in a lot of different spices and yoghurt and thereafter charcoal barbecued. Bertil had shown Linda how to make Chicken Tandoori, on an occasion several weeks ear-

earlier. Now she could make it without any help and the result was really tasty. What a talent.

Benjamin, one of the rainforest guides, came on a visit later in the day. He brought the raw manuscript of a book about the medicinal values of all the rainforest plants. I'd offered to help him write it all down on the computer, to make it easier to edit.

For three years, Benjamin had been interviewing old men and women, medicine men and wizards about their use of plants and trees from the forest, and he'd also found around twenty different medicinal plants just by studying the blue monkeys. When they were ill, they cured themselves with herbs and the juice of vegetables.

As usual, we were very engaged in the planting of rainforest trees on our compound. The ones we'd planted earlier seemed to be doing well and we were just waiting for the rains to plant more. Benjamin and the other guides were very happy that we had set aside part of our land for rainforest, as a compensation for the forest the farmers had cut down on the opposite side of the valley. That rainforest was now only a quarter of the size it had been when we moved to the village.

We placed numbered signs at the different trees and plants, referring to the inventory list I was making of all of them.

One of the most common plants along the roadsides in Western Province is called *Lantana camara*. It multiplied very quickly and in many places formed impassable shrubs. We'd given our plant number 42. When I had a cold, coughing or headache, I made tea from the leaves.

There was also *Ricinus communis* in our garden. I didn't quite like that one. The seeds of that bush belong to the most dangerous seeds in the world, so I feared the day a staff member would use them against an enemy. Castor oil is made from its seeds. Different parts of the plant can be used as a cure for lots of things, like earache, ulcers and intestine trouble, venereal diseases and wounds, or as a skin cream.

Sooner or later, I intended to tackle the folder about the life of the Luhya people in Wuasiva. Veronica had told me, when working for us, quite a lot about the villagers' customs and habits. I wanted to make a presentation of that to hand out to our friends and guests, when they made a village walk through Wuasiva.

Everyone needed our help, regarding us as experts. That was of course good for our egos, so we worked on and were active. Maybe that way we'd, one day, find a buyer.

An email suddenly came from USA. A nasty email from a young couple. They wrote that they'd planned to book their vacations with us. They thought that Riverdale Gardens looked like a paradise, but then they saw a horrible thing on our website, so now they didn't want to come after all. What horrible people Bertil and I were!

What had they seen? They'd seen the photo of two hides from the Colobus monkey, stretched out on the wall on each side of the fireplace. Yes, that was a nasty sight, but there was a reason for them being there.

A chief had given us the monkey hides. You honour a chief and a gift from such a person was highly valued. As permanent settlers in the area, we'd have made a breach of ethics, if we hadn't accepted the hides and put them on the wall.

When that same chief wanted to give us the leopard hide in which he was elected chief, we politely declared that we felt honoured but that we unfortunately couldn't accept the gift because of the general objection to leopard hunting. Happily enough, the chief accepted our explanation.

Worth mentioning is perhaps that the monkey hides and that of the leopard were very old and had been used as far back as when the chief's own father was elected chief. Anyhow, we'd now taken down the monkey hides, hoping the chief wouldn't notice that on his next visit.

With all the problems and stress we'd lately been exposed to, it was important for us to relax once in a while. A chance for relaxation arrived, when an old African, one afternoon, came walking down from the gate. The "mzee" (old man) wanted to sell us some polished stones. We sat down together in the shade to listen to him. He told us that he normally walked on foot - 600 kilometres - north to Turkana and West Pokot in order to get precious stones. Bertil politely explained that we weren't allowed to deal with minerals and precious stones, as we had no license for that, but that we'd be happy to hear more about his rambles.

The mzee explained that he usually brought food on his northbound walks, and that, as a consequence, he now had a lot of friends among the bellicose tribes in the north. We would ourselves like to visit that area, but alas it was said to be dangerous for white people. If you went there, you had to go in convoy with an armed escort.

We offered the old man a soft drink, while he took out his precious stones. We saw green and blue sapphires and even a star sapphire. According to him, he sometimes also found rubies and garnets. What a pity, we couldn't buy anything. If we did, we could be expelled from the country. The afternoon was, in any case, agreeable and the stories we heard were worth remembering.

## 80. Busy as bees

Every afternoon, more and more clouds were piling up. Everyone claimed the dry season was coming to its end and that would actually be good. It was hot but not in any way as hot as earlier during the year. We would, as usual, plant maize and beans, as soon as the rains had started. The vegetable fields had already been dug and were lying in wait. Our neighbours had already sown their maize, and we wondered how they'd manage since, unless the rains started soon, they might have a big problem.

Was there normal weather one single year? When it was supposed to rain, it was dry and vice-versa. It was April and the rainy season should have started long ago, but the drought continued.

We were busy or you could say "bees-y". The bees had decided to make demands on all our time. They'd chosen us – not we them – making sure we couldn't ignore them. So, it wasn't voluntarily we'd become beekeepers.

Twice during the past two weeks, we'd found bee swarms as big as boxing sacks – more than one metre high - in a tree near the house. That was a sign that we needed more beehives. After a lot of searching, we finally found hives in a distant town and bought three of them. The bees seemed to be in a hurry, because they didn't want to wait for the new hives to be hung but instead tried twice that same day to move into our house. It required a lot of commitment and heavy work by all of us, to persuade them to remain at a safe distance from us.

The day after the hive purchase, we found another bee swarm near a crammed hive. The boys quickly prepared one of the new hives. It was hung up and thousands of bees moved into it. A little while later, we needed another hive. It was prepared and hung up. Everything was going fine, we believed; then a lot of bees once more decided to move into the restaurant - in spite of the newly hung beehives. We finished a lot of spray bottles and uttered many swear words, before the bees moved out again and found the last hive.

We now had a total of four beehives and every hive could give honey up to a value of three thousand shillings. Our shamba boys claimed there were several kilos of honey in one of the hives and wanted to harvest it at the next full moon, which would be the coming week.

"Bertil, have you seen this tree earlier?" I asked, standing on the veranda outside our bedroom doors.

"No, well, I actually don't quite know. I haven't thought about it before, anyway," answered Bertil hesitantly. "It might have grown during the night," he added jokingly.

None of us had noticed the tree below the veranda before, between the house and the row of rather tall red bottlebrush trees. This tree had beautiful yellow flowers and tender foliage and was obviously fast growing. What tree was it?

Later in the morning, I took a walk to the upper part of the compound. I suddenly saw a lot of trees like the new one near the veranda. They were really beautiful and gave shade, where it usually was very hot. The strange thing was that they'd appeared so suddenly. We'd never before seen them on our land and I didn't think we'd ever seen them anywhere else. Luckily enough Benjamin would visit us that day.

When he turned up, I asked him about my newly discovered tree. He told me, it was called "Omukhule" in the local language and *Sesbania sesban* in Latin. It could grow up to six metres high and had hairy branches. It was fast growing and the life span wasn't more than a couple of years. The leaves could be crushed, mixed with water and given to cows that had recently calved, in order to increase milk production, and ground leaves could be used as a cure for different stomach problems.

Benjamin was like an encyclopaedia. It was absolutely fantastic to listen to him. Before he left, we put a numbered sign at one of the newly discovered trees and I wrote down the text he'd given me.

When our friend had disappeared, I sat down in a comfortable chair and started paging the folder I had made of all our medicinal plants. I noticed that we already had cures against malaria, prostate cancer and all kinds of stomach illnesses, headache, venereal diseases, children's diseases and intestinal worms. We had furthermore soap plants, tree plants out of which you could weave cloth, medicines for ear inflammations, bronchitis, pneumonia... We had ten different plants for malaria, six for headaches, eleven for coughs, two for measles, two for snakebites and so on. I learned new things every day.

Benjamin would soon bring us many more plants. We'd by now put out 110 signs, which equalled the same number of different medicinal plants. People visiting us were impressed. Riverdale Gardens was starting to look like a botanical garden.

One of the US monkey researchers came on a visit and brought us the thick books about mushroom cultivation we'd ordered in the United States. Now we could start reading how we could get bigger and better harvests, but we were still proud that we'd succeeded in growing nice mushrooms without having any books.

Bertil began to make mycelia. It wasn't easy, since we didn't have a sterile laboratory. Cleanliness was very important. Everything must be absolutely sterile. One single bacteria or mould spore sufficed for everything to fail. Hence Bertil used a glove box of his own design, in order to get a sterile environment. The box cover was of glass and at the front of the box there were two holes with rubber gloves in them. In order to work in the box, you put your hands in the gloves, thus avoiding touching with your own hands the things you'd be working with. Everything you needed was inside the box. To manage under such primitive conditions, without electricity, was quite an achievement.

Mycelia could be produced either through spores or cloning. Bertil worked with both methods. When cloning mushrooms, he created identical copies of an extra fine mushroom which we'd obtained from mycelia made of a tiny piece of that mushroom. In the second case, you grew mycelia from the mushroom spores.

Everyone was enormously interested in the mushroom project. Our Member of Parliament came on a visit. He stayed for quite some time down in the mushroom area. On another occasion, a representative of UNDP visited us and was equally enthusiastic. Our chief wanted to send us a group of ten people to be taught mushroom cultivation and another group of ten would come from the Catholic Church.

If we managed to teach the locals in the region mushroom farming, we could be proud. Africans loved mushrooms, as did all Europeans within the area.

The month of April ended with a Walpurgis fire. It was the neighbour's banda that burned down. The fire started when his still exploded. What a hullabaloo. Musse was scared out of his wits and sought refuge under the big table, turning over a flower vase in his panic.

The neighbour's house burned all night. In the morning, only the mud walls were left. Everything had been lost. Such things could happen, if you were working with illegal brewing. It was forbidden here too.

## 81. Red mercury

One late afternoon when Linda was about to leave, she said, handing over a letter, "I'm sorry, but I forgot to give you this letter."

Since I was closest to her, I received the folded paper.

"Where did you get it from?" I asked.

"I got it from my husband who is working up in Kipkarren River. He got it from another person, who said you should have it."

I unfolded the paper and started reading. Linda had already disappeared out through the gate. Completely bewildered, I handed it on to Bertil.

It was a handwritten document, which started "General Information! The stuff is in strong metallic seal with two wires - positive & negative protruding from the chemical itself…"

The thing being described was a cylinder with a glass window on one side and two wires on the other. The cylinder was, according to the document, marked with the words "Pure Red Mercury – Danger. Sealed in Great Britain 1945."

Bertil was ransacking his memory. Where had he read about red mercury? He connected the computer to the Internet and searched for Red Mercury. Imagine his surprise, when he read that this material could be used as detonator in nuclear weapons; that it was an extremely strong explosive, in great demand among terrorists and similar people.

Bertil printed the web page and declared we must get hold of Linda's husband, so that he could tell us where he'd got the letter. We realized this was a serious matter. We didn't want to have anything to do with it. Why would anyone want us to have it?

Next morning, we asked Linda to bring her husband over. We promised to drive him to the bus stop, so that he wouldn't be late for work. He said he'd received the letter from an unknown person in Kipkarren River, together with the message that the Europeans his wife was working for would probably be interested. That was all the information he had.

Bertil called the Swedish Embassy and informed the person in charge of security about the whole situation. The man asked him to fax the letter to them. They'd make sure the British Embassy got it. The Swedish Embassy also suggested we contact Police Headquarters in Kakamega. Since we knew one inspector at the C.I.D. there, we decided to hand over the case to him.

Arriving at the police station, we asked to be spared registering in the visitors' book. Handing over the letter to the inspector, we said, "We got this letter from our house girl," and then we told him the whole story, straight off. When he'd read the letter with a questioning expression on his face, Bertil handed over the printout from the website, which explained what Red Mercury was. The inspector stared at the text for some time. Then he stood up, opened the door and told his assistant to join us. They seemed quite upset, while discussing the matter in the local language.

The inspector quickly turned to us, declaring, "We'll take over the matter from now. You don't have to worry. We'll drive up north to talk to people in Kipkarren River and we'll see what happens."

Later, we heard that some persons from Uganda had contacted the person who later on contacted Linda's husband, at the marketplace. According to him, they had a box with the described cylinders in their possession but the box was at that time still in Uganda. The men intended to return to the marketplace two weeks later with a couple of samples to show us. The police were now planning an ambush for the Ugandan men when they showed up at the market.

Much later, we heard from the inspector that the sellers had intended to ask us for 3.5 million shillings for each cylinder. In their stupidity, they thought we'd be interested. As white people we of course had unlimited funds.

At our meeting with the inspector, we asked him how his puppy, one of Musse's brothers, was doing. To our horror, we heard that the puppy had been murdered, as had all other dogs he'd had. He'd been poisoned.

It wasn't enough that people murdered each other; on top of that they also killed innocent animals.

## 82. Escalating violence

We spent the evenings sitting in candlelight at our computers. It was cosy but somewhat difficult to see the keys. It was also sweaty. In the kitchen, we had glass jars with wheat continually boiling in the pressure cooker. That was called sterilization. When the jars were cold, they'd be inoculated with oyster mycelia and within a couple of weeks we'd have two kilos of mycelia that, used in the right way, would produce many kilos of mushrooms.

Fred seemed to have been born in a laboratory. He loved to sit with gloves on, working with petri dishes in the glove box. We'd tried to teach Linda and Willy to make mycelia but they weren't as good at it as Fred. All three of them were, however, now so good at growing mushrooms that they were able to start teaching the people in the area.

We decided to visit our friend Elena, to get a break from the mushroom work. We hadn't spoken to her for quite some time and we wanted to catch the opportunity to see her, now that we were in town.

Bertil had to hoot for a while, before the small door at the side of the tall gate was opened.

"Angelina, is Elena here?" I asked.

Elena's youngest daughter seemed embarrassed and reluctant to answer. How strange! She was usually very alert and agreeable, but now she looked like she was on the verge of tears. What had happened?

"Yeees," she answered hesitantly and then she continued, "But she says she doesn't want to see anyone."

I was worried. I'd sent lots of emails to Elena, without getting any answer. I'd called her many times and nobody had answered. I must see her and know what had happened.

"Angelina, you have to let us in anyhow. We are your mother's friends and she might need us."

Just as the gate was opened for us, I saw my little friend in the background. Looking completely wrecked, she walked into our open arms. We held her tight, noticing the tears running down her cheeks.

After a while, she calmed down a little. We sat down in the kitchen, all three of us, and there she told us, in a stuttering, incoherent way, what had happened. It was horrible. Approximately a week earlier, a gang of Africans broke into their house during the night. Elena was subjected to horrifying acts of cruelty and Sebastian was knocked unconscious. Strangely enough, their two dogs didn't react to the break-in. That meant that one of the villains must know the dogs.

Since this occurrence, they'd got anonymous telephone calls with death threats daily, so the family was moving around, sleeping one night at each place. One of their dogs was found dead one morning, having been poisoned, and they were afraid the other dog might die too.

Elena was feeling awful and wanted to leave Kenya, something her husband didn't agree to. In the worst case, she might have to leave alone. She had no relatives alive in her own country and therefore was thinking of maybe going to England where one of her children was studying. What had happened was horrible. She'd been living in the country for twenty years and now had to escape. She had no money and owned nothing. What would she do? To come and live with us was no solution, since many gangs in Kakamega came from

Wulushi, close to us. She wouldn't be any safer with us.

After a while, Elena's husband, Sebastian came home for lunch. During the meal, he informed us that the situation in Kakamega and surroundings had become very unpleasant. One or more gangs were ravaging, plundering, breaking in, cutting up people using machetes and raping. Many people had been assaulted, not only Indians and whites but also Africans. Everyone that the villains believed had money was attacked. At night, the Indians were patrolling town by car. The police did little. Sebastian confirmed that many of the gang members came from our area and that they'd attacked people close to us, down in Wulushi. He asked us to be careful and not to trust anyone.

We heard that not even the orphanage in town had escaped the villains. The nuns had been assaulted and hurt and all the money stolen. What kind of people could do something like that?

Having reciprocally promised each other to keep in close contact, we left for home, feeling completely sickened by the story we'd been told.

All this naturally meant a big change for us. Evening time, we sat with the doors locked. The doors had always been unlocked and the windows wide open, as long as we'd been awake. A night askari now patrolled around our house, all night long. Bertil connected the alarm system, so that we could reach it from the bed. But who would come to our rescue, should the alarm start sounding?

This might appear rather dramatic and pathetic, but it wasn't very funny to sleep with a machete each under the bed and the air pistol between us.

A couple of days later, Elena called. Crying, she told us that the second of her wonderful dogs now had died of poisoning. The family had moved back to the villa and had installed, at tremendous cost, compact steel security gates to the house and thick bars protecting the windows. Elena intended to flee from Kenya, but she still didn't know where to or when.

We decided to pack an emergency suitcase, so that we too were prepared for flight, should something happen in our area. In that case, we'd try to get to the embassy in Nairobi and contact our family from there, asking for money for the flight tickets.

Not only violence but also corruption, was being manifested in new ways. Of course, there were honest people, but to us these seemed few and far between. During the four years we'd lived here, we'd hired more than sixty persons and had fired fifty-four of them for dishonesty. We now had only five employees: time would show whether they were honest.

One example of corruption: one day we went to town to buy food and a crate of beer. The guy receiving the crate with empty beer bottles returned after a moment with an empty bottle, which had a small piece of glass missing at the opening. He declared Bertil had to pay 25 shillings for it. Payment should be made outside, in the street, without any receipt. He had of course a broken bottle of his own that he showed to unsuspecting customers in order to get some extra money.

Another example: A person needing a licence for something went to the Licence Office in the Town Hall to ask for a form for the desired licence.

"Sorry, there aren't any forms," the person behind the counter said. "Come back next week."

Next week, he got the same answer and it would continue like that for months, or years. If, on the other hand, he put a one hundred shilling note on the counter, all the forms in the world were available.

Towards the end of the month, it finally started to rain and we experienced our worst tempest to date. Falling trees pulled down the telephone wires. Around ten banana plants were uprooted. The mango tree was cut in two halves and two big trees were reduced to firewood. The visibility was, at moments, less than a metre. From the apartment in the restaurant building we couldn't even see our car, parked about a metre away.

We missed normal Swedish summer weather so much; sometimes grey, sometimes blue, without the extremes we had in Kenya. We talked and thought; and talked and thought some more. Might we have earned celebrating Midsummer in Sweden? At my parents' summer house in Tyresö? My summer paradise.

It was such a relief, when we'd made up our minds. We needed a breather in all this misery. Regardless of whether we found a buyer beforehand or not, we intended to spend two summer months in Sweden. We would walk in the forest, pick mushrooms, eat blueberries from the bush and just enjoy ourselves. Not one single mean person would be allowed to come close to us; only peace and quiet and relaxation.

On our flight to Sweden, we'd take a couple of wooden crates, containing some objects we didn't want to leave behind, if later we had to leave Kenya in a hurry.

## 83. Mushroom period

While waiting for our summer vacation in Sweden, we dedicated all our time to the mushrooms. Everybody in our region loved mushrooms, but only very few picked them in the forest. Those doing so and selling them in the marketplace said it was difficult to distinguish the good mushrooms from the poisonous ones. Furthermore they said, as we already knew, that "Mushrooms only grow where snakes are breathing." Therefore interest was exceptionally high, when we showed it was possible to cultivate good mushrooms.

The mushroom project was a winner. Our employees had now trained twenty local instructors, spread all over Wulushi; an area of about 200 square kilometres in size with more than one hundred thousand inhabitants. We'd even trained people in far-away Butere. The instructors would train their neighbours in their own villages. Our full-day seminars, free of charge, were highly appreciated and the interest in attending was spreading like an avalanche.

Growing mushrooms was so cheap that the poorest villagers could manage. The market would probably be extensive. The chiefs were smiling and everyone was jubilant, as there were big profits to be made also for the poor villagers. Why hadn't we started this project a couple of years earlier?

One morning, a mushroom grower friend from Butere came on a visit. He told us that Kakamega Agricultural Show would open in two days time. He asked us to help with the exhibition stand for Mumias-Butere district. They'd be showing mushroom cultivation in their stand and wanted to borrow some fine substrate bags they could exhibit. We promised our employees would be at the show with good material before the opening.

On the show's opening day, we sent Linda, Fred and Willy to spend the day there. They were wearing their white Riverdale Gardens T-shirts, looking very smart. We gave them a rather generous sum of money, ordering them to amuse themselves as much as possible. They were extremely happy.

Next day, we went to the Agricultural Show ourselves. Walking around, we saw attractions like the sun-operated cooking cases and amusements such as merry-go-rounds. The Mumias-Butere stand was the one attracting most spectators and, as expected, the stand won first prize for its oyster mushrooms. They were even on the TV news. It wasn't even mentioned that a European couple was behind it all.

One night, Joe knocked at the door, asking if he could pick the "busine" he'd found on the compound. His English wasn't good, so when we asked what "busine" was, he started gesticulating, uttering long sentences in the Luhya language mixed with English. He was such a darling, that man. Finally, we understood he was talking about a local mushroom he'd obviously found on our land. He got permission to pick it, but we asked him to leave a couple of them for us to look at. Joe's expression, when he got a positive answer, was wonderful.

"Much busine, many busine. Thank you!" he emitted, when I gave him a bag to use.

On the following day, we took a look at this local mushroom.

"Goodness, it looks like a champignon," Bertil exclaimed.

Scanning the ground, we saw lots of new mushrooms coming up. Champignons! I'd actually already found puffballs on our compound earlier, but that there were also champignons was nice.

Bertil analysed the mushroom. It was really of the art *Agaricus* – a champignon. Naturally, he took a spore print of it, so that he could also cultivate this mushroom in the future.

A few days later, it was chaos. People from the UNDP, together with people from KEEP, came to visit. Later in the day, the local manager of an international ecological organization arrived and within moments Father Samuel also turned up with two Brothers from the Catholic Church. At the same time, we were having a full-day seminar about mushroom growing for instructors in hut number two. All the visitors became intensely interested in the seminar, staying behind to listen and watch. They seemed extremely impressed.

At the end of the day, Bertil and I tried to summarize the results of the different visits. We arrived at the following conclusion:

KEEP absolutely wanted to buy Riverdale Gardens and we'd be really glad if they could take over, but unfortunately they didn't have any money and were dependent on financial help. Their main donor, the UNDP, wasn't allowed to grant money for buying land.

The catholic Brothers and Father Samuel were very enthusiastic about our property. They were helping street children and were of the opinion that Riverdale Gardens would fit like a glove. Unfortunately, neither did they have any money right now.

The third visitor, the local manager of the international organization, was interested but nor had he any money at present; the budget for the year having already been exceeded.

So there seemed to be a lot of interest, but everybody seemed to be having the same money problem. In spite of having already reduced our price considerably, we still had a problem getting paid. We might have to consider getting the money later. Which one could we trust most?

After a lot of meetings with different parties, we decided we'd sell Riverdale Gardens to the big international organization, but they wouldn't be able to pay us until next fiscal year. Their local manager would move into our main building, when we left for Nairobi on June 10th. We had some issues to take care of in Nairobi before leaving for Sweden, for a two-month long vacation, in the middle of the month.

The agreed amount wasn't high, but the organization worked with praiseworthy projects in Kenya. The sales contract would be signed on our return.

What would we do with our dogs, now that we'd found a buyer? After many long discussions, we concluded that we must find new homes for Rufus and Merry. According to some friends of ours in Kisumu, the RSPCA could find them a good family. One of our conditions was, of course, that both of them should be together. Hence we decided to leave the dogs at a kennel in Nakuru, where the RSPCA would collect them. We would probably be able to find a new home in the area for our youngest dog, Musse.

Under no circumstances whatsoever, would I accompany Bertil to Nakuru. I didn't want to remember my dogs from a tearful parting there. I wanted to remember them from Riverdale Gardens. So I decided to stay at home, letting Fred accompany Bertil.

The farewell on the lawn was horribly difficult. We'd done so much together. They'd been close to dying; we'd delivered their puppies and many other things. At last, I gave them a final hug, walked inside and, lying on my bed, I started crying. I didn't want to see the car leave with them.

## 84. Swedish summer vacation

When Bertil returned from Nakuru, he told me, beaming with joy, that the kennel owner had told him quarantine was no longer needed for dogs coming to Sweden from Kenya. He could arrange cheap air transport for us and we'd then be able to take also Musse with us. Bertil and the kennel owner therefore jointly had decided that the RSPCA wouldn't take care of our dogs. They'd instead stay at the kennel, until all of us could leave for Sweden.

I found this very strange, but on the other hand it was the kennel owner's business to know such things, so he was probably right.

"Linda, please come here a moment," I said, while having lunch with our employees on the veranda. "Look, I'm giving you this as a keepsake."

I hung a silver chain with a small heart around her neck. The boys got similar chains. Fred got one with a shark's tooth and Willy one with a small jade elephant.

Bertil, who had taught them the noble art of growing mushrooms, obviously realized how insecure they felt. "We'll be back at the end of August, so we'll only be gone for a couple of months," he said. "You must take care of the mushroom farming while we are away. Just remember it's important to wash carefully. You have your notes too, so everything will be alright."

"We'll be in contact with you via email all the time. If there is something urgent, we can phone you," I added. "Promise to be nice to Musse."

As if understanding my words, Musse jumped up to lick the tip of my nose.

A couple of hours later, it was time to go to Kisumu to catch our flight for Nairobi. Mr. Muasya had also turned up. He'd keep an eye on Riverdale Gardens for us. On occasions when he couldn't stay overnight, the boys would take turns doing it.

We'd finally told our staff members we were selling. They'd probably already guessed as much, judging by how rapidly rumours spread in this country. As compensation, they'd been told the mushroom cultivation would continue, so they didn't have to fear for their future support.

"See you soon!" After giving Musse a final hug, we entered the car together with Fred, who would drive the car back home from Kisumu.

Then we left Riverdale Gardens behind for a two-month long vacation in Sweden. It would be so wonderful.

## 85. Back home

With a squeaking sound, the Akamba bus pulled out from the bus terminal in Nairobi. We gave a huge sigh. After a lot of chaos and confusion at the terminal, sitting on the bus was an enormous relief, in spite of the long and tiresome full day's journey ahead of us. Well, we were on our way home at last. To Riverdale Gardens.

The hours passed. We sat mostly silent, except when gasping with anxiety as the bus almost slid off the road or narrowly avoided collision. The driver was like a madman. Many more passengers than allowed were pressed in; it was sweaty and stuffy and the noise made it impossible to carry on conversation. Both of us were lost in thought.

My head was full of questions and uncertainty. What would we do now? Was there any other way? How could they? Are they out of their minds? But the manager is European… The thoughts were many and perplexing.

During our vacation in Sweden, we'd been told that the international organization had backed out of the purchase of Riverdale Gardens. They'd got it into their heads that we had planned to pay Mr. Muasya commission on the sale. As if we'd ever talked about that. It was obvious that one of Mr. Muasya's enemies had spread the rumour. Yet nobody had even asked us if it was true.

When we went to the organization's headquarters in Nairobi, after our return from Sweden, the European manager also told us we were terrible people, trying to steal the neighbour's land. We didn't even get a chance to tell him the truth about our neighbour's lies.

It was enough to drive you mad. I felt hopelessly depressed. All the happiness from spending time with Father in Sweden had gone. I wished we'd never heard about Kenya. We were back at square one.

After a short refreshment break in Nakuru, we soon started slowly climbing the mountains west of Rift Valley. Approximately an hour later, I suddenly saw something white at the side of the road and poked Bertil in the ribs.

"Look!" I said. "Snow drifts."

It was the first time I saw snow in Kenya and that was actually a strange feeling. We weren't very high above sea level - only a couple of thousand metres - so seeing snow astonished me. The weather must have been exceptionally cold during our absence.

I managed to doze off for a little more than an hour, but then Bertil woke me, since it was soon time to get off the bus. We'd almost reached Wageya, where Fred would meet us with our Suzuki.

"Mama, I've missed you so much!" Fred exclaimed, hugging me and kissing me on my cheek.

But what was this? An African man and moreover an employee hugging a white woman and moreover his boss in a public place with people around who knew him. Something seemed wrong. Something didn't ring true. It felt like a theatrical performance. Fred and I had certainly never hugged each other before. The closest we'd come to one another was when I had put my hand on his forehead to find out if he had a high fever. This was absolutely not a question of racism, just that men and women, regardless of skin colour, didn't touch each other in public out here in the villages. Among modern Africans in the cities, it might be different.

Soon we were home again. People waved and smiled at us, along the road. A lot of people on the public land outside our gates watched us, as we drove through them into our compound. What a commotion? Had something happened? Or did they just want to continue with the mushroom growing? Why did everyone seem so friendly?

As soon as the car had halted down at the restaurant and I'd opened the car door, a black figure came prancing towards me. He lay down on his back in order to be scratched on his tummy. Then he tried to climb into my arms. He was so lovely, our wonderful little Musse.

Linda, Fred and Willy had a thousand things to tell us, but we asked them to let us sit down for a little while on the veranda to catch our breath. They were shining like suns, all three of them, and it wasn't long before they started insisting on showing us this and this and that…

## 86. Kiss of death

In the evening, we snuggled up on the veranda with lit kerosene lamps. We talked a lot about the oyster mushrooms and the new strain the staff had developed during our absence. According to what they told us and according to the email reports they'd sent us in Sweden, they seemed to have worked diligently. Then why had so much money been spent?

"Bertil, I'm going to transcribe the economic reports into the computer and analyse how much money has been spent on different things. I can't quite understand what has happened financially."

After a while, we heard a knock at the door. Joe and Moses entered, in order to greet us. It was nice to see our night askaris again and we chatted for some minutes.

"Bwana and Bibi, how do you find things here? Are you content with the staff and how we've dealt with things?" Joe asked a little later.

When we answered that we were content, Joe and Moses looked like they wanted to say something but without doing it they disappeared out into the darkness again.

"They've something on their minds," Bertil pointed out. "We'll have to ask them later, if there is anything special they'd like to discuss."

Next morning, I transcribed figures into a spreadsheet in the computer. Bertil checked the mycelia and returned, very upset, saying it was full of contamination - quite impossible to use. We'd have to start all over again. Why hadn't our employees told us that?

Later in the day, we went down to Wulushi to see if we could find our friend Petrus. Strangely enough, he hadn't yet come to greet us. After some searching, we found him and asked how things had been at Riverdale during our absence. He explained that he and the staff had quarrelled and that they'd sent him away. So he hadn't been there much and couldn't tell us how things had been. Petrus also seemed to be withholding information. We were getting worried. Something was very wrong.

I wanted to finish the computer work, balance up the costs and income, before I did any questioning. Perhaps I might find something strange there - and I certainly did. They'd bought petrol corresponding to twenty drives to Nairobi and back; the food costs were preposterous and there were lots of strange out-of-pocket expenses without receipts. One hundred kilos of mycelia was missing, even though we'd deducted the weight of the mycelia that, according to Linda, had been bad. All expenses were astronomical and lots of income entries were missing. This wasn't caused merely by incompetence and carelessness. This must have been done on purpose.

It was difficult to look happy and content in front of the employees, but we'd determined that, before confronting them, we must check through other people what had happened.

As if reading our thoughts, Mr. Ongeri from Butere - one of the mushroom growers in that district - suddenly turned up. He showed us a list of things to buy that he'd received from another man in Butere. It specified different ingredients and things needed for making mycelia. The other man had asked Mr. Ongeri to buy these things and now he had some questions to put to us.

Looking at the list, we saw that, although there were some faults, the things we used for making mycelia were there. Lots of different things could be used, but the exact ones we used were on the list. One of the staff members must actually have given away this secret information. Mr. Ongeri, who was a nice and kind man, was horrified when he heard this and promised to try and find out more about how the list had come about.

Joe was off-duty in the evening and then Moses came to us and said he wanted to tell us something. We sat down together indoors and he divulged what had happened during our absence.

The boys, Fred and Willy, had taken turns in using our bedroom, taking girls there. Evening time, the house had been kept open for all sorts of people and there had been a lot of drinking going on. Our house and our private apartment had been public property. Linda had obviously not been involved in the night activities, but she'd been washing our glasses from the drinks cabinet for hours in the mornings. The boys had also been driving around in all directions in our car. The mushroom cultivation had also started to get a bad reputation, because of the mouldy mycelia they'd sold. Moses asked us not to tell anyone what he'd told us and we promised him that.

We sat numbed after Moses had left to start his night-watch duty. I felt nauseated. Our most private rooms had been used as a porno club. I could kill them.

"OK," said Bertil, "now we know that things have happened here. We can ask Joe and Petrus and pretend we've heard rumours down in the village, so that Moses won't be seen as the one giving them away."

I felt completely frozen inside. Quite empty. I had, with all my heart, given each of them a keepsake. We'd actually been like one big happy family. How could they?

During the following two days, we questioned Joe, Petrus and some other persons we trusted. We heard that my Suzuki had been used as a taxi. Fred and Willy, Simon and one other boy had been going around like kings in it. Joe verified what Moses had told us about the things happening at night, and Petrus informed us about other unpleasant things that had happened in the daytime. Some mushroom growers told us about the mouldy mycelia and we ourselves knew that money had disappeared. Now we had enough facts to confront the trio.

We called a meeting on the veranda. The three staff members arrived, without any suspicions. We hadn't given the game away, showing what we knew. What a shock they'd get.

Bertil and I revealed that we knew what they'd done. We showed them the list of costs and asked for explanations. Where was the driver's log Fred had promised to keep updated? Why were so and so many kilos of mycelia missing? Vegetables for many thousand shillings, how come? Night parties in our apartment? And so on. The three became more and more silent.

We finally asked them, if they had any explanations or wanted to tell us the truth. They just kept silent, refusing to answer, so we told them that they'd have three days to confess. If they confessed, we could discuss a possible continued employment. Anyone not confessing would of course be fired without any letter of recommendation. We pointed out that we hadn't yet determined whether we should turn the issue over to the police or not.

Only Fred came to confess his sins - probably not all of them but some - and of course he blamed the others as much as he could. He had no explanation for a lot of things, but we needed his technical skills, so we let him persuade us to give him another chance. We were, however, very much aware that we could no longer trust him. Each time I saw him, I remembered the kiss he gave me on my cheek in Wageya. Talk about a Judas kiss.

Linda and Willy didn't turn up. That meant they were fired. I felt sorry for Linda whom I really liked. Willy, on the other hand, was a cold individual and I was glad that we'd got rid of him.

## 87. New efforts

We buried our problems in hard work. By the evening, we were completely exhausted and went early to bed. Anything was better than thinking of the treachery we'd been subjected to by our co-workers. The worst of all was that we earlier had regarded them almost as family members.

Fred was now test-working for two months. One single mistake from his side and he'd immediately be kicked out. Our friend Petrus was also working for us and had brought a friend, Bernie, who was helping us with the mushroom project. Macy was our new house girl. She couldn't cook to any great extent, but she was with us primarily to help with the mushroom growing. We'd also employed a young boy, twenty-year-old Tommy, who was a deaf-mute, since he had measles in fourth grade. As he'd been studying at an agricultural school, he'd mainly take care of the garden and the vegetables. We communicated well with him, either through sign language or in writing. He walked around with a notepad and a pencil and understood written English and was delighted to have a job. Our spirits were high and we were having fun together, while toiling with our mushrooms.

The boys took turns with the special Saturday work I'd given them. They actually seemed to like it. Each Saturday, one of the boys had to pick flowers for all the vases and arrange them nicely. Naturally Petrus was fantastic. He was, after all, a gardener but it was nice that also Bernie, Fred and Tommy succeeded - even if not with the same beautiful result. It took them several hours to do this and they knew they were allowed to pick whatever flowers and sprigs they wanted. My only wish was that all my vases were filled and placed in the way they themselves thought most beautiful. But I had to bite my tongue to keep quiet when, one day, Bernie picked all my *Agapanthus Africana*. They'd just started flowering for the first time.

We were drowning in work. Our weeks were fully booked with mushroom meetings in different places, and mushrooms kept pouring in. Everything was to be noted and controlled, as well as sorted according to quality. We also had to take care of the big boxes full of dried mushrooms that Linda had packed during our Swedish vacation. Unfortunately, she didn't care enough to check the mushrooms for worms, before drying them, so I was now trying to check them afterwards, which wasn't easy. All the dried mushrooms were packed in small plastic bags, so that they would be easier to sell.

Bertil and I spent a considerable part of the time driving around in the countryside. We made home visits in distant villages as well as marketing visits in Kitale, Kisumu, Eldoret and Kakamega. Everyone was very positive. Our small plastic bag with dried mushrooms, sealed with the sealing machine and with a beautiful label, was widely acclaimed so now we were waiting for orders. In the pipeline was also the dispatch of a big pile of marketing letters to hotel chains and camps in the national parks.

There was no end to the interest in mushroom farming expressed by the rural people. We'd, among other places, been in the rainforest, in KEEP's meeting room, to give a lecture to a group of Japanese professors and doctors, all specialists in rainforest conservation. I almost felt as if I was giving bread to a baker's children. Japan had such good mushroom farmers, but the difference between cultivating mushrooms in a modern establishment and doing it with primitive methods in banana groves was actually rather big.

A Dutch friend, whom we had got to know on the Internet, came to spend a couple of weeks with us and, during that time, he taught us a lot of tricks in the art of mushrooming. We'd allowed Fred to continue making mycelia, but this time we were cunning. A new and important ingredient was kept secret from him: that way he wouldn't be able to cheat us again.

Bertil built a sun-operated mushroom drier, with a capacity of about ten kilos of fresh mushrooms per day. It dried the mushrooms to perfection and also made it possible to keep a check on hygiene during the drying.

All day long caravans of people carrying home-grown mushrooms came. We received up to five or six kilos per day. The best mushrooms would be sold fresh, while the other mushrooms, being of a slightly poorer quality, were dried and packed.

A big hotel chain was interested in buying fresh mushrooms. They wanted all we could produce. The problem was, however, how to find a method to keep them fresh so that they'd still be good after car transport in cool boxes to Nairobi or the coast.

By now, we'd proved it was possible to grow mushrooms at low cost and that no modern methods were needed for this. We wanted to develop this project into a full-scale aid project for the region. Since we ourselves in the long run couldn't afford to pay all the costs, we tried to find a solution to the question of financing the project. After a tremendous lot of work, we were finally able to send a budget proposal to a large number of prospective sponsors, amongst them UNDP and USAid.

## 88. Our dogs are back

It was obvious, we'd remain in Africa for quite some time and therefore we decided to bring Rufus and Merry back home. We missed them so very much.

The kennel owner in Nakuru hadn't wanted anyone to take over the dogs. The reason was, "The people here are not right in the head. They just kill dogs and all other animals." He kept forty dogs in his kennel that nobody paid for. On top of that, he kept eleven other lame and maimed dogs and a lot of homeless cats in his own home and, furthermore, at night all the donkeys in the neighbourhood were allowed to graze for free in his garden.

After all, you were absolutely forbidden to bring dogs from Africa to Sweden, without a long stay in quarantine. We'd checked the rules while in Sweden, so the kennel man was wrong on that issue. This meant that we wouldn't be able to bring the dogs, the day we left Kenya. Consequently, we must try to enjoy their company as long as possible.

It was a fond reunion. Seeing us, our dogs started howling. When we arrived home, Rufus and Merry immediately recognized the place. Since we didn't know how Rufus and Musse, both of them male dogs, would react, we kept Musse chained to begin with. Merry walked up to him and started licking and grooming him, as she'd always done. Rufus didn't take any notice at all of Musse and quickly recovered his position as ruler of the roost. Musse withdrew without any problem at all. In other words, everything was back to normal in the pack.

Some days after the dogs' return, I was on my way to the toilet at the lower part of the compound. Our employees were having lunch and Bertil was in Kakamega. I whistled to the dogs and went down to open the gate. Suddenly I was sitting on the ground, wondering how on earth I could get up. The dogs had collided in the gate opening and, at high speed, continued slipping downwards and into my right leg and knee. Sixty-seventy kilos of dog at full speed. That was an impact you noticed alright.

After a while, I got up again. At least it wasn't a fractured thighbone. But my knee was enormous. All the muscles had received a heavy blow, but with liniment, painkillers and bandage I was, a few days later, able to start walking again. And, happily enough, the meniscus hadn't been injured. From that moment on, I always carried a spray bottle with water in one hand, when walking. Any dog trying to force its way past me immediately got a shower.

We worked intensely with the production of new mushroom mycelia, as our former employees had managed to ruin the lot. It took time to make mycelia. Every day, lots of people came to buy - even wanting to pay in advance – but were disappointed. They had to return home empty handed, because we didn't yet have enough to start selling.

A big newspaper wanted to write an article about the mushroom project. The TV would perhaps do a feature and we were invited to a big happening with official "planting" of mycelia in Butere. All V.I.P.s were invited, so we naturally hoped our mycelia would be ready in time.

Meanwhile, we made mushroom bags for ourselves, in order to have at least enough fresh mushrooms to cover the petrol cost for our trips to Kisumu. The dried ones, we delivered nicely packed to a store in Kakamega, where the hotels bought them.

For a long time, we'd been trying to solve the problem of how to keep the fresh mushrooms fresh, but in spite of a lot of different tests we hadn't arrived at a solution. Now we decided to build a big refrigerator. It would be operated without electricity, petrol or kerosene and instead work by evaporation through charcoal.

Outside the kitchen, we had a cement pool – 3.5 x 1.2 metres - that we'd earlier used for guests' children to practice gold panning. Now we constructed a superstructure on top of it and that way we got a cold store almost two metres high. In it there would be space for lots of fresh mushrooms and other kinds of food.

The walls were made of chicken net on both the inner and outer sides, with a 30 centimetre space between the walls. We filled that space with charcoal. On the roof, we put a layer of charcoal and on top of that a big tin tray with an elevated brim, filled with charcoal and water. Bands of jute cloth led the water from the tray down into the charcoal walls. When the water evaporated in the sun, the temperature was lowered inside the cold store.

In order to make the cold store work, we needed enough water. It remained to be seen if we'd get that.

One day, the waterman asked for some money to buy fuel for the water pump - again. We gave him money but, as expected, everyone else - who had never paid for water and who had arbitrarily connected themselves to the water pipe - took the opportunity to draw water for free. Since Riverdale was at the end of the pipe, as usual no water was left for us. The chances of being able to use our newly built refrigerator weren't good. Would we never learn from experience? We should, by now, have realized this wouldn't be allowed to function without interference.

We couldn't sell mycelia unless we had a continuous water supply for the cold storage. The storage was needed for keeping the fresh mushrooms in good shape. We would get a good profit selling fresh mushrooms and we needed that income to pay the villagers for the mushrooms they sold to us. Hence, unless we got water, it was impossible for us to continue paying people.

At the last Water Committee meeting, the old waterman was fired. A new meeting took place and at that one the chief, over the head of the whole committee, decided to reinstall the old man in his job. Subsequently he now officially had the chief behind him and he wouldn't let us persuade him to turn on the water; not even if he was paid. It was that simple to destroy the idea behind our new refrigerator. It meant only one thing. It was obvious; we were being forced to leave.

There was approximately a one-kilometre long telephone wire, hung on poles and trees, leading to our telephone. The villagers often needed to fell a tree. Then they usually felled it over the wire. In total there were 123 joints on this one thousand-metre wire. Twisted open joints with all the humming and crackling that meant. At times, we'd only been able to communicate on the Internet, using 1,200 Baud instead of 14,400 and the telephone often didn't work at all. Our visits to the Telephone Company in town had, as a result, been rather frequent but now some changes had been made there.

The Post Office, that earlier included the telephone company, had been commercialised. The only tangible result was that you now saw nice new signposts in Kakamega, with the name TelCom Kenya. Subheadings on the posts included, amongst others, 'Customer Care and Complaints Desk'. Inside the building, these functions didn't exist. TelCom had obviously decided it worked well without such things. As a complaining subscriber, there was no longer anyone to contact.

After many attempts, Bertil, however, finally, on a Thursday, succeeded in getting a meeting with the Assistant Manager at TelCom Kenya in Kakamega. Bertil reminded the man of the promise he'd been given two and a half years earlier that the drop wires would be replaced. The manager promised to have it done the next day; at the latest on the Saturday. Imagine, they really came the following day and replaced one thousand metres. Everything was working much better now. The next day someone felled a tree across the telephone wire …

The chief had a harambee again, in order to get money to finish his office, but evidently only around twenty persons attended in contrast to the usual several hundred. At the last harambee, when we'd donated a large amount of money, he'd received more than enough for building his new office, but it had never been finished. Doors and windows were still missing. On the other hand, he suddenly had enough money to move into a newly constructed nice private house. Consequently, we chose to let the harambee pass in silence.

The chief's total inability to see to the best for the village by helping us instead of upsetting our plans, made us see red. That he was so corrupt didn't make us feel any friendlier. One Friday, I caused a rumpus in Wulushi. In public, I reprimanded the chief and even asked him to shut up. That was probably the first time anyone had dared to say such a thing to him since he was elected chief.

After the scene, we went straight to the District Officer's office. We handed over a long list of complaints about the chief. The District Officer looked pale, when he'd finished reading the list.

We told him that, according to witnesses, the chief, one night outside the bar in Wushiye, had been overheard saying, "The Europeans that live in my village are bad people. They employ people, don't pay them any salary and thereafter send them away. If any villager should attack the wazungu at night, I don't want any neighbours to come to their rescue."

We would try to persuade the witnesses to give a written testimony, but the question was whether they dared to. With such a paper, the chief would surely immediately lose his position as a chief. Maybe we'd also be expelled from Kenya? But we didn't care any longer.

A new ingredient in the threats against us was that certain people, although not many, started turning against us simply because we were Europeans. This seemed to be founded in the hatred towards the immigrants during the colonization era and was influenced by the atmosphere in Zimbabwe. In spite of most villagers being positive towards us, a few could do a lot of damage by spreading mean and untrue rumours. We'd seen earlier, how easy it was to enrage a mass of people.

The chief's "Go-ahead-harm-the-wazungu"-message in combination with the anti-colonial feelings made me really scared. I, once again, started having nightmares and categorically refused to leave the compound on foot. When out with the car, we no longer stopped to chat with people along the road, even if they made signs that they wanted to talk to us. It would be too dangerous to do that. It was a very strange feeling not knowing who our true friends were and who weren't. During the years we had so many times trusted the wrong people so now we dared not trust anybody, except our closest staff.

## 89. Illegal brewing now legal

Like so many times before, we established that this country was strange. Suddenly, the President declared that illegal brewing, as of now, was no longer illegal. This occurred just as 140 people died from consuming home-brew; and a lot of more were dying in and around Nairobi.

In our area, a lot of brewing was done in the bushes. Violence among people was extensive, getting increasingly worse, due to the said home brewing. One of the few more honest assistant chiefs was in a coma. He was cut in the head with a panga when, a couple of days earlier, together with some village elders, he'd tried to close an illegal brewing nest in Wulushi. The owner got angry, grabbed a panga and slashed the sub-chief across his head several times. This incident took place a couple of days before the President's announcement. The poor assistant chief and his family would probably not get any help as they'd almost certainly be told brewing was now legal.

We got a lot of answers to our mailing to the embassies and help organizations, regarding the financing of the mushroom project. Unfortunately, several of the international organizations told us they were withdrawing from Kenya: very few new projects would be sponsored because of the extensive corruption. The UNDP hadn't yet come with any definite answer but they'd asked us whether it was possible to move the project to another part of Kenya. We'd answered that it depended on the climate, closeness to the market and accessibility to primary produce. Suddenly one day, however, a

UNDP representative came to look a little closer at the project. Unfortunately, we were in Kisumu that day.

On the other hand, the administration in Western Kenya was hoping to get a lot of aid for alleviating the situation of the AIDS victims. As a consequence, we tried with renewed vigour to find a buyer wanting to turn Riverdale Gardens into an orphanage.

One morning, there was no milk left for the dogs. We did, as our employees usually did for their tea: we bought milk in Njombo's kiosk. He once again had his kiosk in his father's house. We got something watery, almost transparent, in a plastic bag.

Bertil checked the milk with his density-meter and found that fifty percent was water. For this we'd paid our staff a lot of money, every day for several years. We wondered about the quality of the water Njombo mixed in. After this, we started buying milk in town also for the staff breakfasts. We gave them half the amount of milk they'd received earlier, but it still contained more real milk than they were used to.

When buying milk in town, we usually bought only a couple of fresh milk cartons and the rest so called UHT (high pasteurised milk). We bought one big box of UHT milk at a time, so all the cartons had the same date. Sometimes we discovered that a UHT-box was sour and unusable. Then we returned the whole box and showed the sour milk to the shop owner. Don't think they'd put away the sour milk to be returned - not at all. It went directly into the milk department to be sold again. If we were unlucky, we could actually get back the same sour milk.

Talking of possible poisoning, one day we met our plumber, who was looking somewhat down, and I asked him what had happened. He told us someone, probably envious, had poisoned both the pigs he'd bought when they were still piglets, and had been fattening for slaughter at Christmas. He'd counted on making a lot of money on them and now they were dead.

In spite of the setbacks, this late autumn was a good period. All of us were getting along well; the work was fun; the villagers were happy and the staff were all friends. You could hear a lot of laughter from our compound.

The rainy season, however, was one of the worst so far. A Swedish annual precipitation in one hour. All the roads were flooded and mostly looked like big muddy lakes. The sun didn't come out much, which meant we couldn't charge our batteries sufficiently. Our water tanks, on the other hand, were spilling over daily so we didn't suffer from any water shortage.

It was maybe because of the intense rain that we had ten centimetre sized fruit on one of our many avocado trees. We'd planted the seeds two and a half year earlier - and already fruit. That was unbelievable, the villagers said. It usually took at least seven years, before the trees gave fruit. This tree was now five to six metres high and full of flowers and fruits.

When suddenly we had a one-day interruption in this eternal raining, we took the opportunity to drive south to Kisumu to do some urgent shopping. As we were walking along the main street, a car suddenly braked at our side. The driver asked us to go to his electrical shop. He informed us he'd just returned from the head office in Canada. He now wanted to give us a new electric transformer instead of the one we'd returned broken more than two years ago. The reason for his offer was probably the angry email Bertil had sent to the head office lodging a complaint against the shop in Kisumu. During this long wait, we'd had time to get another transformer but the staff broke that one while we were in Sweden. Now we felt as if we were getting a Christmas present and really looked forward to finally being able to watch a video.

But things never turned out the way we hoped for. Five days of continuous rain, so no charging through our solar panels. Then came a short dry spell with sunshine, but then we discovered that the battery was ruined. We didn't feel like investing in yet another one. So now we had a transformer for solar power but no battery.

## 90. Rat invasion

The kitchen stove hadn't been working as it should and we hadn't been able to use the oven for a long time. We decided to remove the stove from the kitchen in order to clean it. Cleaning should remedy that problem. For two whole days, we worked. Meanwhile, we had to cook our meals on a "jiko" (charcoal stove) and, as we weren't accustomed to using it, we didn't have much food during those days.

While cleaning, we found that rats had eaten all the cables in the oven and built a lot of nests there. Disgusting. Now we had a gas stove without an oven. The same thing had happened to our refrigerator: all the electric wiring had been gnawed at. It now also operated only on gas. The microwave oven was stacked away in the container. It didn't work at all, but as far as that was concerned, we had to blame a stroke of lightning and not the rats.

The rats that appeared were irritating. At night we heard them padding about in the walls and, once in a while, a gnawing sound. Bertil had drilled small holes here and there in the inner walls and at times we sprayed acetic acid into them. Rats don't like acetic acid.

After each spraying, it was quiet for a few hours. When the acid had evaporated, the animals unfortunately returned. They attacked everything. They even made holes in the big plastic containers with vegetable oil. They usually gnawed the holes in the bottom so that all the oil ran out. Even the can containing acetic acid was attacked. Revenge perhaps?

In the evenings, Bertil made us tea and then Merry quietly accompanied him into the kitchen to start the big hunt. She was phenomenal at catching and killing.

You could almost believe she was a cat. She stole up on them and finished them off in a flash.

We regretted that we hadn't, right from the start, bought a house-cat to keep the rats in check. Now we dared not do that, since our dogs would certainly kill the cat. Since rats attracted snakes, we shuddered at the thought that the compound cobras would follow the rats into our house. Bertil had recently told me that, sometimes at night he heard a slithering sound in the walls. He thought it came from snakes. I wished he hadn't told me.

Having fixed the disgusting rat removal, we started clearing out our things. Come the day of our return to Sweden, we wouldn't, alas, have any memories at all of our earlier life. Unfortunately, the container was included in the places that needed to be cleansed and cleared. Everything in it smelled of mould. We sneezed and coughed and continued working. It was important for us to be in a position where we could literally stand up and steal away, if necessary.

Now that we'd been so efficient and energetic, we needed a change. Since we'd heard so many good things about the small Brazilian orphanage outside Kakamega, we decided to go there.

The Brazilian nun, Sister Augusta, who was in charge, was a wonderful person. She had between fifty and sixty children in her care, from seventeen years down to a day old. She regarded them all as her own children. She blew their noses and washed and comforted them. Sometimes she had to bury them; two newly born infants were dying during one of our visits. The infants were often found in ditches, in the rainforest or in the sugarcane fields, abandoned by their mothers.

The older boys were mostly former street children, whom she'd convinced they'd be better off at her orphanage than in the street. Every Saturday, she gave these boys some pocket money and permission to spend the day with their old friends in town. They were allowed to put on their old rags and spend the day living in the street. They returned voluntarily around suppertime, often accompanied by a new street child wanting to move into Sister Augusta's home. I thought this was a very nice and pedagogical way to treat them.

We brought a box with children's jigsaw puzzles that the American missionary family, moving back to the US a year earlier, had given us. We had many boxes with toys, but we had to check that they worked before giving them away. Hence, I laid puzzles and played with toys in the evenings. We also brought seven or eight banana stems, since the orphanage's banana plants were still small, and we intended to give Sister Augusta a lot of pawpaw and paprika plants as well. She was overwhelmed with joy when she got all that plus some big bags with dried oyster mushrooms for her and the children. She wanted to pay us for all the things she received, but since her engagement in those poor children was payment enough for us, we refused to accept any money.

Elena and Sebastian were also close friends of Sister Augusta and helped the orphanage through fund raising. Sister Augusta now asked us how Elena was doing. Very downhearted, we told her that she'd left the country some days ago, all alone; immigrating to England, where one of her children was living. She'd left Kenya without a shilling in her pocket and without any belongings. It was so awful.

## 91. Christmas time

We had four beehives. One day, just before Christmas, three of them were ready to harvest. By tradition, you normally did that at night. You took off almost all your clothes and lit some torches. Then you removed all the honeycombs from the hive and cut off the wax into a big basin. The hive was of course destroyed that way, but that was obviously not so important, and you usually got a lot of bee stings, since all the bees were in the hive at night.

This time, our shamba boys wanted to harvest daytime. They made head covers of old hats and mosquito nets. The covers would have worked very well, if only they'd tied them better around their bodies. When they started working on the first beehive, some bees nestled down under Fred's and Petrus' nets. Fred kept a cool head and opened the net to let them out without any problem. Petrus, on the other hand, was seized with panic when three bees landed on his face. He killed them and lifted the net. Immediately the friends of the killed bees swarmed in. When you kill a bee, it actually sends out a smell signal, which puts the whole colony into an aggressive mood.

Petrus got around thirty stings on his face and fled down to the shower, where he fell unconscious. When I found him, he was getting weaker and weaker. Bertil came rushing after me and got about ten stings. (I was lucky getting only one.) Bertil ran up to the car and drove to the shower, through bushes and flowerbeds. We loaded Petrus into the car and put him on Fred's lap. Bertil drove, with the accelerator pressed down to a maximum, to the Missionary Hospital. The distance was about eight kilometres of bad road; the drive only took seven minutes instead of the normal twenty-seven.

At the hospital, Petrus was given intravenous cortisone and after five to ten minutes he started coming round. After half an hour, he'd recovered considerably and wanted to return home, so the doctor allowed him to leave. However, when we got home, he got worse again after only ten minutes. We had no alternative but to return to the hospital at the same high speed. This time, however, Petrus was put under observation for the night.

Petrus hadn't told us he had malaria. This is dangerous in combination with bee stings. However, by the following day he was feeling a new man and Bertil could collect him from the hospital.

This episode really put a damper on the Christmas rush. Thank God it ended in a happy way.

"Christmas time is here again…." (Swedish Christmas carol: "Nu är det jul igen…")

Our Christmas was, as usual, not a normal one. No Christmas decorations except for a few candlesticks with red candles, some cypress twigs stolen from the neighbour's hedge and a lot of flower bouquets in red, yellow and green. In the morning, a thick fog enveloped the valley and it was cloudy and raining most of the time. According to the calendar, the dry season had now started.

We had ham and spare-ribs as Christmas food and Bertil had pickled a tin of herring. His homemade mulled wine with local spices was in fact much better than the mulled wine you bought in Sweden. Otherwise nothing special.

Unfortunately, "our friends" had stolen our Christmas gift from Father. We had to comfort ourselves with a five-litre bag-in-box of wine and a couple of newly bought pocket books.

On Christmas Eve, we sat on the veranda in the light of the kerosene lamps and candles. On my side table, I had a cup of coffee and a glass of homemade cognac. The temperature was 23 degrees Celsius - and no snow to shovel. It was romantic and exotic. As Victor Rydberg wrote in his poem 'Tomten', "... and the stars sparkle and gleam..."

Between Christmas and New Year, Fred and I harvested around twenty-five kilos of yellow paprika. All weren't quite yellow yet, but after a couple of days in the house they ripened. It was impossible to leave them on the plant any longer, since then they became shrivelled and burnt by the sun.

What could you do with so much paprika? We decided, as a test, to shred and put them in the mushroom drying device. We asked Petrus to test three paprika fruits to see how fast they dried and then we went to town to do some shopping.

When we returned, we found that Petrus had shred all twenty-five kilos and put them in the dryer. We would obviously not have stuffed paprika for dinner, as planned. The dryer needed sunshine to work so, of course, we had a heavy rainstorm in the afternoon. We could only hope there would be sunshine next day. Otherwise, we'd soon only have mouldy and rotten paprika.

Just before New Year, a big package arrived from the USA from the Dutch mushroom expert who had visited us in September. He'd bought a big pressure cooker from an American company; a very large cooker that could hold more than forty litres. A gift for us. We sterilized sawdust and wheat, at full speed. We used that to make mycelia. With the new device, we could produce up to seventy-five kilos of mycelia per week.

One day, I discovered something unexpected, when picking flowers for the vases. Yet another tasty mushroom was growing on the compound. It was King Stropharia, a kind that gets enormous; up to a metre in diameter. It should be harvested as soon as it is the size of a golf ball. It looks like a red champignon and is delicious.

After a long discussion, we came to the conclusion that we must be responsible for the existence of these mushrooms on our plot. Our Dutch friend actually gave us a small amount of King Stropharia mycelia. Since we thought we'd failed with the cultivation of it, which was done in quite a different way to that of oyster mushrooms, we dumped the substrate under some bushes. Then we forgot about it. It was that substrate that had come to life during the rainy season and now grew so unbelievably fast.

## 92. A big order

We moved into the year of 2001.

In the countryside, people celebrated New Year a little differently. At sunset everyone started beating drums, tins, tanks and everything else that could make a sound. Noise and racket sounded for an hour, until it had become completely dark. After that it became silent.

We waited on the veranda for the church bell in Wushiye to strike midnight. It did so at ten minutes to twelve. We celebrated with a shrimp sandwich (made from tinned shrimps) and cold white wine.

Earlier in the day, a man from Nairobi had visited us. He told us he had some connections, who might want to buy dried mushrooms. He'd talk to them and then come back to us by email. Now it remained to be seen, if that was only empty boasting or if the visit would really give a positive result.

One morning, we got the email. He'd arranged a contract of one hundred kilos dried mushrooms per month! Converted into fresh mushrooms, that meant more than one ton per month. A big multinational food company had found our dried mushrooms to be of high quality. They'd passed all their laboratory tests with the highest possible score.

Now we had to produce a lot of mycelia quickly, so that the growers could start cultivation on a larger scale. The grower got 1,500 shillings per kilo of dried mushrooms. That was more than a normal annual income. Quickly, we called a meeting with some growers and instructors to discuss the news. We really hoped we'd succeed. We needed some success after all the adversities. Most Europeans were forgotten when they left the country so we wanted to leave something behind. Something people would remember. Something positive. We thought we were on our way to do that now.

Owing to the mushroom contract, we had to engage many more groups. So, Bertil and I drove off one Saturday to find another party wanting to start mushroom farming. The trip was along narrow roads. Being almost at our destination, we unfortunately had to turn back to the main road to get some more petrol. After that, back into the bush. We didn't find the group, but we arrived at a small village at the very foot of a big mountain range where we informed the people that we taught the art of growing mushrooms. They laughed heartily at us. It wasn't possible to cultivate mushrooms. There were no seeds, were there?

Our project was thrilling once more, now that we had such a big order. Fred sat all day long making mycelia, while Bertil and I were out in the villages searching for interested groups. We organized a lot of seminars for the people we found.

Willy and Linda, whom we'd fired when we returned from Sweden, had started helping a man who thought he'd quickly become rich on mushroom growing. The man was sure he'd be able to drive us out of the market. He was free to think whatever he wanted, but we didn't want him to spoil the work with the big order.

The man had tried to send people to us to buy our mycelia. He wanted to multiply it, but since all our growers had an ID-card, we'd for a long time been able to stop the man's friends from buying. Now someone had obviously got hold of our mycelia and one day we saw a small notice outside a village shop with the text, "We sell mushroom seeds and buy mushrooms."

We sent a friend with some money to buy mushroom "seeds". On opening the bag, we felt the smell of rotten meat. Bertil analysed the contents and found it completely unusable. The stench was getting stronger, attracting a lot of flies. Mushrooms would never grow out of that mycelia. We were pretty sure the man didn't care that he cheated his friends out of their money, trying to sell this crap to them.

In the middle of January, we suddenly got Christmas gifts. In our absence, the package had been opened by Customs in Kisumu. It contained lots of luxury toiletries and also small Christmas gnomes, tea and candles. It was only to be expected that the spare parts for the converter, for which Christian had been searching for months, had disappeared in Customs. But not even that could drown our Christmas spirit, when we had our new Christmas tea.

After a non-existent dry season, which should have started at the beginning of December and stretched out until the end of March, a day without rain was nice. Otherwise it had been raining from morning to night over the past months, with few exceptions. Without any sunshine, the solar panels hadn't been giving much electricity. Hence we'd been living for quite some time with power rationing. It was also icy cold. When we got out of bed in the morning, it was only between thirteen and fifteen centigrade: who would have thought we'd be using our down quilts in Africa. It was fortunate we'd brought them to Kenya.

## 93. Why?

Days and weeks passed rapidly. It was now February again. During almost the whole month of January, we'd been without a functioning telephone as lightning had struck the line in lots of places. However, it seemed that the dry season had started a couple of days ago, after a delay several month's long.

I'd finally recovered from a severe ache in all my joints, fatigue and a lot of coughing. My problems had probably been caused by the extremely cold and humid weather. I'd drunk large quantities of homemade tea from plant number 41, mixed with our own honey, to alleviate the cough. My only consolation had been to go to bed as early as seven in the evening, covering up with a lot of blankets. In bed, I'd been reading in the light of the gas lamp we'd bought this year. It both heated and gave a good reading light. Why hadn't we bought it several years ago?

The catholic bishop didn't want to buy Riverdale Gardens after all so we continued searching for a buyer, now at a ridiculously low price; a real bargain price. We really must solve this issue soon, as our entry permits would expire in May.

One night, the dogs fought with a wild dog outside the house. Joe was hiding on top of the shower water tank. He thought it was a leopard, fighting the dogs. Musse got a wound in his ear but otherwise the dogs seemed okay. To be on the safe side, we washed ourselves with disinfectant and spirits after touching our dogs. We had to be careful, as some dogs in the area had rabies.

A few days later, the dogs ran away, like so many times before. We could hear them down in the valley, making an awful row. They returned after a long time. Rufus, like the retriever he was, was proudly carrying the prey Merry had killed: a dead cat. We couldn't scold them. It was just their hunting instinct.

The lack of water was getting really acute. The dry season had now been going on for two to three weeks, and we were totally dependent on water to keep our mycelia cold and alive. Our refrigerator was too small for the mycelia bags produced in our big pressure cooker.

Our newly constructed refrigerator would have helped us very much, but we were still without water in the tap. We gave the waterman five litres of diesel for the water pump and watched him filling and starting the pump. We saw water going into the 60 cubic metre big communal water tanks. After a while, the water was turned on and according to the waterman everybody along the pipeline had been shut off. When we'd had eight hundred litres, the water stopped coming. After a check with the waterman, he said "hakuna maji" (no water). Out of the thirty thousand litres that five litres of diesel could pump, we got less than one cubic metre. The waterman sold the rest to other consumers. That way, he got double payment for the water. This happened week after week.

It was alright during the rainy season, when we got rain now and then. During the dry season, our shamba boys had to go to the spring three hundred metres away to fetch water for the kitchen, toilet, shower, washing up and everything else for which water was needed. It was, to summarize, frustrating.

On top of that, the waterman didn't speak English. To scold someone through an interpreter didn't always give the right effect.

Talking of water, this dry season was really dry. We'd bought a hygrometer to measure the humidity. In the afternoons, the relative air humidity was between zero and ten percent. At night it went up to fifty.

The road leading to the main road between Kisumu and Kakamega had been levelled with a scraper. It had now a ten centimetre thick layer of dust, which meant that you had to use four-wheel drive in order not to slide off. The heat made it impossible for us to have the car windows closed, so everything became quite dusty. The only remedy was to take a shower once you were home again, and then the boys had to fetch more water... So, in other words, we had an eternal cycle of problems.

We informed the chief that the order we'd received for dried mushrooms would mean an economic lift for the whole region, if we could meet it. In order to achieve the required quantity, lots of people must grow mushrooms and for that purpose we needed water. It was as always with Chief Weaky. No arguments worked on him. He obviously preferred to see us gone rather than help the people he was elected to help.

Our neighbour still refused to finish the dividing up of his land. He'd twice stopped us from selling by spreading lies regarding the ownership issue. He seemed to think that, if he continued to refuse, he'd get Riverdale Gardens for free when we'd left.

The District Officer, who was also the Chairman of the Land Control Board, had given our neighbour an ultimatum: if he hadn't resolved the issue by March

15th (we'd signed all the documents already two years earlier) he and his family would be evicted from the land by court order. We'd also told the neighbour that if anything should happen to us our sons would inherit our land.

Once again, we had a prospective buyer for the property. A Catholic fraternity wanted to buy Riverdale Gardens, in order to turn it into a home for street children and AIDS orphans. The only problem was the usual one: money. We'd already gone down more than sixty percent on a price that was very low already at the start. In spite of that, they might have problems finding the money. Maybe we'd have to trust them and leave before any payment had been made.

At the same time, we had a new nasty surprise. Our dear neighbour summoned us to appear in Kakamega Court. He claimed that he, as far back as 1981, had bought one entire plot from the former owner of our two plots. In reality, he'd only bought a small part of it. Our night askari Joe was one of the people present on that sales occasion and he was willing to witness, if necessary, that the neighbour had only bought a small piece of the land.

So, it was the same old story that had been going on for a long time. Our neighbour counted on getting the entire plot the day we left, but rather than letting him have it, we would, unless we could sell it, give it away to someone in need.

It was our wedding anniversary. We tried to celebrate, despite the difficulties. For dinner we had a chicken stew with fresh basil, lemon and a touch of white wine. It was 35 degrees hot on the veranda with four percent humidity.

After dinner, we walked up and took photos of the neighbour's boundary. We made sure yesterday's newspaper was included in the photo, to be able to prove when it had been taken. Our neighbour was constantly trying to change the borderline, by cutting his cypress hedge towards our side, so that the branches grew into our plot. During the past few years, he'd probably gained at least half a metre of land. At the same time, our land had been cut into also at the lower end, where cunning neighbours, at the bottom of the valley, little by little had moved the reaches of the stream. We just didn't have the energy to care.

We felt so depressed. We wished we'd never heard about Kenya. Most of all, we'd like to be at the coast in a house with electricity, writing a book about Kenya and the Kenyans. A couple of days off, dedicated to gold panning, would surely have cheered us up, but nowadays we had no time for such luxury. Petty issues that shouldn't actually even exist consumed all our time.

My head was swirling with the never-ending insoluble questions I was constantly asking myself. Why? Why? Why did they treat us like this? Why didn't they understand we cared for them and liked them? Why couldn't they see the human being in us and not only our white skin? Why didn't they understand that we wished them all the good things in the world and wanted to help? The only thing they cared about was stealing and destroying; in fact, in the long run, spoiling things for themselves. What they exposed us to was sheer racism.

## 94. What impudence!

We had arranged a meeting with our friend Timothy at his home. He helped us when we bought the land and he was now also going to help us with the subdivision problem.

Just outside his home, we met a big crowd of people. We passed them and asked if they'd seen Chief Timothy. As we heard that he was in the crowd on the road, we turned and caught up with it. A man with a bloody head was pushed to the centre of the group. People had big canes and clubs in their hands. Timothy told us they were taking a thief to the Police Headquarters in Kakamega and that we, in the meantime, could wait for him on the pavement café of Hotel Franka. We later heard the man died in his cell; probably clubbed to death by the mob.

Having a soft drink at Franka, we suddenly saw "the potato bag". That was what we called a tall and handsome man, who usually walked around in town only clad in a potato bag. Sometimes, he thought he was wearing too much clothing and then he took off the jute bag and walked around stark naked. The man was usually out on the central traffic island of the main road, where everybody dumped their refuse. You could see him lying asleep there, quite unconcerned about the stench and all the donkeys and goats poking amongst the refuse. The difference this day was that we saw him, stark naked, kneeling on the pavement, writing a political manifesto in English. Who would have guessed that such a man hadn't only learned to write with beautiful handwriting but also had the gift of words?

After a very frustrating three hour wait for Timothy in the dust and heat, we gave up and returned home.

Hopefully, he'd look us up at home, as soon as he had time to help us with our problem.

"A society without reasonable communication is dreadful," Bertil said the following day, when we drove north towards Khasili in order to, hopefully, fetch Timothy. We'd received a message that he might have time for us today.

"In Sweden, you only have to lift the receiver and dial the number in order to know if someone is at the agreed place."

Chief Timothy was at his office and we only had to wait a short while, approximately an hour. Then we were finally on our way to town, to the Registrar at the Lands Office.

Suddenly, Timothy exclaimed, "The chiefs in Wulushi were wrong."

"What do you mean?" Bertil looked questioningly at him.

"Well, when you moved to Wulushi, they made a bet you'd only stick it out for one year, but it seems you're stronger than they thought."

So Timothy had known all along, that our own chief had made a bet with other chiefs in the region that we wouldn't last more than a year before running away.

They'd obviously not been thinking about the advantage for the village to have Europeans, willing to invest, living in the area.

It was good to know that we would now soon be leaving. These people didn't seem to want any help. It was so low to make a bet about something like that. By the way, hadn't something like this happened before in Wulushi? I turned to Chief Timothy and asked, "Wasn't there a Japanese woman, a teacher, living in Wulushi some years ago, that the villagers frightened into leaving? On several occasions, different persons have mentioned that, but nobody wants to tell us what happened to her."

No, not even Timothy wanted us to know what the Japanese woman had been exposed to. He looked embarrassed and immediately changed the topic of conversation, without denying the existence of the Japanese teacher. Something really terrible must have happened to her.

We now had to put a stop to the issue of our neighbour and the subdivision, by taking care of it, including title deeds, ourselves. It had taken us a week with a lot of waiting and frustration, since the documents we'd earlier signed had become too old and thus had had to be redone, but now everything was settled. The neighbour of course didn't yet know that we'd already accomplished what he himself hadn't managed to do for two years. And our neighbour would naturally have to pay us for the costs we'd had for his title deeds. No money, no title deeds.

We had booked a meeting with the neighbour's lawyer as we wanted to give him a copy of the plea we'd sent to Court, with our refutation of the neighbour's lies. Having waited in vain for him for two hours at his office, we finally gave up and went to Franka to quench our thirst before returning home.

While we sat there with a beer, reading the newspaper, Noah came. He'd earlier helped us to sell our second-hand things. He told us Fred and Willy had contacted him, while we were in Sweden last year, and asked him if he wanted to buy an electric welding set. They told him that they also had a petrol operated water pump and a video camera for sale. The boys had been driving around in my Suzuki, offering our things for sale. Noah added that, as late as about a week earlier, that is in March 2001, our welding set had still been up for sale in Malava, some thirty kilometres from here, in a workshop belonging to Fred's brother.

We sat dumbstruck. What a cheek!

The water pump was stolen on June 14th 1997 and the welding set and the video camera disappeared during November-December 1998. We'd always been suspicious of Fred, but without proof, we hadn't been able to do anything. Since Noah had a licence for buying and selling second-hand items, he had to report to the police all offers he got on stolen property. Consequently he must notify the police at once, so that he didn't get into trouble.

Fred was sympathetic and intelligent. According to our plans, he'd have continued producing mycelia after our departure from Kenya, but once again it seemed as if the mushroom project was back to square one. The villain was still working for us but we wouldn't accept more. Now he must be caught.

Noah promised to try to find the workshop in Malava. He'd report to us that same evening. Next day, we planned to go to the C.I.D. where we knew some inspectors.

The following evening, an unmarked police Land Rover arrived with four police officers and Noah. Under cover of darkness and armed with three AK-47 and one Uzi, they stole, together with Bertil, down the valley and across the river in order to surprise Fred and his brother. They searched all the houses for evidence. The action was successful and they collected a lot of stolen things but didn't find the more expensive objects. Fred and his brother were handcuffed and marched down through the valley and up to us. The captives were loaded into the back of the Land Rover. Thereafter, the police officers and Bertil drove on to the village where they searched Willy's house, finding some incriminating evidence. Willy was also handcuffed and loaded into the car. Since it was half past eleven at night and very dark, the police car left for the Police Headquarters in Kakamega without Bertil.

Next evening, the same procedure was repeated. This time, the destination was Linda's home, since Fred had said she was involved in the thefts. Again they found evidence in the form of stolen objects.

We spent a lot of time at the police station, identifying property and giving statements. According to Kenyan law, theft carries a sentence of three years in prison, but stealing from an employer gives up to seven years. Trafficking stolen property gives a minimum of seven and a maximum of fourteen years of hard labour.

In other words, we were having quite a busy and turbulent time: quarrelling with our neighbour about the plot; the sale of Riverdale Gardens to the Brotherhood and now, on top of that, a court trial in which we had to witness.

## 95. Critical days

One Saturday morning, we went to Kakamega to talk to the police. Passing the tea plantation along our road, we saw a man felling a tree. We stopped and asked the man to be careful with the telephone wire. He answered he knew his job. We continued in full confidence that he did.

When we returned in the afternoon, the line looked normal. The tree had been properly felled but the telephone was dead. Bertil asked the night askari on duty, Moses, to accompany him out to repair it. When they arrived, they found that the wires had been knotted together. They talked to the woman, who had hired the "clever" tree feller. She explained, "There was a wind." OK, accidents could happen, but why had they tried to hide the fault by knotting the wires together? No answer.

Bertil and Moses walked down between the tea plants and asked a boy to climb the pole and lift the wires down. The repair continued, while a very fat woman started to yell at them in the local language. Moses translated for Bertil.

The woman said, "You shouldn't come like gods and arrest people for no reason." Furthermore, she yelled, "You haven't asked for permission, before putting up the telephone poles and those wires." She really sounded annoyed.

Several witnesses testified to what she'd said. Bertil and Moses didn't pay any attention to the upset woman and continued with the repair. Soon the wires were back up again thanks to the lithe little boy, who got twenty shillings for his help. They walked back home contentedly. We checked email and made some calls. Everything was working fine.

On Sunday morning, Bertil, as usual, checked the telephone. Dead. He asked Moses to check if the wires looked normal and then call the Telephone Company to notify them about the fault.

A quarter of an hour later, Moses returned and told us the wires were gone. Well, somebody seemed to be in need of a clothes-line again. A little later, one of our neighbour's sons came to inform us that, coming home from church, he'd noticed that the telephone wires had been cut between each pole. A piece of it was also missing, so it was obviously sabotage. We began to worry, since the atmosphere around us had become very nasty.

In the afternoon, we sent a messenger for the other night askari, Joe. When he arrived, we locked the dogs into the house and drove to Father Samuel in the Catholic Church. He was the closest person with a telephone; about 500 metres from us. This drive, a few hundred meters long, seemed to take an eternity. I had a horrible feeling we'd be attacked any second by a horde of enraged villagers and begged Bertil to step on the accelerator.

As soon as Father Samuel had calmed us down, we got in contact with TelCom Kenya and reported the sabotage to a dumbfounded operator, "The wires have been cut in eleven places."

At the same time, we called Police Headquarters' help line and informed them about the sabotage. The policeman on duty promised to forward this information to the detective in charge. We returned home and sent Joe away to eat. It was important he was alert during the night watch. Danger might be imminent!

Around eight in the evening, a white Land Rover came to the gate and Joe let it in. The car was full of policemen, armed with AK47 and Uzi. The chief detective declared they'd stay overnight.

"We regard this as a serious matter," he said.

When I asked them if they were hungry, he answered, "We haven't had dinner yet."

I fried sausages, bacon and ten eggs, took out a whole bread loaf, made a pot of tea and put out some soft drinks. Mattresses were brought up from the huts, together with the same number of blankets.

I went to bed early, having secretly removed as many valuable things as possible. Not even police officers were to be trusted in Kenya. Bertil sat talking to the policemen until around eleven, when they went to bed. The detective advised us against going outdoors during the night, not even to the toilet as the policemen intended to shoot at everything moving.

The night passed quietly, but the dogs were nervous as they heard unknown voices from the adjacent dining room.

Morning arrived without any drama. The policemen complained that it had been cold, during the night. Temperature at night was about 12-13 degrees and with only one blanket, I could understand it was a little cool for them. Before leaving, the detective pulled us aside and declared he'd be back in the afternoon to fetch his gift.

A little later in the morning, we went to Kakamega Law Court to be present at the court proceedings regarding the issue of an arrest warrant. It was now time for the suspects - Fred, Willy and Linda - to have their indictments read out.

It was the biggest audience from one place the police had ever seen. The courtroom was filled with people from Wulushi, our neighbourhood. We were thus sitting in the centre of a mass of hostile people. I felt extremely stressed by the threatening atmosphere. That inexplicable hatred was so close. Someone could, any minute, put a knife in my back or Bertil′s. We were completely alone and exposed.

When the indictments had been read out loud and the three suspects, as expected, had declared their innocence, the judge decided bail would be set at 100,000 shillings each, plus an insurance of the same amount.

We quickly slipped away from the courtroom and continued to the C.I.D. to wait for our detective. When he arrived, he told us, completely unconcerned, that the police had still not interrogated two of the most important witnesses. We understood by this action and his lack of commitment, that we could expect those witnesses would never be summoned to the hearing on April 18th. The detective, in any case, promised to try to arrange the court hearing to be held behind locked doors. He'd also noticed the threatening atmosphere in the courtroom.

Thereafter, we proceeded to TelCom Kenya to see the assistant manager. We explained the situation and emphasized our need of communication, caused by the threats against us. He promised work would be started by two o'clock that same afternoon.

As promised, the detective appeared in the evening to receive his gift. We felt it would be risky to deny him anything. He pointed at a tape recorder and a pair of binoculars, which we reluctantly handed over. Sadly, we forgot that inside the recorder was the tape with the birds' morning concert, which we often listened to on the veranda.

In spite of everything, some days later we had to hand over the neighbour's title deed to him, without getting as much as one shilling in payment of all our costs. The neighbour's lawyer told us, with a smile, that the alternative would be that they started a civil case against us. That process could stretch out for five years. The lawyer didn't doubt at all that we'd win, but we would have to wait for several years. Well, we wouldn't lose more than 14,000 shillings and peace was worth that. However, we'd of course delay signing the transfer documents, until things around us had calmed down a bit.

Both of us were now physically and mentally worn out. We dared not drink water, buy vegetables or leave the compound. Several times a day, we checked along the whole fence, if someone had put out rat poison for our dogs. We lived in real mortal fear. Policemen were patrolling outside the fence, armed with AK47s. Several of these men were close friends and relatives to Willy, one of our villains. If someone attacked us, not one single person would come to our rescue. We were completely alone.

Those faces so full of hatred. In the courtroom, I'd noticed threatening glances from at least fifty persons that for certain wanted us dead. Violence was so natural. Recently, a man was murdered around 500 metres from us; the body parts, including his genitals, had been spread over a large area. It was probably over a triviality.

Our first priority was to try to get out of the country, before being murdered. Linda, Fred, his brother Boniface and Willy, were the ones that would be in the front line, wanting to kill us. Unfortunately only Fred was still in custody. The others had bailed themselves out, so we no longer had the security of them being in jail. They could just as well be on the other side of our fence, on their way into the compound.

All this time is blurred for me, but I remember thinking that Petrus and our house-girl Macy were so brave. In spite of the threatening scenario, they faithfully came to work every day, although there wasn't much work to do, now that we'd stopped the mushroom farming and just planned to leave the place. The night askaris, Joe and Moses, were also kind and loyal. We asked them to concentrate the patrolling around the main building. If anyone should want to burn down the huts, it wasn't the end of the world. The most important thing was that we and the dogs survived.

One late afternoon, Sebastian, Elena's husband, appeared together with a female friend. The woman had got it into her head that the village medicine man had put a curse on Bertil and me. She brought her own wizard. We couldn't believe it! This wizard put spells on us to cure any possible curses. We were so taken aback by this that we couldn't even protest and we didn't bother to ask if the wizard found anything. The essential thing was to get rid of all three of them, as fast as possible.

How was it possible that Sebastian, a modern well-educated man, believed in witchcraft? I couldn't understand it but maybe this mixture of a modern life and old traditional beliefs was what made it so difficult for an outsider to live in Kenya. You never knew what to expect; what would come next.

In Court, the judge decided on a new adjournment: until April 27th. The police didn't seem to have done their job at all. Several persons and witnesses had never been contacted, in spite of us reminding them time after time. We had ourselves, together with Noah, gone to Malava a couple of times to look for the man who, as late as in March this year, had tried to sell our electric welding equipment. The police hadn't even bothered to go there.

Rumour had spread that our entry permits would expire soon and it seemed as if they wanted to drag out all court proceedings beyond our time limit.

One morning, we had a meeting with one of the very top-level police inspectors at the C.I.D. to forward our complaints against the police. It was quite unbelievable, how rudely this man behaved towards us. Bertil got into a rage, flew out of his chair, pounded his fist on the table and yelled. Then we walked out of the room.

The Brothers had now come with the down payment. Nine percent of the already too low sales price was all they'd been able to scrape together in a short time. They intended to send a subsidy application to some of their sponsors, so we hoped we'd one day be paid more.

On May 3rd, one of the Brothers would move into one of our huts. He needed to study our routines and it was also important he got to know the dogs. The Brothers would take over Rufus and Merry and had promised to take good care of them. Musse would move to the home of Petrus, who was very fond of him.

## 96. Massacre

Oh, I ardently hoped Linda would pull through. The thoughts were whirling in my head, where I was sitting huddled up in a chair on the veranda. I felt sick and indeed nothing felt right. Rufus and Merry kept poking at me with their noses. Musse jumped onto my lap and wanted to be scratched behind his ears. My lovely dogs, not even their presence could help me. I felt as if the roof had fallen in on me. How could people be this cruel?

We'd just come from the hospital. I'd been sitting close to Linda, who was lying there quite unrecognisable, shaved and with a bandage all around her head, moaning in pain. In spite of all the terrible things she and the others had done to us, I couldn't help but feel a deep compassion and grief over her and her family's fate.

I believed she felt my presence, since she muttered in English, "I've such pain, please help me!"

I tucked the blanket round her, caressed her cheek and deeply wished I could help her with something more than money. Poor, poor Linda!

I fetched a blanket, snuggled deep into it and continued brooding. I thought of that horrible morning, a few days ago. When Petrus turned up, very much delayed, I joked with him and asked if he'd had a lie-in.

Instead of joking back, he looked quite devastated and exclaimed, "So much blood, so much blood, I'll never be able to forget it."

"What do you mean? What's happened? Tell me, Petrus, you look so strange."

"Well, I come from the village down there, from Linda's home. It's terrible, it's awful!" our friend continued.

"But what's happened?"

"There are dead people and hurt ones everywhere... and there is blood all over the place."

"Please Petrus, try to calm down. Try to explain what's happened. Has anything happened to Linda?" I asked, now suddenly very afraid.

Petrus seemed to be in shock. What could have happened?

"There are a lot of dead people. It's too much, I can't bear it." Petrus was almost crying.

I persuaded Petrus to sit down and called for Bertil. I told him something awful had obviously happened down in the village. After a while, Petrus calmed down a little and could tell us, though rather incoherently, what had happened.

Late the night before, one of Linda's male relatives had had an attack of insanity. Nobody yet knew why. Some believed, it was about a land dispute. He took his panga and chopped his pregnant wife and his children to death. After that, he managed to lure his relatives in the other bandas around to open their doors and then attacked also them with his weapon. Having attacked all his relatives, he continued to the home of our assistant chief, Nixon and tried to lure him outside. Nixon, however, smelled a rat and didn't open the door. The man ran away to hide in a banana grove, where he took some rat poison.

In the morning, a search for the man was organized and they found him. He was taken to the hospital and there he quickly recovered from the dose of rat poison. The police then arrested him.

The man had in total wounded or killed sixteen relatives. It was still not clear in what condition some of them were. Everybody had been slashed, several times, with the machete-like panga.

According to Petrus, Linda had been severely cut in her head. Her sister-in-law, who had earlier been active in our mushroom project, had brain damage and was in critical condition. Furthermore, the man's wife and children had already died. Nobody yet knew how many persons would die, but it was a horrible tragedy that had befallen this family and our village.

Some hours later, Moses turned up, quite bloody and very upset by what he'd seen. He'd also been down helping to sort out dead and injured people. He asked for permission to wash himself as he, according to local customs, was neither allowed to see his wife nor to enter his house until he'd been cleaned of all the blood.

A couple of days later, we visited Linda again at the hospital. She'd now passed the most critical stage but was in very great pain. Linda had received three cuts in her head and she was completely unrecognisable. They said, however, that she'd survive, even though the convalescence would be long. Linda's husband and children hadn't been harmed during the massacre, but most of her other relatives had been badly hurt or killed.

We asked Linda's husband to come and see us. We explained to him that, together with my family in Sweden, we'd succeeded in collecting enough money for the payment of her stay in hospital. The money would also probably cover some of her relatives' hospital bills.

When I thought of the court hearing the previous day, I shuddered. We'd been face to face with the two traitors, Willy and Fred. It was hard to believe that Bertil and I had actually gone to the prison to pay Fred his salary, in spite of his being there because he'd stolen from us. We were such idiots. Damn Swedish behaviour and ethics!

The hearing was this time behind closed doors in the judge's room. Both Bertil and I told the judge we pardoned Linda for what she'd done and that we'd be happy if the legal proceedings against her were dropped. The judge seemed to agree that Linda had enough problems as it was and thanked us for our attitude.

We had no idea when the verdict would be announced, but it would probably be after our departure. It wouldn't surprise me, if they started the whole procedure all over again and then withdrew the case, since we wouldn't be able to be present. Nothing was impossible in this godforsaken country.

It was our last day at Riverdale Gardens.

It was quite unbelievable. How would I ever have the strength to start all over again somewhere else? How would I be able to live without our dogs? How would I cope with the rest of my life in pain; one of the reasons for emigrating was, after all, to escape the Swedish climate which made my fibromyalgia worse.

But, on the other hand, I couldn't live like this either; with this violence and complete absence of ethic norms. Not knowing what would happen the next minute; if someone would attack us or poison us or burn our house down at night. This constant fear was tearing me apart. I couldn't stand it any longer.

I’d been thinking, ever since the massacre on Linda’s family, that the guilty man could have continued to our home to slaughter also us since he obviously thought life had been unfair to him. There had been so many possible scenarios in my head – all of them about what could happen to us. We were really lucky to get out of here now, before the thoughts had driven me insane.

We’d decided to say good-bye to our paradise in a magnificent way. We’d leave Wuasiva with our heads high. Hence, our last gesture was to give a farewell lunch. Around twenty people; employees, Father Samuel, the Brothers and the local administration in the form of chiefs, assistant chiefs and district V.I.P.s had been invited. Lunch was good and the atmosphere amicable. We put on a good face, in spite of knowing that some of the persons present had done everything in their power to destroy things for the villagers and us. I smiled and joked while talking to the chief, but within I had quite another feeling.

Of all the people we had invited to lunch there was only one person we felt was a true friend. That was Father Samuel who was a really good man. Not even Chief Timothy, whom we had now known for many years and who had always helped us when we had problems, could be trusted. From the very first moment he had known about the bet the chiefs had made, without telling us about it. He might actually have joined them in the bet. When looking at the laughing and joking lunch guests I wondered if they would let us leave alive. Maybe they had arranged an ambush? We wouldn't be safe until we were in Kisumu.

When lunch was finished, we handed over a new guest book to the Brothers which we inaugurated, writing down a wish for a good future. Then I lay down on the lawn and cuddled my beloved dogs. Musse would accompany Petrus to his home the same day, but the other two would be left with the Brothers. I hoped they would get a lot of love.

Farewell and gifts to Petrus, Macy, Bernie, Tommy, Joe and Moses. A farewell to the others and then we left.

The Brothers would drive us to the Hotel Imperial in Kisumu. We'd decided not one single person would be told where we were going. Officially we'd, before our return flight to Sweden, go on a vacation to northern Kenya, as we hadn't yet seen that part of the country. We felt threatened and were afraid someone or something would throw a spanner into the works for our departure. It was better nobody knew our whereabouts.

At the gate, I turned around and had a last long look at our home that we were now leaving forever. What a paradise – unfortunately with a touch of hell.

# Epilogue

(May 2006)
I feel so good! After five years of depression and nightmares, I now feel as if I have gone through an internal cleansing. During the writing of the book, I have been forced to face all that I had hitherto been evading. Things that earlier I had refused to think or even talk about, I have now been addressing in my text. I have read through all the old diary notes, emails and faxes to both near and dear. I have been forced to relive old traumatic and sad experiences. Sometimes, I have cried lakes of tears; sometimes been blaspheming so that my office has been reeking of sulphur, but now I am through it and I feel like a new person.

It was really not easy to return to Sweden. We had, after all, mentally said goodbye when we decided to emigrate. Emotionally our home was still in Kenya. We also returned quite destitute, without either a place to live or work; forced to rebuild a new life from scratch, though we did not want to be here.

The years in Kenya were not easy either. Now, afterwards, I feel as if the pieces are starting to fall into their right place. It is easier to be happy for the persons we managed to help than mourning all the persons we could not help, hindered by corruption and criminality. It is perhaps actually not so strange that the villagers acted the way they did: to live during a transition period between new and old, a life marked by ancient local traditions and modern corruption, can't be easy.

www.ingramcontent.com/pod-product-compliance
Lightning Source LLC
Chambersburg PA
CBHW030212170426
43201CB00006B/60
*9781907756597*